D1117649

SHAKESPEARE SURVEY

ADVISORY BOARD

PETER ALEXANDER	KENNETH MUIR
H. S. BENNETT	GEORGE RYLANDS
H. B. CHARLTON	I. A. SHAPIRO
R. W. DAVID	CHARLES J. SISSON
SIR BARRY JACKSON	F. P. WILSON
	J. DOVER WILSON	

Secretaries and Assistants to the Editor: B. A. HARRIS and N. J. SANDERS

PANEL OF CORRESPONDENTS

Argentine:	M. DE VEDIA Y MITRE	*Israel:*	REUBEN AVINOAM
Australia:	H. J. OLIVER	*Italy:*	MARIO PRAZ
Austria:	S. KORNINGER	*Japan:*	JIRO OZU
Belgium:	DOM. DE GRUYTER	*Mexico:*	RAFAEL H. VALLE
Brazil:	EUGENIO GOMES	*Netherlands:*	A. G. H. BACHRACH
Bulgaria:	MARCO MINCOFF	*New Zealand:*	I. A. GORDON
Canada:	ARNOLD EDINBOROUGH	*Norway:*	LORENTZ ECKHOFF
Ceylon:	R. K. BRADY	*Poland:*	STANISŁAW HELSZTYŃSKI
China:	CHANG CHEN-HSIEN	*Portugal:*	PAULO QUINTELA
Czechoslovakia:	B. HODEK	*South Africa:*	A. C. PARTRIDGE
Denmark:	ALF HENRIQUES	*Spain:*	LUIS ASTRANA MARÍN
East Africa:	A. J. R. MASTER	*Sweden:*	NILS MOLIN
Finland:	RAFAEL KOSKIMIES	*Switzerland:*	GEORGES BONNARD
France:	JEAN JACQUOT	*Turkey:*	NUREDDIN SEVIN
Germany:	WOLFGANG CLEMEN	*Uruguay:*	C. SABAT ERCASTY
	KARL BRINKMANN	*U.S.A.*	LOUIS MARDER
Greece:	GEORGE THEOTOKAS	*U.S.S.R.*	IU. SHVEDOV
Hungary:	LADISLAS ORSZÁGH	*Yugoslavia:*	B. NEDIĆ

SHAKESPEARE SURVEY

AN ANNUAL SURVEY OF
SHAKESPEARIAN STUDY & PRODUCTION

13

EDITED BY
ALLARDYCE NICOLL

Issued under the Sponsorship of
THE UNIVERSITY OF BIRMINGHAM
THE UNIVERSITY OF MANCHESTER
THE SHAKESPEARE MEMORIAL THEATRE
THE SHAKESPEARE BIRTHPLACE TRUST

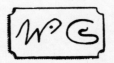

CAMBRIDGE
AT THE UNIVERSITY PRESS
1970

Published by the Syndics of the Cambridge University Press

Bentley House, 200 Euston Road, London N.W. 1

American Branch: 32 East 57th Street, New York, N.Y. 10022

ISBN 0 521 06426 0

First published 1960
Reprinted 1966 1970

822.332
N645
v. 13

Printed in Great Britain
at the University Printing House, Cambridge
(Brooke Crutchley, University Printer)

CONTENTS

[*Notes are placed at the end of each contribution. All line references are to the 'Globe' edition, and, unless for special reasons, quotations are from this text*]

List of Plates viii

The Catharsis of *King Lear* by J. STAMPFER I

Lear's Last Speech *by* J. K. WALTON II

Albany *by* LEO KIRSCHBAUM. 20

Madness in *King Lear by* KENNETH MUIR 30

The Influence of *Gorboduc* on *King Lear by* BARBARA HELIODORA CARNEIRO DE MENDONÇA 41

Some Aspects of the Style of *King Lear by* WINIFRED M. T. NOWOTTNY . . . 49

Keats and *King Lear by* D. G. JAMES 58

King Lear on the Stage: A Producer's Reflections *by* ARNOLD SZYFMAN . . . 69

Costume in *King Lear by* W. MOELWYN MERCHANT 72

The Marriage-Contracts in *Measure for Measure by* ERNEST SCHANZER 81

Tom Skelton—A Seventeenth-century Jester *by* E. W. IVES 90

Illustrations of Social Life III: Street Cries *by* F. P. WILSON 106

An Elizabethan Stage Drawing? *by* R. A. FOAKES and R. T. RICKERT III

Was there a Music-room in Shakespeare's Globe? *by* RICHARD HOSLEY . . . 113

International Notes 124

Shakespeare Productions in the United Kingdom: 1958 134

Three Adaptations *by* JOHN RUSSELL BROWN 137

The Year's Contributions to Shakespearian Study
   1. Critical Studies *reviewed by* BERNARD HARRIS 146
   2. Shakespeare's Life, Times and Stage *reviewed by* R. A. FOAKES 154
   3. Textual Studies *reviewed by* JAMES G. MCMANAWAY 162

Books Received 170

Index 172

71271

LIST OF PLATES

PLS. I–IV ARE BETWEEN PP. 32 AND 33

I–II. Costumes for productions of *King Lear*

III. The Town Crier, etc.
      (British Museum)

IV. A. 'I haue Screens if you Desier'
      (Huntington Library)
   B. 'What kichin-stuffe'
      (Huntington Library)
   C. The bookvendor: 'I haue Ripe Strawburyes'
      (British Museum)
   D. The Common Cryer
      (Bodleian Library)

PLS. V–VIII ARE BETWEEN PP. 144 AND 145

V. A. Tom Skelton
      (Muncaster Collection: photo: *Country Life*)
  B. Tom Skelton
      (The Shakespeare Institute)

VI. *All's Well That Ends Well*, Shakespeare Memorial Theatre, 1959. Directed by Tyrone Guthrie, designed by Tanya Moiseiwitsch
   A. The Widow, Diana and Helena
   B. The Countess and Rinaldo
   C. Parolles unmasked
      (Photos: Angus McBean)

VII. *All's Well That Ends Well* (*cont.*)
   A. The King and Helena
   B. Bertram and Helena

   A Midsummer Night's Dream, Shakespeare Memorial Theatre, 1959. Directed by Peter Hall, designed by Lila de Nobili
   C. Titania and her attendants
   D. Oberon and Puck
      (Photos: Angus McBean)

VIII. A. Frontispiece from *The Tempest, by Mr Dryden* (1735)
      (Photo: John Cope)

   B. *The Tempest: or The Enchanted Island*, The Old Vic, 1959. Directed by Douglas Seale, costumes and scenery by Finlay James, choreography by Peter Wright. Masque of Neptune and Amphitrite
      (Photo: Central Press Photos Ltd.)

THE CATHARSIS OF *KING LEAR*

BY

J. STAMPFER

The overriding critical problem in *King Lear* is that of its ending. The deaths of Lear and Cordelia confront us like a raw, fresh wound where our every instinct calls for healing and reconciliation. This problem, moreover, is as much one of philosophic order as of dramatic effect. In what sort of universe, we ask ourselves, can wasteful death follow suffering and torture? Nor is this concern an extrapolation from our own culture. It is, rather, implicit in Lear's own image, when he calls for tongues and eyes to howl 'That heaven's vault should crack' (v, iii, 259), and in his despairing question:

> Why should a dog, a horse, a rat, have life,
> And thou no breath at all? (v, iii, 306–7)

The problem becomes more overwhelming when we consider that, unlike the problems Shakespeare may have inherited with the plot of *Hamlet*, this tragic ending was imposed by Shakespeare on a story which, in its source, allowed Cordelia's forces to win the war. Moreover, the massive intrusion into *King Lear* of Christian elements of providence, depravity, and spiritual regeneration make it impossible to shunt aside the ending as a coincidence of its pre-Christian setting. The antiquity of setting may have had the irrelevant effect of releasing certain inhibitions in the playwright's mind; but the playgoers in Shakespeare's audience did not put on pagan minds to see the play. Rather, the constant references to retributive justice, perhaps greater here than in any other of Shakespeare's tragedies, make it an issue in a way that it is not in such 'pagan' plays as *Timon of Athens*, *Antony and Cleopatra*, and *Coriolanus*. Indeed, part of the poignance of *King Lear* lies in the fact that its issues, and the varieties of evil that it faces, are so central to Christianity, while it is denied any of the mitigation offered by a well-defined heaven and hell, and a formal doctrine of supernatural salvation.

The impression of unreconciled savagery and violence in the ending has been mitigated, in our generation, by a critical reading that would interpret Lear's last emotion as one of joy, even ecstasy, rather than one of unbearable agony. Bradley advances this reading, though hedged with a considerable qualification, in the following passage:

And, finally, though he is killed by an agony of pain, the agony in which he actually dies is not one of pain but of ecstasy. Suddenly, with a cry represented in the oldest text by a four-times repeated 'O', he exclaims:

> Do you see this? Look on her, look, her lips,
> Look there, look there!

These are the last words of Lear. He is sure, at last, that she *lives*: and what had he said when he was still in doubt?

> She lives! if it be so,
> It is a chance which doth redeem all sorrows
> That ever I have felt!

I

To us, perhaps, the knowledge that he is deceived may bring a culmination of pain: but, if it brings *only* that, I believe we are false to Shakespeare, and it seems almost beyond question that any actor is false to the text who does not attempt to express, in Lear's last accents and gestures and look, an unbearable *joy*.[1]

Some recent critics[2] have gone much further than Bradley in an attempt to build from Lear's momentary emotion at death a 'chance which doth redeem all sorrows', and make the play's ending a transfigured vision of attained salvation.

Before disputing the weight this penultimate moment in Lear's life can bear in counter-balancing all that precedes it, one must first consider whether the reading itself is defensible; for, in a sense, everything in the play hangs in the balance with Lear's death. If it is one of transfiguring joy, then one might, for all the enormous difficulties involved, affirm that a species of order is re-established. If not, however, then the impression is irresistible that in *King Lear* Shakespeare was confronting chaos itself, unmitigated, brutal, and utterly unresolved. The problems of justice and order, however interpreted, finally rest in the mystery of Lear's last moment, and not in the ambiguity of whether Edgar will or will not take over, by default, the throne of England. Like the news of Edmund's death, the problem of the succession is 'but a trifle' (v, iii, 295) alongside the supreme issue of whether any 'comfort' was applied by Shakespeare to the 'great decay' of Lear, as was evidently applied by him to the deaths of Hamlet and to a lesser extent Othello.

Bradley and those who follow him in this matter rest their case on the observation that Lear died persuaded that Cordelia still lived. He leaves unremarked, however, the fact that this illusion is not a new and sudden turn, but recurs three or four times in the last scene. It is, indeed, the main concern of Lear's first three speeches on re-entering the stage, before he goes temporarily out of his mind:

> She's gone for ever!
> I know when one is dead, and when one lives;
> She's dead as earth. Lend me a looking glass;
> If that her breath will mist or stain the stone,
> Why, then she lives. (v, iii, 259–63)

The tension here, and it is the underlying tension in Lear until his death, lies between an absolute knowledge that Cordelia is dead, and an absolute inability to accept it. Lear 'knows when one is dead, and when one lives'. His very faculties of reason and knowledge would be in question if he could not distinguish life from death. 'She's gone for ever...She's dead as earth', he repeats over and over. If he is to grasp reality in the face of madness, it is the reality of Cordelia's death that he must grasp. But this is the one reality that sears him whenever he attempts to grasp it, and so he tries, by the test of the looking glass, to prove that she lives, despite his emphatically underlined knowledge to the contrary.

Three brief speeches by Kent, Edgar and Albany intervene between this and Lear's next speech. One would guess that Lear is very active on stage at this point, possibly getting a looking glass, holding it up to Cordelia's lips, registering either momentary hope or immediate despair, then, when this test fails, snatching a feather and trying a second test. He would seem to be oblivious to all reality but Cordelia's body and his attempts to prove that she is alive. His second speech shows what is at stake in the effort:

> This feather stirs; she lives! If it be so,
> It is a chance which does redeem all sorrows
> That ever I have felt. (ll. 265–7)

This effort, too, fails, and Kent's painful attempt, on his knees, to wrest Lear's attention away from Cordelia only makes Lear momentarily turn on his companions with the savage outcry of 'murderers' and 'traitors' before trying again to prove her alive, this time by putting his ear to her lips in the thought that she might be speaking:

> A plague upon you, murderers, traitors all:
> I might have sav'd her; now she's gone for ever!
> Cordelia! Cordelia! stay a little. Ha!
> What is't thou say'st? Her voice was ever soft,
> Gentle, and low; an excellent thing in woman.
> I kill'd the slave that was a-hanging thee. (ll. 269–74)

His outcry, 'Ha!', like his cry 'This feather stirs', registers an illusion that Cordelia has spoken to him. This is a wilder self-deception than the thought that she has breathed, and remains with him beyond the end of the speech. His 'I kill'd the slave' is said almost lovingly and protectively to Cordelia's body, as if she heard him. Thus he struggles simultaneously for sanity and for the belief that Cordelia lives. Under the strain of these two irreconcilable psychic needs, his mind simply slips and relaxes into temporary madness:

> He knows not what he says; and vain is it
> That we present us to him. (ll. 293–4)

But agonized sanity breaks through Lear's madness once more, as the words of Kent, Albany and Edgar could not. Albany sees it rising, ominously convulsing Lear's features, and exclaims, 'O, see, see!' (l. 304) as Lear cries out:

> And my poor fool is hang'd! No, no, no life!
> Why should a dog, a horse, a rat, have life,
> And thou no breath at all? Thou'lt come no more,
> Never, never, never, never, never! (ll. 305–8)

The repeated cries of 'Never!' are the steady hammering of truth on a mind unable to endure it. Lear's life-blood rushes to his head. He chokes, and asks someone to undo the button of his collar (l. 309). Then, against the unendurable pressure of reality, the counterbalancing illusion that Cordelia lives rushes forth once more. Once again, it is at her lips, breathing or speaking, that he seeks life and dies:

> Do you see this? Look on her, look, her lips,
> Look there, look there! (*dies*) (ll. 310–11)

Who is to say, given this cycle of despair, insanity, and the illusion of hope, if it really matters at what point of the cycle Lear expires, or even if his last words establish it decisively? On the contrary, on purely aesthetic grounds, we have an indication from another point in Act v

3

that all of Lear's emotions have been gathering to an unendurable head at the moment of death. Gloucester, the counterpart to Lear in the subplot, was, like him, driven out by his false offspring, tormented in the storm, and finally preserved by a faithful, though rejected child. And Gloucester's death, which is described in considerable detail by Edgar, contains just such a welter of conflicting feelings as does Lear's, and might well be the model for understanding Lear's death:

> Never,—O fault!—reveal'd myself unto him,
> Until some half-hour past, when I was arm'd.
> Not sure, though hoping, of this good success,
> I ask'd his blessing, and from first to last
> Told him our pilgrimage; but his flaw'd heart,
> Alack, too weak the conflict to support!
> 'Twixt two extremes of passion, joy and grief,
> Burst smilingly.
>
> (v, iii, 192–9)

Gloucester's heart burst from its inability to contain two conflicting emotions, his psyche torn apart by a thunderclap of simultaneous joy and grief. And such, by aesthetic parallel, we may presume was the death of Lear, whose 'flaw'd heart', too, as is evident throughout the last scene, was

> Alack, too weak the conflict to support!

But the similarity only serves to accentuate the basic difference between the two deaths. Gloucester died between extremes of joy and grief, at the knowledge that his son was miraculously preserved, Lear between extremes of illusion and truth, ecstasy and the blackest despair, at the knowledge that his daughter was needlessly butchered. Gloucester's heart 'burst smilingly' at his reunion with Edgar; Lear's, we are driven to conclude, burst in the purest agony at his eternal separation from Cordelia.

There is, then, no mitigation in Lear's death, hence no mitigation in the ending of the play. On the contrary, either the play has no aesthetic unity, or everything in it, including Lear's spiritual regeneration, is instrumental to the explosive poignance of Lear's death. Nor can there be any blenching from the implications of Lear's last sane question:

> Why should a dog, a horse, a rat, have life,
> And thou no breath at all? Thou'lt come no more.
> Never, never, never, never, never!

It is only by giving Lear's death a fleeting, ecstatic joy that Bradley can read some sort of reconciliation into the ending, some renewed synthesis of cosmic goodness to follow an anti-thesis of pure evil. Without it, this is simply, as Lear recognized, a universe where dogs, horses, and rats live, and Cordelias are butchered. There may be mitigations in man himself, but none in the world which surrounds him. Indeed, unless Lear's death is a thoroughly anomalous postscript to his pilgrimage of life, the most organic view of the plot would make almost a test case of Lear, depicting, through his life and death, a universe in which even those who have fully repented, done penance, and risen to the tender regard of sainthood[3] can be hunted down, driven insane, and killed by the most agonizing extremes of passion.

The plot of *King Lear* is generally not read in this fashion. On the contrary, its denouement is generally interpreted as another 'turn of the screw', an added, and unnecessary, twist of horror to round out a play already sated with horrors. If it is defended, it is generally on grounds like those of Lamb,[4] who contended that it was a 'fair dismissal' from life after all Lear had suffered, or those of Bradley, that Lear's death is a transfiguration of joy to counterbalance all that has preceded it. Neither reading is satisfactory, Lamb's because it makes the ending, at best, an epilogue rather than a denouement to the main body of the action, Bradley's because the textual evidence points to the opposite interpretation of Lear's death. If Lear's spiritual regeneration, however, with the fearful penance he endures, is taken as the play's 'middle', and his death, despite that regeneration, as its denouement, then the catharsis of *King Lear*, Shakespeare's profoundest tragedy, has as yet escaped definition. This catharsis, grounded in the most universal elements of the human condition, can be formulated only when one has drawn together some of the relevant philosophical issues of the play.

Thus, the ending is decisive in resolving the plethora of attitudes presented in the play concerning the relationship between God and man. Set side by side, out of context, and unrelated to the denouement, these attitudes, and their religious frames of reference, can be made to appear an absolute chaos. Certainly almost every possible point of view on the gods and cosmic justice is expressed, from a malevolent, wanton polytheism (IV, i, 38–9) to an astrological determinism (IV, iii, 34–5), from an amoral, personified Nature-goddess (I, ii, 1) to 'high-judging Jove' (II, iv, 231). But the very multitude, concern, and contradictory character of these references do not cancel each other out, but rather show how precarious is the concept of cosmic justice. Surely if the play's ending is an ending, and cosmic justice has hung in the balance with such matters as Goneril's cruelty (IV, ii, 46–50), Gloucester's blinding (III, vii, 99–100), and Edmund's death (V, iii, 174), it collapses with Lear's ultimate question: 'Why should a dog, a horse, a rat, have life, / And thou no breath at all?' Despite the pagan setting, the problem of theodicy, the justification of God's way with man, is invoked by so many characters, and with such concern, that it emerges as a key issue in the play. As such, either the denouement vindicates it, or its integrity is universally destroyed. In point of fact, this is implied in the deaths of Lear and Cordelia.

The force of evil, perhaps the most dynamic element in the Christian tragedies, is extended to wide dimensions in *King Lear*, where two distinct modes of evil emerge, evil as animalism, in Goneril and Regan, and evil as doctrinaire atheism, in Edmund. These modes are not to be confused. Goneril, in particular, is, from the point of view of conscience, an animal or beast of prey. She and Regan never discuss doctrine, as does Edmund, or offer motives, as does Iago. Their actions have the immediacy of animals, to whom consideration never interposes between appetite and deed. It is in this spirit that Lear compares Goneril, in a single scene (I, iv), to a sea-monster, a detested kite, a serpent and a wolf, and Albany, in another (IV, ii), to a tiger, a bear, a monster of the deep, and a fiend, as though, through them, animalism were bursting through civil society.

Edmund, on the other hand, is a doctrinaire atheist, with regard not only to God, but also to the traditional, organic universe, a heterodoxy equally horrifying to the Elizabethans. This doctrinaire atheism involves an issue as basic in *King Lear* as that of a retributive justice, and that is the bond between man, society and nature. Here, there is no plethora of attitudes, but two positions, essentially, that of Cordelia, and that of Edmund. Cordelia's position is perhaps best expressed by Albany, after he learns of Goneril's treatment of Lear:

> That nature which contemns its origin
> Cannot be bordered certain in itself.
> She that herself will sliver and disbranch
> From her material sap, perforce must wither
> And come to desperate use. (IV, ii, 32–6)

According to Albany, an invisible bond of sympathy binds human beings like twigs to the branches of a tree. This bond is no vague universal principle, but closely rooted in one's immediate family and society. This is natural law in its most elemental possible sense, not a moral code, but almost a biochemical reaction. Hierarchical propriety is a necessity for life, like sunlight and water, its violation an act of suicide or perversion. It is Cordelia, in response to this law, who says firmly, 'I love your majesty? According to my bond; no more nor less' (I, i, 94–5). This bond, the central concept of the play, is the bond of nature, made up at once of propriety and charity.

In contrast to this concept of Nature is Edmund's soliloquy affirming his doctrinaire atheism (I, ii, 1–15), where natural law is summed up in two phrases, 'the plague of custom', and 'the curiosity of nations'. The bond of human relations, as understood by Cordelia and Albany, is a tissue of extraneous, artificial constraints. Edmund recognizes a hierarchy, but rather than growing out of society, this hierarchy goes wholly against its grain. This is the hierarchy of animal vitality, by which 'the lusty stealth of nature', even in the act of adultery, creates a more worthy issue than the 'dull, stale, tired bed' of marriage. And in response to Gloucester's superstitious references to the larger concept of the organic universe, Edmund repudiates any relationship between the 'orbs from whom we do exist' and his own destiny (I, ii, 139–45).

Strangely enough, however, while the denouement seems to destroy any basis for providential justice, it would seem to vindicate Cordelia with regard to the bond of human nature. Thus, the deaths of Cornwall, Goneril, and Regan are, as Albany prophesied, the swift and monstrous preying of humanity upon itself. Cornwall is killed by his own servant; Regan is poisoned by her sister; and Goneril finally commits suicide. Even more is Cordelia vindicated in Edmund, who is mortally wounded by his brother, and then goes through a complete, and to this reader, sincere repentance before his death. Critics have expressed bewilderment at Edmund's delay in attempting to save Lear and Cordelia. They do not, however, remark the significance of the point at which Edmund acts. For it is not until Goneril confesses the poisoning of Regan and commits suicide, thus persuading Edmund that he was loved, that he bestirs himself to save Lear and Cordelia if it is not too late. Intellectual assent is not sufficient. Only to those wholly caught up in the bond of love is charity possible:

> *Edm.* Yet Edmund was belov'd:
> The one the other poison'd for my sake,
> And after slew herself.
> *Alb.* Even so. Cover their faces.
> *Edm.* I pant for life. Some good I mean to do,
> Despite of mine own nature. (V, iii, 239–44)

Herein, however, lies a sardonic paradox; for Edmund deceived himself. He was the object of lust, but was not encompassed by love. Goneril slew Regan for his sake, but it was out of lust and ambition; she was incapable of that love which brings to self-transcendence, such as Cordelia's love of Lear, or his own act of 'good', in spite of his 'own nature'. And far from killing herself for Edmund's sake, she committed suicide, utterly alone, at the implicit threat of arrest for treason. Edmund, ever the doctrinaire logician, took false evidence of the bond of love at face value, and died as isolated as he lived. The two forms of evil in *King Lear* were ultimately opaque to one another.

But an even more sardonic paradox is implicit in Edmund's death. For Edmund, by abandoning his atheistic faith and acknowledging the power of love, accepts Cordelia's instinctual affirmation of natural law. But the denouement itself, with the gratuitous, harrowing deaths of Cordelia and Lear, controverts any justice in the universe. Chance kills, in despite of the maidenly stars. It would seem, then, by the denouement, that the universe belongs to Edmund, but mankind belongs to Cordelia. In a palsied cosmos, orphan man must either live by the moral law, which is the bond of love, or swiftly destroy himself. To this paradox, too, Shakespeare offers no mitigation in *King Lear*. The human condition is as inescapable as it is unendurable.

To so paradoxical an ending, what catharsis is possible? This question can be answered only by re-examining the structure of the plot. There can be observed, in *Hamlet*, a radical break from the mode of redemption in such earlier plays as *Romeo and Juliet*. In *Romeo and Juliet*, redemption comes when the tragic hero affirms the traditional frame of values of society, love, an appropriate marriage, peace, and the like, though society has, in practice, ceased to follow them. The result is to enhance the *sancta* of society by the sacrifice of life itself. In *Hamlet*, redemption only comes, finally, when the tragic hero spurns and transcends the *sancta* of society, and appeals to a religious mysticism into which human wisdom can have no entry, and in which, at most, 'the readiness is all'. The final result, however, is none the less the redemption of society and the reconciliation of the tragic hero to it; for Hamlet's last act is to cast a decisive vote for the next king of Denmark. Even *Othello*, domestic tragedy though it is, ends with the reconciliation of the tragic hero and society; and Othello's last act is an affirmation of loyalty to Venice and the execution of judgement upon himself. *King Lear* is Shakespeare's first tragedy in which the tragic hero dies unreconciled and indifferent to society.

The opening movement of *King Lear* is, then, not merely a physical exile from, but an abandonment of the formal *sancta* and institutions of society, which is pictured as even more bankrupt than in *Hamlet*. In *Hamlet*, only one man's deliberate crime corrupts the Danish state, 'mining all within'; in *King Lear*, animalism, atheism, brutal ambition, superstition, self-indulgence, and lethargy all contribute to society's decay. In this opening movement of abandonment, Lear is stripped of all that majesty and reverence clothing him in the opening scene, of kingdom, family, retainers, shelter, and finally reason and clothing themselves, until he comes, at the nadir of his fortunes, to 'the thing itself...a poor bare forked animal' (III, iv, 111–12). Romeo found his touchstone of truth against the rich texture of the Capulet feast, Lear in an abandoned and naked madman. Romeo and Juliet formed, from the first, an inviolate circle of innocence that was the fulfilment of their previous lives; Lear found no innocence until all his previous life had been stripped away from him.

In contrast to this movement of abandonment, and the basis of the second, counter-movement, stands not, as in *Hamlet*, religious mysticism, but an elemental bond that we can, in this play, indifferently call charity or natural law, one that binds man to man, child to parent, husband to wife, and servant to master almost by a biological impulsion. From first to last, charity is discovered, not as the crown of power and earthly blessing, but in their despite. This theme is enunciated by France in taking Cordelia for his wife:

> Fairest Cordelia, that art most rich being poor,
> Most choice forsaken, and most lov'd despis'd!
> Thee and thy virtues here I seize upon,
> Be it lawful I take up what's cast away.
> Gods, gods! 'tis strange that from their cold'st neglect
> My love should kindle to inflam'd respect. (I, i, 253-8)

The same affirmation is made by Kent, in entering the impoverished Lear's service:

> *Lear.* If thou be'st as poor for a subject as he's for a king, thou art poor
> enough. What wouldst thou?
> *Kent.* Service.
> *Lear.* Who wouldst thou serve?
> *Kent.* You.
> *Lear.* Dost thou know me, fellow?
> *Kent.* No, sir; but you have that in your countenance which I would fain
> call master.
> *Lear.* What's that?
> *Kent.* Authority. (I, iv, 22-32)

Indeed, organized society dulls people to an awareness of charity, so that it is only in Lear's abandonment that he becomes bound to all men:

> Poor naked wretches, wheresoe'er you are,
> That bide the pelting of this pitiless storm,
> How shall your houseless heads and unfed sides,
> Your loop'd and window'd raggedness, defend you
> From seasons such as these? O, I have ta'en
> Too little care of this! Take physic, pomp;
> Expose thyself to what these wretches feel,
> That thou may'st shake the superflux to them,
> And show the heavens more just. (III, iv, 28-36)

Shakespeare could, of course, have used this more elemental level of charity or natural law as he used the force of love in *Romeo and Juliet*, to redeem and renew society. Had he chosen to do so, it would have become politically effective in Cordelia's invading army, overwhelmed the corrupt elements then in power, and restored the throne to Lear, as is suggested in Shakespeare's conventionally pious source. But society, in Shakespeare, is now no longer capable of self-renewal. And so the counter-movement of the play, the reclothing of Lear, by charity and natural law, with majesty, sanity, family and shelter, after the most terrible of penances, does not close the play. At its close, the completion only of its dramatic 'middle', Lear is utterly purged of soul, while the hierarchy of society is reduced, as at the end of *Hamlet*, to an equation of 'court news' with 'gilded butterflies' (v, iii, 13–14). At this point, if the universe of the play contained a transcendent providence, it should act as in the closing movement of *Hamlet*, mysteriously to redeem a society unable to redeem itself.

Shakespeare's pessimism, however, has deepened since *Hamlet*, and the deaths to no purpose of Lear and Cordelia controvert any providential redemption in the play's decisive, closing movement, so that another resolution entirely is called for. Narrowing our problem somewhat, the catharsis of any play lies in the relationship of the denouement to the expectations set up in the play's 'middle'. In *King Lear*, this middle movement has to do primarily with Lear's spiritual regeneration after his 'stripping' in the opening movement of the play. These two movements can be subsumed in a single great cycle, from hauteur and spiritual blindness through purgative suffering to humility and spiritual vision, a cycle that reaches its culmination in Lear's address of consolation to Cordelia before they are taken off to prison (v, iii, 9–17). The catharsis of *King Lear* would seem to lie, then, in the challenge of Lear's subsequent death to the penance and spiritual transcendence that culminates the play's second movement. This challenge can be described as follows:—

All men, in all societies, make, as it were, a covenant with society in their earliest infancy. By this covenant, the dawning human consciousness accepts society's deepest ordinances, beliefs, and moral standards in exchange for a promise of whatever rewards and blessings society offers. The notion of intelligible reward and punishment, whether formulated as a theological doctrine and called retributive justice or as a psychological doctrine and called the reality principle, is as basic to human nature as the passions themselves. But given the contingency of human life, that covenant is constantly broken by corruption within and without. A man's life and that of his family are at all times hostages of his limited wisdom, his tainted morality, the wayward-ness of chance, and the decay of institutions. Indeed, social ritual, whether religious in character, like confession or periodic fasting, or secular, like the ceremonial convening of a legislature, is an attempt to strengthen the bond of a covenant inevitably weakened by the attrition of evil and the brute passage of time. These are all, in a sense, acts of penance, that is, acts whose deepest intent is to purge us of guilt and the fear of being abandoned, to refresh our bond with one another and with our private and collective destiny.

Lear, at the beginning of the play, embodies all that man looks forward to in a world in which, ultimately, nothing is secure. He has vocation, age, wealth, monarchy, family, personal fol-lowers and long experience. Like Oedipus and Othello, he would have seemed to have attained, before the play begins, what men strive for with indifferent success all their lives. In this sense, Lear engages our sympathies as an archetype of mankind. And just as Othello discovers areas of experience which he never cultivated and which destroy him, Lear discovers that even in those areas he most cultivated he has nothing. Thus, like Oedipus and more than Othello, Lear activates the latent anxiety at the core of the human condition, the fear not only of unexpected catastrophe but that even what seems like success may be a delusion, masking corruption, crime and almost consummated failure.

This opening movement, however, leads not to dissolution, exposure and self-recognition, as in *Oedipus* and *Othello*, but to purgation. And Lear's purgation, by the end of the play's middle movement, like his gifts and his vulnerability at its start, is so complete as to be archetypal. By the time he enters prison, he has paid every price and been stripped of everything a man can lose, even his sanity, in payment for folly and pride. He stands beyond the veil of fire, momentarily serene and alive. As such he activates an even profounder fear than the fear of failure, and that is the fear that whatever penance a man may pay may not be enough once the machinery of destruction has been let loose, because the partner of his covenant may be neither grace nor the balance of law, but malignity, intransigence or chaos.

The final, penultimate tragedy of Lear, then, is not the tragedy of *hubris*, but the tragedy of penance. When Lear, the archetype not of a proud, but of a penitential man, brutally dies, then the uttermost that can happen to man has happened. One can rationalize a passing pedestrian struck down by a random automobile; there is no blenching from this death. Each audience harbours this anxiety in moments of guilt and in acts of penance. And with Lear's death, each audience, by the ritual of the drama, shares and releases the most private and constricting fear to which mankind is subject, the fear that penance is impossible, that the covenant, once broken, can never be re-established, because its partner has no charity, resilience, or harmony—the fear, in other words, that we inhabit an imbecile universe. It is by this vision of reality that Lear lays down his life for his folly. Within its bounds lies the catharsis of Shakespeare's profoundest tragedy.

NOTES

1. A. C. Bradley, *Shakespearean Tragedy* (1924), p. 291.

2. Harold S. Wilson, *On the Design of Shakespearean Tragedy* (Toronto, 1957), p. 204; Geoffrey Bush, *Shakespeare and the Natural Condition* (Cambridge, Mass., 1956), p. 128.

3. L. L. Schücking, in his *Character Problems in Shakespeare's Plays* (New York, 1922), p. 186, cites most, though not all the evidence that can be offered to document a spiritual regeneration in Lear, only to deny it any validity in the play because, by the comparative method, he finds no similar concern elsewhere in Shakespeare for *charitas*, or social justice. Aside from a number of relevant passages that leap to mind from other plays, the most striking parallel is in *King Lear*, itself, where Gloucester, Lear's counterpart in the subplot, makes a speech similar to Lear's prayer, though not as profound, on the poor and the wretched (IV, i, 67–74). Whatever may or may not be true in other plays, charity is apparently a prime consideration in *King Lear*; and, if so, Lear's regeneration in charity is, by Schücking's own evidence, part of the play's aesthetic movement.

4. New Variorum edition of *King Lear* (Philadelphia, 1880), p. 421.

LEAR'S LAST SPEECH

BY

J. K. WALTON

The suggestion that Lear dies from an unbearable joy induced by the belief that Cordelia is alive was first put forward by A. C. Bradley,[1] and has been adopted by some subsequent critics.[2] It deserves perhaps a fuller consideration than it is usually given.[3] The point, after all, is not a small one. If he dies from joy thinking that Cordelia still lives he dies, unlike all other tragic heroes, not aware that any tragedy has taken place, for the other deaths are not to be thought of as tragic. Nor is the problem one which can be considered independently of an interpretation of the play as a whole. The question of Lear's final consciousness is clearly part of the larger question of the interpretation to be given to the general theme of ignorance and knowledge which has an important role throughout the drama. I hope to show that an analysis of the various stages and forms which this theme takes helps in the interpretation of Lear's last speech.

A recurring situation throughout the play is that of a belief, assumption, or hope which is quickly shown to be false by the impact of events. Lear is at first repeatedly made to acquire knowledge in this manner, and since he rejects the advice of Kent, it is the sole means by which he is able to learn. The process by which he acquires knowledge—his treatment by Goneril, his discovery that fifty of his followers have been dismissed, his finding Kent in the stocks, and his reception by Regan—is brought into all the clearer focus since at this stage he is alone in learning by this method. It is only later, from near the end of Act III onwards, that other characters are subjected to a similar process. We should, however, remember that while in the first two acts Lear is suffering continuously, he is not a passive character in a physical sense. To a considerable extent he has physically the initiative. He gives away his kingdom, rejects Cordelia, and banishes Kent. He could, if he wished, have submitted to Goneril's demands, but instead he chooses to go to Regan. His decision to go into the storm is his own; here again he could have capitulated. Nor is he passive in the storm. He contends 'with the fretful elements', and 'Strives in his little world of man to out-storm / The to-and-fro-conflicting wind and rain' (III, i, 4 ff.). But during the storm the nature of his initiative changes. Hitherto his initiative has consisted in various deeds. His mind, at least in its acquisition of knowledge, has been more acted upon than acting. During the storm he loses initiative so far as action is concerned, but his mind ceases to be passive in regard to learning. The active role of his mind, which with an awakened imaginative sympathy now begins to generalize his own experience, is first displayed[4] when he shows pity for the Fool (III, ii, 68), and declares that

> The art of our necessities is strange,
> And can make vile things precious.[5]   (III, ii, 70-1)

Formerly his utterances (apart from his talk with the Fool) have consisted mainly of orders, denunciations of others, or appeals to the heavens.

From now on Lear's capacity to acquire knowledge goes together with an ability to perceive the sufferings of others. The prayer 'Poor naked wretches...' (III, iv, 28 ff.), which he utters on his next appearance, is based on his recognition of the existence of 'houseless heads and unfed sides', with their 'loop'd and window'd raggedness', of which earlier he has taken 'Too little care'. The arrival of Edgar disguised as mad Tom—which is the last of the blows which Lear is to receive in the first stage of his education and that which causes him on one level to lose his sanity—is also the one which decisively sets his mind on its quest of knowledge. Henceforth he progresses not only from having knowledge inflicted on him to a capacity for summing up the implications of his experience; he also actively seeks knowledge out by the use of 'reason in madness'. He sees Edgar as the image of truth—'unaccommodated man is no more but such a poor, bare, forked animal as thou art' (III, iv, 109–11)—and proceeds to tear off his own clothes in an action expressive of his desire to find reality. His quest for truth is carried further by his questionings of Edgar, who from being the image of truth has now become its source:

> First let me talk with this philosopher.
> What is the cause of thunder? (III, iv, 158–9)

and he declares that 'I'll talk a word with this same learned Theban' (l. 161), and 'I will keep still with my philosopher' (l. 180).

The 'trial' of Goneril and Regan, which takes place when Lear next appears (III, vi), represents an extension of his newly acquired attitude of mind. He is no longer content merely to denounce; he wants an investigation into the matter which will weigh the evidence and judicially establish its finding. But the justice which he imagines does not work. Goneril, whom he has arraigned, escapes and he perceives corruption in the 'False justicer'. He continues the inquisition with a medical rather than a judicial image in his mind. Almost his last words in the storm scenes are, 'let them anatomize Regan, see what breeds about her heart. Is there any cause in nature that makes these hard hearts?' (III, vi, 80–81).

Lear's search for knowledge has not yet been able to achieve a resolution. In the account of him which Kent is given in IV, iii, we hear that the condition of his mind prevents him from meeting Cordelia:

> A sovereign shame so elbows him: his own unkindness,
> That stripp'd her from his benediction, turn'd her
> To foreign casualties, gave her dear rights
> To his dog-hearted daughters, these things sting
> His mind so venomously that burning shame
> Detains him from Cordelia. (IV, iii, 43–8)

The next development of Lear's capacity for acquiring knowledge occurs when he meets Gloucester (IV, vi). The last time we saw Lear he had attempted to obtain justice, but he had sensed its inadequacy. In this scene he is able to proceed to an analysis of justice and authority which includes in its scope his own exercise of them in the initial action of the play. He can now summarize all that he has already learned, and develop his knowledge still further. His mind is recalled to what he once was, in fact as well as in name, by Gloucester's 'Is't not the King?' (l. 110). Lear's imagination is now able to comprehend both the authority he had as King and the knowledge which he has gained by his decision to abandon that authority. His full expres-

sion of this knowledge does not come at once. The way is, however, prepared for it by his
answer to Gloucester:

> Ay, every inch a king:
> When I do stare, see how the subject quakes.
> I pardon that man's life. What was thy cause?
> Adultery?
> Thou shalt not die: die for adultery! No:
> The wren goes to't, and the small gilded fly
> Does lecher in my sight. (IV, vi, 110–16)

The thought is already present, if only as yet indirectly expressed, that none offends because
everyone offends, especially those who are most ostentatious in their virtue ('yond simp'ring
dame'). What generates Lear's final development of the knowledge he has gained is, appropriately, the continued presence of Gloucester who, on a lower level, has had an experience
similar to his own.[6] Prompted by Gloucester's physical blindness—'A man may see how this
world goes with no eyes' (ll. 151–2)—Lear makes his culminating analysis of the reality that
underlies the appearance of things:

> Look with thine ears: see how yond justice rails upon yond simple thief. Hark, in thine
> ear: change places, and, handy-dandy, which is the justice, which is the thief? Thou hast
> seen a farmer's dog bark at a beggar?
> *Glou.* Ay, Sir.
> *Lear.* And the creature run from the cur? There thou might'st behold
> The great image of Authority:
> A dog's obey'd in office.
> Thou rascal beadle, hold thy bloody hand!
> Why dost thou lash that whore? Strip thine own back;
> Thou hotly lusts to use her in that kind
> For which thou whipp'st her. The usurer hangs the cozener.
> Thorough tatter'd clothes small vices do appear;
> Robes and furr'd gowns hide all. Plate sin with gold,
> And the strong lance of justice hurtless breaks;
> Arm it in rags, a pigmy's straw does pierce it.
> None does offend, none, I say, none; I'll able 'em:
> Take that of me, my friend, who have the power
> To seal th'accuser's lips. (IV, vi, 152–72)

The conclusion is that there can be no real justice in a society where inequality of conditions
exists. Lear himself had been a victim even while he had exercised authority. He has earlier
told how he was blinded by flattery—'They flattered me like a dog...they told me I was
every thing'—and how he did not find them out until 'the thunder would not peace at my
bidding' (ll. 97 ff.). The conclusion 'None does offend, none, I say, none' follows from his newly
won knowledge. He ceases to demand that justice be executed on Goneril and Regan. He is
now ready to be freed from the conflict in his mind which arises from the co-existence of a desire

for punishment for those who have injured him and a feeling that he himself is guilty. This is not to say that when his meeting with Cordelia takes place he does not feel guilty. He is 'bound / Upon a wheel of fire' (IV, vii, 46–7), and he tells her 'If you have poison for me, I will drink it' (l. 72). But his mind is now in a condition in which he is capable of receiving her forgiveness. The sleep from which he wakes is the immediate cause of his restored sanity, but we impoverish the play if we see him on regaining his wits as merely enfeebled by what he has been through. He describes himself, admittedly, as 'a very foolish fond old man' (l. 60), but it is a necessary part of his present greatness that he should be able to see himself in this light. His simplicity is the result not so much of weakness as of the resolution of tension which he himself, through his pursuit of knowledge, has achieved. His thought has been raised to a higher level by his struggles, a level which includes, unalloyed with madness, the knowledge he has gained.

Lear's newly developed strength is shown as soon as he is once more exposed to adversity. When he and Cordelia are captured, she asks 'Shall we not see these daughters and these sisters?', and he replies:

> No, no, no, no! Come, let's away to prison;
> We two alone will sing like birds i' th' cage:
> When thou dost ask me blessing, I'll kneel down,
> And ask of thee forgiveness: so we'll live,
> And pray, and sing, and tell old tales, and laugh
> At gilded butterflies, and hear poor rogues
> Talk of court news; and we'll talk with them too,
> Who loses and who wins; who's in, who's out;
> And take upon's the mystery of things,
> As if we were Gods' spies: and we'll wear out,
> In a wall'd prison, packs and sects of great ones
> That ebb and flow by th'moon.   (V, iii, 8–19)

We must not, like Bradley,[7] think of this speech as showing Lear's pathetic blindness to his position now that he and Cordelia are prisoners, and as an actual plan, soon to be rendered impossible, of how he is to spend the remainder of his old age. That he is not speaking literally is shown by the declaration that 'we'll wear out, / In a wall'd prison, packs and sects of great ones / That ebb and flow by th'moon'. Lear has always been conscious of his age, and he can hardly be here taken as actually expecting a further long lease of life. His mind is now raised far above the immediate events by which he is assailed, because of the knowledge he has acquired, a knowledge that enables him to evaluate the 'packs and sects of great ones' at their true worth. What unites him for ever to Cordelia is their active interest in truth: they will 'take upon's the mystery of things, / As if we were Gods' spies'. The difference between the old and the new Lear is further emphasized in his next speech when he says, 'The good years shall devour them, flesh and fell, / Ere they shall make us weep' (ll. 24–5). These words recall his blustering threats to Goneril just before he goes into the storm, when he speaks of the terrors he shall inflict on her before he will weep (II, iv, 280 ff.). Here, however, he is not making an empty threat but a prophecy, for when he does next weep Goneril and Regan are in fact both dead.[8]

We have seen how, until a change takes place in the storm, Lear has been forced to acquire knowledge through the impact of events, and how during this period he is alone in so acquiring it. But at the same time as Lear is changing from one on whom knowledge is inflicted to one who seeks it out, other characters begin to have to learn in the way he had to learn, by being subjected to sudden blows which destroy their illusions and hopes. The first to undergo this form of education is Cornwall and, ironically, the lesson is administered by one of the humble, a recognition of whose existence has been the earliest sign of Lear's awakened and now active mind. When the servant takes Cornwall to task for blinding Gloucester, he exclaims incredulously 'My villain!' (III, vii, 77), and he is echoed by Regan's 'A peasant stand up thus!' (l. 79). For Cornwall 'Untimely comes this hurt' (l. 97). It is almost immediately after Cornwall has been attacked that Gloucester learns from Regan that it was Edmund who betrayed him. An experience similar to Cornwall's awaits Oswald when he jubilantly exclaims on seeing Gloucester,

> Most happy!
> That eyeless head of thine was first fram'd flesh
> To raise my fortunes. (IV, vi, 227–9)

He too is incredulous at being withstood by one of apparently base degree ('Slave, thou hast slain me'), and dies exclaiming 'O! untimely death' (l. 252).

Like Cornwall and Oswald, the other evil characters experience a swift overtaking by events. Regan is struck untimely down by her sister's poison just when she hopes to gain Edmund. Goneril herself displays, by the inadequacy of her remark on Edmund's overthrow ('thou art not vanquish'd, / But cozen'd and beguil'd'), an incredulous refusal to face the fact of his defeat, which is also her own. With Edmund the acquisition of knowledge is more complex—appropriately, since he is the most intelligent of the evil characters—but in his case also its acquisition proceeds only step by step with events. He does not reveal, any more than the others, an active power to acquire it. When he realizes that he is dying he echoes Edgar's

> The Gods are just, and of our pleasant vices
> Make instruments to plague us;
> The dark and vicious place where thee he got
> Cost him his eyes. (v, iii, 170–3)

with

> Th'hast spoken right, 'tis true.
> The wheel is come full circle; I am here.

Edgar then goes on to give his account of how he has looked after their father, Gloucester, and describes his death. Edmund tells him that

> This speech of yours hath mov'd me,
> And shall perchance do good; but speak you on;
> You look as you had something more to say. (ll. 199–201)

Here, clearly, Edmund is toying with the idea of revealing that he has ordered the deaths of Lear and Cordelia; his human feeling is aroused by hearing how Edgar has looked after their father. But Edmund is not able to learn mercy merely by word or reason. In order to bring

15

him to act mercifully an act is necessary; and this consists in the bringing in of the bodies of Goneril and Regan.⁹ This makes him realize

> Yet Edmund was belov'd:
> The one the other poison'd for my sake,
> And after slew herself. (ll. 239–41)

The actual presence of the dead bodies, by bringing home to him that he was after all 'belov'd', gives him the good will which makes him, but only when it is too late, try to perform his good deed.

> I pant for life; some good I mean to do
> Despite of mine own nature. Quickly send,
> Be brief in it, to th'castle; for my writ
> Is on the life of Lear and on Cordelia.
> Nay, send in time. (ll. 243–7)

Edmund's delay, which has caused so much puzzlement, can thus be seen as part of the theme of the acquisition of knowledge.

But in the latter part of the play the evil characters are not alone in being instructed by the impact of events. So also are the good, the difference being that the events which cause an extension of their consciousness are provided by Lear and Gloucester themselves. Here the role of Lear, and to a lesser extent of Gloucester, changes into its opposite. From being the recipients of knowledge they come eventually, by their appearance at dramatically important points, to instruct others. Thus Edgar is congratulating himself that 'The lamentable change is from the best; / The worst returns to laughter' (IV, i, 5–6) when he sees the blinded Gloucester, and learns that 'the worst is not / So long as we can say "This is the worst"' (ll. 27–8). Edgar's later comment on witnessing the scene between Gloucester and Lear—'I would not take this from report; it is, / And my heart breaks at it' (IV, vi, 142–3)—explicitly affirms that the knowledge which it conveys is only to be acquired from direct experience.

The final appearance of Lear represents a further development of this change of roles. Earlier in the play his appeals to the heavens have, as a part of his tragic initiation, met with 'the sternest of replies'.¹⁰ At the end Albany, on hearing of the danger to Cordelia, exclaims 'The gods defend her!', and his prayer is at once answered by the entry of 'Lear, *with* Cordelia *dead in his arms*'. Lear from being the instructed has become the instructor, causing Kent to liken the scene to the Last Judgment (l. 263). Far from trying to delude himself, Lear emphasizes the fact that Cordelia is dead:

> She's gone for ever.
> I know when one is dead, and when one lives;
> She's dead as earth. (ll. 259–61)

He tries, however, to find out, by objective evidence, whether there is a chance that she is still alive ('Lend me a looking-glass'), and seeing the movement of a feather thinks for a moment that she may have survived, but soon perceives that she is indeed 'gone for ever' (l. 270). He once more wonders momentarily if she lives—'Ha! / What is't thou say'st?'—but he receives no answer. His last appearance in the role of instructor occurs when Albany declares that a just settlement is to be established:

> All friends shall taste
> The wages of their virtue, and all foes
> The cup of their deservings. (ll. 302–4)

An ending of this kind may be adequate for, say, *Macbeth* (the ending of which it indeed resembles), but for this play it will not do. It is Lear himself who in his last speech and death demonstrates its inadequacy, so that Albany comes to realize that 'Our present business / Is general woe' (ll. 318–19):

> And my poor fool is hang'd! No, no, no life!
> Why should a dog, a horse, a rat, have life,
> And thou no breath at all? Thou'lt come no more,
> Never, never, never, never, never!
> Pray you, undo this button: thank you, Sir.
> Do you see this? Look on her, look, her lips,
> Look there, look there! (ll. 305–11)

If we take it that Lear finally believes that Cordelia is alive, we alter the direction of the whole movement which has been taking place throughout the play, a movement by which he attains to an ever greater consciousness and eventually becomes the agent who brings about an enlargement of the consciousness of others; and we are also guilty of confusing together Lear and the evil characters, for it is especially they who remain incapable of adequately assessing events. There is, in fact, nothing in his speech from the five-times repeated 'Never' to his last words 'look there!', which indicates a transition from grief to joy. Bradley thought that there was a cry 'represented in the oldest text by a four-times repeated "O"',[11] but since it occurs only in the Quarto it is presumably an actor's interpolation,[12] a fact of which Bradley in the then existing state of textual studies could not be expected to be aware. Cordelia's lips might, by a change in colour, give a sign of death but hardly one of life; and it is appropriate that Lear's attention should be finally concentrated on her organ of speech. As at the beginning of the play she says nothing, but this time Lear dies with the effort of realizing to the full the implications of her silence. That, and not merely despair, brings about his death. The extent of his consciousness, as well as of his sufferings, is emphasized in the concluding speech:[13]

> The oldest hath borne most: we that are young
> Shall never see so much, nor live so long.

We should remember that Bradley's interpretation of Lear's last speech finds its logical development in the view proposed by William Empson, who regards Lear in the last scene as mad again, and as, finally, the eternal fool and scapegoat who has experienced everything and learned nothing.[14] This is an interpretation which makes it difficult to regard *King Lear* as a tragedy at all. Moreover, it is only by bearing in mind the active role of Lear's progress towards knowledge that we can see the later part of the play as having a convincing dramatic form. D. G. James, who interprets the whole drama as a process of discovery not so much by Lear as by Shakespeare himself, follows Granville-Barker in thinking that in the last two acts the best things 'will be incidental and not germane to the actual story'.[15] If we see the active and central role as residing elsewhere than in Lear, the last two acts are indeed dramatically unconvincing, with the main emphasis on Edgar as a fighting man and Cordelia as the leader of an army. James remarks that 'the souls of Cordelia and Edgar are not in the stage figures who in battle and combat thus serve the purposes of a plot which a dramatist has to get on with and bring to a conclusion'.[16] But Cordelia and Edgar appear unreal only if we see the active roles they are given as occupying the centre of the dramatic movement. With the main interest concentrated on the development of Lear, the presentation of Edgar as a fighting man and Cordelia as the leader of an army does not have to be any less perfunctory than it actually is; and 'the soul of the play and the body of the plot' do not, as James suggests,[17] fall apart.

NOTES

1. In *Shakespearean Tragedy* (1904; ed. 1905), p. 291.

2. It has, for example, been accepted by H. Granville-Barker, *Prefaces to Shakespeare: First Series* (1927), p. 185, n. 1; R. W. Chambers, 'King Lear', *W. P. Ker Memorial Lecture* (1939; Glasgow, 1940), pp. 44 ff.; William Empson, *The Structure of Complex Words* (1951), pp. 151 ff.; Kenneth Muir, The New Arden ed. (1952), p. lix.

3. In three recent extensive studies of *King Lear*—see R. B. Heilman, *This Great Stage* (Louisiana State University Press, 1948); J. F. Danby, *Shakespeare's Doctrine of Nature* (1949); D. G. James, *The Dream of Learning* (Oxford, 1951) —the suggestion is not discussed at all. Heilman (p. 54) remarks non-committally that Lear 'strains frantically, possibly convinced that he does see life'. Danby merely observes (p. 195) that Lear in the last scene is 'mad again'. James does not refer to Bradley's suggestion.

4. Already, just before going out into the storm, Lear replies to Regan's 'What need one?' with

      O! reason not the need; our basest beggars
      Are in the poorest thing superfluous: (II, iv, 266–7)

but while this may to some extent announce his later capacity for generalizing his experiences, here the generalization is merely part of the argument with which he attacks Regan.

5. Quotations are from *King Lear*, ed. K. Muir.

6. One indication of Gloucester's lesser stature is that he has to be helped in his acquisition of knowledge by Edgar, whereas Lear learns essentially through his own efforts. The comments of the Fool, though illuminating, only emphasize those things which Lear already suspects. These comments in no way represent an equivalent to Edgar's guidance of Gloucester.

7. *Shakespearean Tragedy*, p. 290.

8. See Muir, ed. cit. p. 201. In a sense Lear's words in II, iv, 286–8 ('this heart / Shall break into a hundred thousand flaws / Or ere I'll weep') are also true—he does go mad rather than weep and capitulate—but in the context these words are associated with his empty threats of revenge.

9. It is true that Albany has already (l. 237) asked Edmund where Lear and Cordelia are, but the dying Edmund need not have answered, and it is only after the speeches in ll. 239–42 that he gives the necessary information. Moreover, it is clear from the speech, quoted below, in which he tells of their danger that he is now genuinely anxious that the reprieve should reach them in time.

10. The phrase used by Bradley, *Shakespearean Tragedy*, p. 274.

11. *Ibid.* p. 291.

12. See *King Lear*, ed. G. I. Duthie (Oxford, 1949), p. 44. The four-times repeated 'O' occurs after 'thank you, Sir' (l. 309). Far from representing a transition to Lear's last words the 'O's are meant to be his dying groans; they, in fact, take the place of his last words (ll. 310–11) which are found only in the Folio. It is these last words in ll. 310–11 which Bradley thinks express the ecstasy of joy from which Lear dies. If the Quarto version gives anything approximating to the stage presentation of his death, he clearly cannot have been presented as dying from joy rather than grief.

13. In the Folio the last speech is given, correctly, to Edgar; in the Quarto it is given to Albany.

14. See *The Structure of Complex Words*, pp. 151 ff. Empson, referring to Lear's 'And my poor fool is hang'd!', suggests (p. 152) that 'Lear is now thrown back into something like the storm phase of his madness, the effect of immediate shock, and the Fool seems to him part of it'. But 'fool' was a term of endearment (see *O.E.D.* 'Fool', sb.¹, 1 c), and even if we think that there is an association in Lear's mind between the Fool and Cordelia, the connection is natural, for the Fool like Cordelia has the merit of speaking the truth. Lear's earlier remoteness, after his entry with Cordelia dead in his arms, from what is taking place around him is the result of his new-found union with her. His sense of this union has been given expression in his 'Come, let's away to prison' speech, and makes all the greater his concentration on the fact of her death.

15. See *The Dream of Learning*, p. 112.

16. *Ibid.* p. 113.

17. *Ibid.* p. 112. Bradley himself, since he sees Lear as essentially passive, is driven to the unsatisfactory conclusion that 'it is impossible...from the point of view of construction, to regard the hero as the leading figure' (*op. cit.* p. 53). From the viewpoint of construction he thus regards Goneril, Regan and Edmund as the leading characters. This suggests that there is in *King Lear* a serious discrepancy between form and content.

ALBANY

BY

LEO KIRSCHBAUM

Many regard themselves, and want us to regard them, as professional on the subject of that species of drama conveniently covered by the term 'tragedy'. Listen, they say, and we shall tell you what *Agamemnon* or *Othello* is about. But it is my view that the actual spiritual economics of a particular tragedy is not easy to apprehend or to grasp. Is there gain or loss in *Macbeth*? Gain in what, loss in what? Because we are what we are, pain and death are focal, and we cannot help recalling *King Lear* as the blinding of Gloucester and the death of Cordelia, as though these had constituted the totality of our reactions to the play. But we also sometimes remember that always at the end of every Shakespeare tragedy there is a kind of recovery. The least emotional reaction we have had, then, *at that moment*, is that the preceding events *were* terrible but they are *now* over. However, I have always felt that this is too simple, not completely true to our experience of the tragedy. Our final ease in the theatre or in the armchair (I think we all have it, to a greater or lesser degree), is due to some realization, conscious in a greater or lesser degree, that *all* that has happened in the drama we have just witnessed or read was not depressing. Sometimes it is the spiritual growth of the protagonist or an enemy—Macbeth or Macduff— that we sense or acknowledge. Sometimes it is the ineluctable surprise that evil seems productive of good, that the worse the degradation of humanity on the stage, the greater the consequent exaltation. Shockingly, blood and pain and death and betrayal appear to be the dung that makes the flower grow. How great Emilia is in the last act of *Othello*! But she would have remained a menial, the play seems to say, had no destruction occurred. Watch her as she develops stature, depth, complexity, courage: she becomes more real, more fine, as the scenes break and darken around her. Therefore I ask: Does anyone dare to say that Emilia's final apotheosis is not worth Desdemona's death?—Or that Albany's growth from nonentity to greatness in *King Lear* is not worth Gloucester's eyes? I hope I am not so stupid as to give an answer to these impossible questions. I am merely demanding that before you come to absolute convictions about Shakespeare's tragic macrocosm you stare sufficiently long at the coarse fingers and the coarse balances you are employing.

I think the lack of comment on Albany in discussions of *King Lear* is probably due to the complexity of the play. Yet he bulks so large finally in the plot that what he is and what he signifies cannot safely be disregarded. But Shakespeare has deliberately made our progressive knowledge of him difficult. As with Emilia, we do not at first know with Albany whether we are witnessing a weak character or a lightly sketched characterization, which the dramatist will not deepen till it suits his purpose. That is, because he appears for so long to possess no colour at all, we do not definitely know till the fourth act where to put Goneril's husband— whether among the black characters (Goneril, Regan, Cornwall, etc.) or among the white or relatively white (Kent, Lear, Gloucester, etc.). But if in order to see the operation of the whole drama better, we temporarily disengage a part of the design to study it more closely, we shall see that Albany was meant by Shakespeare to be observed carefully. Such observation may be both simple and not simple. We can be satisfied merely with observing him when he appears. Or we can constantly, never for a moment, forget that he is Cornwall's counterpart. (The grouping and splitting of groups are important devices in the dramatic technique of *King Lear*.) We start with two bad daughters, Goneril and Regan. We start, in this first scene, with their two wholly unportrayed husbands. Relatively soon, we discover what Cornwall is. Concerning him and Regan we feel as we feel concerning him and Edmund, that evil innately chooses evil, that it likes it and prefers it. But what about his counterpart, Albany? Is he choosing Goneril's viciousness? being demolished by it? or sitting on a fence while the new scythe sweeps its way? Because he is a prominent but not immediately perceivable part of the play's architecture, because Shakespeare at first purposefully makes him two-dimensional (if one-dimensional would not be a better word for his weak impression), because at times the play appears to utilize him (that is, he does apparently what the play requires, not what he as a character might choose), Albany is by no means the easiest to write about of the imitations of human beings in *King Lear*.

Albany is mentioned in the first line of the play, which actually poses the problem of his qualities versus Cornwall's. Gloucester tells Kent that Lear seems to be still pondering which of the two dukes is preferable. But although the play begins with this question, although the first scene defines the daughters, defines the king, defines Kent, France and Burgundy, it does not tell us anything conclusive about the two dukes. The scene does suggest that Albany and Cornwall must have or should have moral and psychological problems arising from the nature of the strong, forceful, bad woman to whom each is married. Is the moral grouping to be Goneril-Regan, as it is? Or Goneril-Albany plus Regan-Cornwall? Or what? It is dramatically significant that the dukes share one line, 'Dear Sir forbear', when Lear seems about to strike Kent with his sword. It is also significant that the king treats them as one:

> Our son of Cornwall,
> And you, our no less loving son of Albany,
> We have this hour a constant will to publish
> Our daughters' several dowers, that future strife
> May be prevented now.

and

> Cornwall and Albany,
> With my two daughters' dowers, digest the third.

Gloucester's remark on his entrance in I, ii, that 'France in choler parted' is not unconnected with our memory of the first scene, that the King of France stood up against destructive ego-centric power whereas the Dukes of Cornwall and Albany remained uncommitted, or, rather, willy-nilly because of Lear's largess appeared committed—and to the viewpoint of their wives as well. But sufficient particularities for any decision concerning either duke have not as yet been given.

We first are able to measure Albany's stature in I, iii. He is not prepossessing. Goneril has been treating Lear like a bad child, has lied insufferably about the manners of his retinue, has threatened to reduce his train—and the king is wild with anger. Albany enters. Lear immediately asks, 'Is it your will, speak sir?' but does not even wait for a reply, turns to one of his knights and orders horses to be saddled. Albany does not know at all what has just been occurring. (Why not? We have heard earlier in the scene from one of Lear's retainers that 'there's a great abatement of kindness' not only in Goneril and the dependants but 'in the Duke himself also'.) He begs Lear to 'be patient'. The king does not even listen deeply to him but begins to curse Goneril. Albany at this outbreak seems truly perturbed, but also woefully undominant:

> *Albany.* My lord, I am guiltless, as I am ignorant
> Of what hath moved you.
> *Lear.* It may be so, my lord.

And Lear continues to curse his daughter. After his exit,

> *Albany.* Now, gods, that we adore, whereof comes this?
> *Goneril.* Never afflict yourself to know the cause;
> But let his disposition have that scope
> That dotage gives it.

Note that neither the king nor his daughter grant Albany the character status which each acknowledges, however malevolently, in the other. We get the same pattern again when Lear re-enters:

> *Lear.* What, fifty of my followers at a clap!
> Within a fortnight!
> *Albany.* What's the matter, sir?
> *Lear.* I'll tell thee: life and death, I am ashamed
> That thou [Goneril] hast power to shake my manhood thus.

The negative, uninformed, inconsiderable husband, whom the situation portrays as powerless, is brushed aside here by confronting father and daughter. After Lear's departure,

> *Albany.* I cannot be so partial, Goneril,
> To the great love I bear you,—
> *Goneril.* Pray you, content. What, Oswald, hoa!

As Goneril speaks bitterly about the danger of Lear's hundred knights and calls for her steward again, Shakespeare underscores her husband's non-intervention:

> *Albany.* Well, you may fear too far.
> *Goneril.* Safer than trust too far:
> Let me still take away the harms I fear.

Note the *me* in this last line, while remembering that the man before you is the presumptive ruler of half of England! After giving orders to Oswald, Goneril turns to her mate:

> No, no, my lord,
> This milky gentleness and course of yours
> Though I condemn not, yet, under pardon,
> You are much more attask'd for want of wisdom
> Than prais'd for harmful mildness.

Albany. How far your eyes may pierce I cannot tell;
    Striving to better, oft we mar what's well.
Goneril. Nay, then—
Albany. Well, well; th'event. *Exeunt.*

This man, we are ready to affirm, may be good, but he appears a weakling; there is no strength in him, no impulse to lead or control. He is dominated by his wife.

We do not see him again until IV, ii, when most of the evil in the play has been accomplished. And therein lies the reason for his non-appearance. For when we are allowed to observe him once more, he will be very different. He will be shown as one whom the fact of evil is changing from a negative personality into a positive one, who is now the psychological and moral equal of his wife. But though he is not on the stage in the interim, his now revealed terrible counterpart, Cornwall, is, but not allowing *his* terrible mate, Regan, to dominate; and Albany's terrible mate, Goneril, is, too, doing whatever her fiend-like nature wishes—and some query in us, some place, must be wondering where Albany is; what he would say and do *now*, facing the evil wrought by the above three and Edmund; whether and when he will return and with what characteristics. That he has not accompanied Goneril to Gloucester's castle accentuates his nonentity. But as often with Shakespeare, artifice accompanies the art. Both negatively and positively there are reasons why Albany cannot appear in the events in Gloucester's home. *Negatively*: To have Albany there would mean that he would, one way or another, have to declare himself morally; he could not evade decision before the treatment of Lear and Gloucester. For him to acquiesce in any way would make the dramatist's later particular use of him impossible; he could never be transmuted into decency. For him to object in any way would impede the mode of the play—evil is not to have a single let in *King Lear* until Gloucester's eyes are ejected, when the servant gives Cornwall a death wound. *Positively*: Shakespeare utilizes the fact of Albany, but not his character, to illustrate the consequences of Lear's fatuousness in dividing the kingdom 'that future strife / May be prevented now'. Albany's reported disagreement with Cornwall does nothing, I believe, to establish the former's moral superiority. For one thing, most of what we hear about it in II, i, occurs before we discover what Cornwall really is. No, it is there for the play's pattern, not for characterization. In the above scene, Curan tells Edmund of 'ear-kissing' rumours of 'likely wars toward 'twixt the Dukes'. Edmund utilizes this information in getting Edgar to flee. And Cornwall seems to be referring to future strife when he seizes upon Edmund because 'Natures of such deep trust, we shall much need'. The next reference to the dukes' quarrels, in the first of the storm scenes, III, i, does come perilously near to placing a co-operative Albany in the category of the greatly evil. Kent is speaking to the Gentleman, whom he is sending to Dover:

                            There is division,
Although as yet the fact of it is cover'd
With mutual cunning, 'twixt Albany, and Cornwall;
Who have—as who have not, that their great stars
Thron'd and set high?—servants, who seem no less,
Which are to France the spies and speculations
Intelligent of our state; what hath been seen,
Either in snuffs and packings of the dukes,

Or the hard rein which both of them have borne
Against the old kind king; or something deeper,
Whereof perchance these are but furnishings;
But true it is, from France there comes a power....

'Both of them!' Is Shakespeare implying that in the circumstances Albany's non-assertiveness is as criminal as Cornwall's action? I do not pretend to clarity on the problem, though I am inclined to think that Albany's character is still not involved, that artifice is employing his name and position for plot purposes. (However, when we approach the end of the play and find Albany on the side against Lear and Cordelia, a position that perhaps raises important moral issues, we may remember the above puzzling lines.) The last reference to the dukes' quarrel is in III, iii, in Gloucester's revelation to Edmund:

Go to; say you nothing. There's a division betwixt the dukes, and a worse matter than that: I have received a letter this night; 'tis dangerous to be spoken; I have locked the letter in my closet: these injuries the king now bears will be revenged home; there's part of a power already footed: we must incline to the king.

Coming as it does immediately after Gloucester's account of Regan's and Cornwall's 'unnatural dealing', this glance at the dukes' opposition might be taken as implying, once more, Albany's superiority, but I do not think this would be justified. It is again the ironic motif of internal conflict, which, as in Kent's speech, is now supplying a cause for France's invasion.

In III, vii, when Cornwall tells Edmund to travel back with Goneril, he seems to take Albany for granted concerning France's army: 'Advise the duke where you are going to a most festinate preparation.'

At IV, ii, after such a length of time, after we have supped full of terror, pain, and pity, we meet Goneril's husband once more. And, as sometimes happens in Shakespeare, he possesses full emotional knowledge, if not factual knowledge, of the terrible scenes which we, the spectators, have witnessed but which he has not. It is these preceding scenes that, finally, have been decisive in Albany's moral constitution. Within the *King Lear* tragic world there has occurred a melioristic phenomenon of the utmost spiritual importance. That which was weak and ineffective has been changed through the very fact of evil itself into something ethically aware and strong—but not quite yet in active leadership. His transformation is recorded at the very beginning of the scene. In the presence of Edmund, Goneril asks Oswald where her 'mild husband' is:

> *Steward.* Madam, within; but never man so chang'd.
> I told him of the army that was landed;
> He smiled at it: I told him you were coming;
> His answer was 'The worse': of Gloucester's treachery,
> And of the loyal service of his son,
> When I inform'd him, then he call'd me sot,
> And told me I had turn'd the wrong side out:
> What most he should dislike seems pleasant to him;
> What like, offensive.

Goneril, now totally attracted to her husband's opposite, Edmund, reacts with lines that come uncomfortably close to the Albany whom we have hitherto observed:

> It is the cowish terror of his spirit,
> That dares not undertake: he'll not feel wrongs
> Which tie him to an answer.

How sardonic is her irony concerning him when she says farewell to her lover: 'I must change arms at home, and give the distaff / Into my husband's hand.' For to such as Goneril, Oswald's account of Albany but denotes the latter's usual weakness. We see presently how wrong she is. The steward's words, 'Madam, here comes my lord', are prescient. His first words destroy Goneril's domination forever. She is 'not worth the dust which the rude wind / Blows in [her] face'. One who has rejected her parent as she has 'must wither, / And come to deadly use'. These words are packed. Goneril is not to be trusted in any human relationship—toward husband, toward sister, toward herself. Of course, she is incapable of understanding the 'Wisdom and goodness' which are directing his present speech. She and Regan are 'vile', 'filths', 'tigers', 'Most barbarous, most degenerate'. Their father is a 'gracious aged man', to be treated with 'reverence'. Albany is certainly feeling the wrongs which have tied him to an answer! And in the clearest manner now he makes the moral distinction between himself and Cornwall:

> Could my good brother suffer you to do it?
> A man, a prince, by him so benefited!

By appealing to the 'heavens...to tame this vile offence', Albany for the first time, but not the last, shows his great piety. Goneril sneers at him as 'milk-liver'd', 'a moral fool', but he refuses to consider, at this moment, her emphasis on France's threat. He will not stop speaking of her fiendish behaviour to her father. She laughs at his 'manhood'. To her he is still a weakling. When the messenger tells Albany that Cornwall has been slain while putting out Gloucester's eyes, he has not a word of pity for Cornwall, only for his victim. And he prayerfully recognizes the heavenly justice in this quick striking down. The messenger's information concerning Edmund's role in this 'wickedness' to his father prompts him to exclaim:

> Gloucester, I live
> To thank thee for the love thou show'dst the king,
> And to revenge thine eyes.

So ends this significant scene.

Now, how much the play requires us to pay attention to Albany's queer moral dilemma—loving Lear but yet fighting Cordelia and her army who are there for Lear's rescue—I do not know. There is some stress on this, but not enough to make it a certain central issue. Perhaps, Shakespeare's shortness with the problem is evidence that the exigencies of plot are paramount. Albany's reluctance is mentioned at the beginning of IV, v:

> *Regan.* But are my brother's powers set forth?
> *Steward.* Ay, madam.
> *Regan.* Himself in person there?
> *Steward.* Madam, with much ado:
>   Your sister is the better soldier.

This is the scene that announces the splitting of the sisters' attachment: they are now rivals for Edmund, but Regan does not seem to trust Albany as an efficacious stay to Goneril's wishes, and we are strongly reminded of Albany's negative culpability by Lear's words in his great mad scene, IV, vi:

> It were a delicate stratagem, to shoe
> A troop of horse with felt: I'll put't in proof;
> And when I have stol'n upon these sons-in-law,
> Then, kill, kill, kill, kill, kill, kill!

Contrariwise, we are reminded of Albany's goodness by Edgar, after he has read Goneril's murder letter to Edmund:

> O undistinguish'd space of woman's will!
> A plot upon her virtuous husband's life.

Just before we see Albany again in v, i, his irresolution in the present war situation is once more noted:

> *Bastard.* Know of the duke if his last purpose hold,
> Or whether since he is advis'd by aught
> To change the course; he's full of alteration
> And self-reproving: bring his constant pleasure.

Albany's solution is given to the sisters and Edmund in his first speech:

> Our very loving sister, well be-met.
> Sir, this I hear; the king is come to his daughter,
> With others, whom the rigour of our state
> Forced to cry out. Where I could not be honest,
> I never yet was valiant; for this business,
> It toucheth us, as France invades our land,
> Not bolds the king, with others, whom, I fear,
> Most just and heavy causes make oppose.

I have never found this a wholly satisfactory explanation, and I can only repeat my point, that the plot needs Albany on a side to which morally, being what he is now, he simply cannot belong. It may be too, though I am reluctant to suggest this, that the theme of invasion of England was so offensive to an English audience of Shakespeare's time, the dramatist could rely on the spectators not questioning Albany's position. Edgar, too, seems involved in a similar necessity of plot. We hear him in v, i, after giving Goneril's epistle to her husband, speaking to Albany as though the victory of the anti-Cordelia army, that is, Albany's, was necessary for his own settling of accounts with Edmund (as the unknown 'champion'). (Is it that the destruction of the Goneril-Edmund-Regan trio has to come from within the group, to emanate from the leadership of Albany, who will call on Edgar?) However, when just before the battle, v, ii, Edgar tells his father, 'Pray that the right may thrive', I confess I do not know to which army he is referring. And when, soon after, he announces 'King Lear hath lost', it sounds as though he is speaking of his own side! But v, iii, one of the greatest suspense scenes in drama, fully, I assert, justifies whatever machination Shakespeare has been employing. In this scene, the necessity of an Albany who is militarily on one side, morally on the other, is more than fully excusable. The same can be said of Edgar.

We had wondered in v, i, before the battle, about the conjunction of Albany and Edmund as leaders of the British. We had not forgotten the former's promise to revenge Gloucester. What would be the final outcome of the relationship between the two? Edmund had tended to dismiss the other:

> Now then we'll use
> His countenance for the battle; which being done,
> Let her who would be rid of him devise
> His speedy taking off. As for the mercy
> Which he intends to Lear and to Cordelia,
> The battle done, and they within our power,
> Shall never see his pardon; for my state
> Stands on me to defend, not to debate.

But the Albany who enters in v, iii, has a markedly increased spiritual stature. He is now, and feels he is, the one dominant figure on the stage—and convinces us immediately too. I find my own reaction to Albany's intense irony to Goneril in this scene quite meaningful. It is not until Albany is able himself to speak scornfully to this woman who has spoken so scornfully of and to him that I acknowledge myself wholly satisfied with his conduct. It is as though he were taking over a power which the evil group have hitherto arrogated to themselves. Albany's first words to Edmund are semi-satirical:

> Sir, you have shown to-day your valiant strain,
> And fortune led you well.

He demands of Edmund this day's captives, Lear and Cordelia, concerning whose fate we are much on edge after the Bastard's murderous instructions to the Captain. 'I do require them of you', says Albany. This man is not to be trifled with. Edmund makes an excuse,

> The question of Cordelia and her father
> Requires a fitter place.

But Albany at last and for all time puts the conscienceless fortune-seeker in his proper niche:

> Sir, by your patience,
> I hold you but a subject of this war,
> Not as a brother.

As, then, Regan and Goneril quarrel, with obvious jealousy, concerning Edmund's status, Albany watches, perhaps ironically smiling at his wife's effrontery. Finally, she cannot contain herself:

> *Goneril.* Mean you to enjoy him?
> *Albany.* The let-alone lies not in your good will.
> *Bastard.* Nor in thine, lord.
> *Albany.* Half-blooded fellow, yes.

No more are words or acts to deter this strong leader, who is gladdening our hearts. He immediately arrests Edmund for treason—and scornfully reveals that he is aware of Goneril's adulterous love. She tries to speak scorn herself: 'An interlude!'—but Albany this time turns his back on her and orders Edmund to defend himself in trial by combat; if a champion does not appear, Albany himself will fight him. And by 'many treasons', Albany must mean not merely what Edmund intended to Albany but also what he did to Gloucester and was accessory in doing to Lear. Albany, now acting the sole king, tells Edmund,

> Trust to thy single virtue; for thy soldiers,
> All levied in my name, have in my name
> Took their discharge.

When Edmund falls to Edgar's sword, Albany exclaims, 'Save him, save him'. This is not pity. Albany wants Edmund to live long enough to confess. And he shows the incriminating letter to both the dying man and Goneril. She underlines the tremendous transformation that has occurred in Albany by asserting *now* that she can destroy the letter if she wishes, *now* when her husband has wholly taken over the power she once possessed:

> Say, if I do, the Laws are mine not thine:
> Who can arraign me for't?

Albany, knowing how 'desperate' she is, sends someone to 'govern her' after her exit. The word *govern*! He embraces the revealed Edgar: 'Let sorrow split my heart, if ever I / Did hate thee or thy father.' And Edgar replies, 'Worthy prince, I know't.' At Edgar's account of himself and Gloucester, Albany evinces deep and tender sensitivity,

> If there be more, more woeful, hold it in;
> For I am almost ready to dissolve,
> Hearing of this.

But the fineness of his ethos is, perhaps, best displayed by his speech after the Gentleman rushes in and tells of the sisters' deaths:

> Produce the bodies, be they alive or dead:
> This judgement of the heavens, that makes us tremble,
> Touches us not with pity.

Aristotle himself could not have been more discriminating in moral reactions.

It is at this moment that the leadership of Albany in this scene is peculiarly emphasized. It was upon him that the saving of Lear and Cordelia depended, but his initial concern was put in abeyance by the necessity of dealing with the evil trio—and so our almost unbearable apprehension for the king and his daughter had likewise temporarily to be suppressed; but our concern, I believe, is never wholly out of attention. In fact, I believe, it builds up. Now, at Kent's question on the whereabouts of Lear, Albany exclaims 'Great thing of us forgot!' But even now there is interruption as the dead daughters' bodies are brought in. After Edmund at last reveals his death plan for Lear and Cordelia, Albany cries, 'Run, run, O, run...Haste thee for thy life'. He prays for Cordelia, 'The gods defend her'. His piety in this scene is noteworthy.

They are too late. At the sight of Lear with the dead Cordelia in his arms, Albany's emotions are almost beyond endurance: 'Fall and cease.' But his pervasive control of the scene once more asserts itself:

> *Messenger.* Edmund is dead, my lord.
> *Albany.* That's but a trifle here.
> You lords and noble friends, know our intent.
> What comfort to this great decay may come
> Shall be appli'd: for us we will resign,
> During the life of this old majesty,
> To him our absolute power: you, to your rights;
> With boot, and such addition as your honours
> Have more than merited. All friends shall taste
> The wages of their virtue, and all foes
> The cup of their deservings.

Strength, charity, justice, lack of sentimentality are all illustrated here. And after Lear's death we see that along with Albany's moral greatness goes a corresponding humility. To Kent and Edgar he says,

> Our present business
> Is general woe. Friends of my soul, you twain
> Rule in this realm, and the gor'd state sustain.

And this great man, great in psychological strength, great in physical power, great in speech, great in piety and morality, was the nonentity with whom the play began! And *King Lear* is often described as totally dark!

MADNESS IN *KING LEAR*

BY

KENNETH MUIR

Shakespeare has many portraits of madness, real and assumed, and he returned to the theme again and again. Dr Pinch tries to exorcise Antipholus of Ephesus; Titus Andronicus is driven mad by his sufferings; Feste, disguised as Sir Topaz, pretends to exorcise Malvolio; Hamlet, unbalanced as he is, feigns madness, and Ophelia is driven mad by grief; Constance is driven distracted by her loss of Arthur; Portia, and perhaps Lady Macbeth, commit suicide while of unsound mind; and in *The Tempest* the three men of sin are maddened by the workings of conscience, so that their brains are as useless as a tumour.[1] It says much for Shakespeare's powers of observation or for his intuitive understanding of the human mind that his depiction of madness, though based no doubt on sixteenth-century theory, has satisfied medical opinion of later ages. J. C. Bucknill in his *Remarks on the Medical Knowledge of Shakespeare*[2] (1860) and H. Somerville in *Madness in Shakespearian Tragedy*[3] (1929) illustrate the fact that our increasing knowledge of madness during the past century has served only to justify Shakespeare's intuitions. Ella Freeman Sharpe, indeed, was so impressed by the depiction of Lear's madness that in her *Collected Papers on Psycho-Analysis* (1950) she argued that the play reflected the traumatic experiences of Shakespeare himself and that 'psychically he regressed to the loves and hates of early childhood', re-enacting his infantile desire not to share his mother's love either with her husband or with other children.[4] This theory is worth referring to, not because it is anything but wildly improbable, but because it shows that the madness depicted in the play has not been rendered false by the passage of time.

We may assume that the relation of the poet to his work is different from that posited by Ella Freeman Sharpe. The greater the artist, Eliot assures us, the wider the gulf between the heart that suffers and the mind that creates. But we may agree with D. G. James who argued that

Lear was contained in the Shakespeare who gave him birth; his passions, and the passions of the other characters, were felt and realized in Shakespeare who suffered in them. Therefore, the idea of *King Lear* we have is also the life of Shakespeare as he was then; and in contemplating the play we become what we behold; as he was what he created.[5]

There is no madness in the old play of *King Leir*, none in the story of Lear as told by Holinshed, Spenser, in *The Mirror for Magistrates*, or in any other version before Shakespeare's time, and none in Sidney's story of the Paphlagonian King. If the madness was suggested by the contemporary story of Brian Annesley[6] and his three daughters—the older ones being harsh, and the youngest, Cordell, kind—we may be sure that it was not merely the desire for topicality that made Shakespeare take the suggestion as a cat laps milk. Maeterlinck believed[7] that Shakespeare deliberately unsettled the reason of his protagonists, and thus opened

the dike that held captive the swollen lyrical flood. Henceforward, he speaks freely by their mouths; and beauty invades the stage without fearing lest it be told that it is out of place.

Orwell, on the other hand, regarded[8] Lear's madness as a protective device to enable Shakespeare to utter dangerous thoughts. Shakespeare, he says, is

noticeably cautious, not to say cowardly, in his manner of uttering unpopular opinions. Almost never does he put a subversive or sceptical remark into the mouth of a character likely to be identified with himself. Throughout his plays the acute social critics, the people who are not taken in by accepted fallacies, are buffoons, villains, lunatics or persons who are shamming insanity or are in a state of violent hysteria. *Lear* is a play in which this tendency is particularly well marked. It contains a great deal of veiled social criticism...but it is all uttered by the Fool, by Edgar when he is pretending to be mad, or by Lear during his bouts of madness. In his sane moments Lear hardly ever makes an intelligent remark. And yet the very fact that Shakespeare had to use these subterfuges shows how widely his thoughts ranged.

Against Maeterlinck's view it must be objected that the mad scenes of *King Lear* are no more lyrical than the rest of the play; and against Orwell's view of Shakespeare as the subversive sceptic without the courage of his own convictions it must be pointed out that none of his characters should be taken as his own mouthpiece. Ulysses' views on Order are shared by Rosencrantz, whom Shakespeare treats with scant sympathy, and considerably modified by the King in *All's Well that Ends Well*.[9] We cannot even be certain that the *Sonnets* are autobiographical. We cannot tell whether Shakespeare was a cowardly sceptic or a natural conformist. His acceptance of the 'establishment' and his criticism of it are equally in character. This is not to say that no point of view emerges from each play and from the canon as a whole; but the point of view is complex, subsuming both the anarchical and the conformist. The Shakespearian dialectic is not a reflection of the poet's timidity but of his negative capability.

In the dialogue with Gloucester in IV, vi, Lear's invective has a double target—the hypocrisy of the simpering dame and the hypocrisy of the law. There is no evidence to show that Shakespeare was sheltering behind a mask. The attack on lechery can be paralleled in the diatribes of Timon and the attack on authority and law is no more extreme than that of the eminently sane Isabella or that of the praying Claudius who knew that

> In the corrupted currents of this world
> Offence's gilded hand may shove by justice,
> And oft 'tis seen the wicked prize itself
> Buys out the law.

Lest the audience should be tempted to dismiss what Lear says as mere raving, Shakespeare provides a choric comment through the mouth of Edgar:

> O, matter and impertinency mix'd!
> Reason in madness!

Lear's mad speeches, moreover, are all linked with other passages in the play. The revulsion against sex, besides being a well-known symptom of certain forms of madness,[10] is linked with Lear's earlier suspicion that the mother of Goneril and Regan must be an adultress,[11] with Gloucester's pleasant vices which led to the birth of Edmund and ultimately to his own blinding, and to Edmund's intrigues with Goneril and Regan. The attack on the imperfect instruments of justice, themselves guilty of the sins they condemn in others, is merely a reinforcement of Lear's speech in the storm, before he crossed the borders of madness:

> Let the great gods,
> That keep this dreadful pother o'er our heads,
> Find out their enemies now. Tremble, thou wretch,
> That hast within thee undivulged crimes,
> Unwhipp'd of justice: hide thee, thou bloody hand;
> Thou perjur'd, and thou simular man of virtue
> That art incestuous: caitiff, to pieces shake,
> That under covert and convenient seeming
> Hast practis'd on man's life: close pent-up guilts,
> Rive your concealing continents, and cry
> These dreadful summoners grace.[12]

Here, as in the mad scene, the justice of the gods, from whom no secrets are hid, is contrasted with the imperfections of earthly justice.

One of Lear's first speeches after his wits begin to turn consists of a prayer to 'houseless poverty':

> Poor naked wretches, wheresoe'er you are,
> That bide the pelting of this pitiless storm,
> How shall your houseless heads and unfed sides,
> Your loop'd and window'd raggedness, defend you
> From seasons such as these? O, I have ta'en
> Too little care of this! Take physic, pomp;
> Expose thyself to feel what wretches feel,
> That thou mayst shake the superflux to them,
> And show the heavens more just.[13]

It has not escaped notice that Gloucester expresses similar sentiments when he hands his purse to Poor Tom:

> heavens, deal so still!
> Let the superfluous and lust-dieted man,
> That slaves your ordinance, that will not see
> Because he does not feel, feel your power quickly;
> So distribution should undo excess,
> And each man have enough.

This repetition is of some importance since Schücking has argued[14] that it is not really consistent with Shakespeare's philosophy to see in the play a gradual purification of Lear's character. Shakespeare, he argues, nowhere associates compassion for the poor 'with a higher moral standpoint'. The point is not whether Lear's pity was intended to arouse the audience's sympathy for him, nor even whether Shakespeare himself agreed with Lear's sentiments, but whether the audience would understand that his newly aroused concern for the poor was a sign of moral

PLATE I

(*a*) From Rowe's frontispiece, 1709 (*b*) From Rowe's frontispiece, 1714 (*c*) From Hayman's frontispiece for Hanmer's Shakespeare, 1744

(*d*) From McArdell's mezzotint after Benjamin Wilson: 'Garrick as Lear' (*e*) From van Bleeck: Mrs Cibber in Nahum Tate's adaptation of *King Lear*

(*f*) From John Runciman's 'Lear in the Storm', 1767 (*g*) Alexander Runciman, 'Lear on the Heath'

COSTUMES FOR PRODUCTIONS OF 'KING LEAR'

PLATE II

(a) Fuseli's 'Lear and Cordelia',
Rivington's edition, 1805

(b) James Barry, from a painting for
the Boydell Gallery, engraved by Legat

(c) Mulready drawing for Lamb's
Tales from Shakespeare

(d) From Ford Madox Brown's 'Lear and Cordelia'

(e) Bernard Partridge: Irving as Lear

(f) Sir John Gielgud, *King Lear*, Stratford, 1956

(g) Robert Colquhoun, *King Lear*, Stratford, 1953

COSTUMES FOR PRODUCTIONS OF 'KING LEAR'

PLATE III

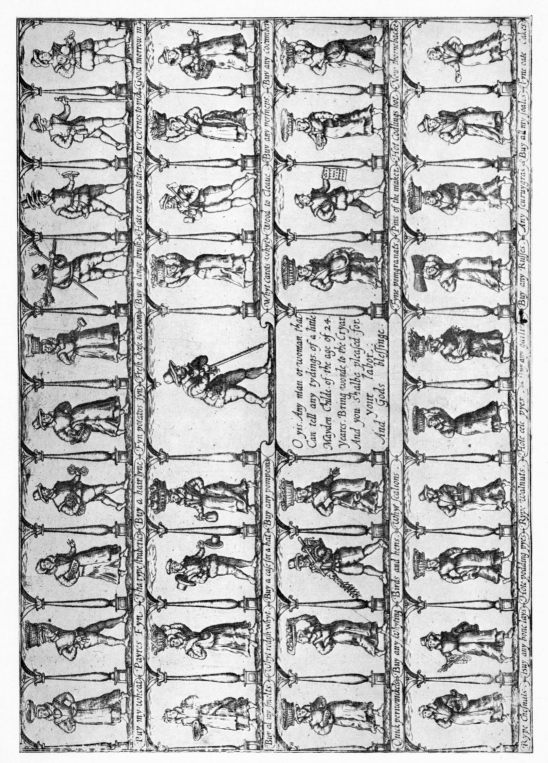

THE TOWN CRIER, ETC.

PLATE IV

A. 'I HAUE SCREENES IF YOU DESIER'

B. 'WHAT KICHIN-STUFFE'

C. THE BOOKVENDOR; 'I HAVE RIPE STRAWBURYES'

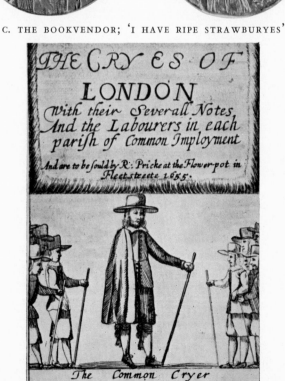

D. THE COMMON CRYER

improvement. Here, surely, there can be no doubt. Shakespeare's audience was not so cut off from the Christian tradition as not to know that charity was a virtue; and the fact that similar sentiments are put into Gloucester's mouth is a reinforcement of Lear's words. If Lear were mad at this point—and he has not yet crossed the frontier—he would be expressing reason in madness. Even Schücking is constrained to admit that Lear's later criticisms of society show profound insight; but he claims that this does not exhibit a development of Lear's character, because it is dependent on a state of mental derangement. The Lear who welcomes prison with Cordelia

is not a purified Lear from whose character the flame of unhappiness has burnt away the ignoble dross, but a nature completely transformed, whose extraordinary vital forces are extinguished, or about to be extinguished.

But, as I have pointed out elsewhere,[15] the three moments in the play crucial to Bradley's theory of Lear's development—his recognition of error, his compassion for the poor, and his kneeling to Cordelia—occur either before or after his madness; and Schücking seems insufficiently aware of the 'reason in madness' theme so essential to the play's meaning.

Shakespeare was only following tradition in making fool and madman the vehicle of unpopular truths;[16] and Lear's Fool disappears from the play at the moment when his master, as madman, can carry on the Fool's role. But whereas the Fool's criticism is mostly directed against Lear himself, Lear's is directed against the hypocrisies and injustices of society.

It is sometimes asserted that Shakespeare and Webster were the only two dramatists of the period to treat madness as other than matter for mirth. But, in fact, Kyd's portraits of Isabella and Hieronimo, and especially the anonymous Painter scene in *The Spanish Tragedy*, are quite serious in intention; and though the mad scene in *The Honest Whore*, Part I, may have aroused some laughter, as indeed the mad scenes in *King Lear* may have done, Dekker was careful to prepare the way for a more sympathetic reaction on the part of the audience. Anselmo remarks:

> And tho twould greeue a soule, to see Gods image
> So blemisht and defac'd, yet do they act
> Such anticke and such pretty lunacies,
> That spite of sorrow they will make you smile.[17]

Later in the scene the First Madman rebukes the visitors for their laughter:

Do you laugh at Gods creatures? Do you mock old age you roagues? is this gray beard and head counterfet, that you cry ha ha ha?

But neither Kyd nor Dekker, nor even Webster, use their madmen for any fundamental criticism of society. Bucknill was right when he pointed out that Lear's madness releases his imagination.

It is only when all the barriers of conventional restraint are broken down, that the native and naked force of the soul displays itself. The display arises from the absence of restraint, and not from the stimulus of disease.[18]

Joseph Warton and others have argued that Lear was virtually mad when he divided his kingdom; but the steps of his descent into madness are clearly marked by Shakespeare. When Kent, after Cordelia has been banished, tells the King:

> be Kent unmannerly,
> When Lear is mad...

it is obvious that Kent does not regard his master as insane; and when Regan and Goneril discuss their father at the end of the scene, they complain that his age is full of changes, that he has shown poor judgement, that even in his prime 'he hath ever but slenderly known himself'; and that they must

look to receive from his age, not alone the imperfections of long-engraffed condition, but therewithal the unruly waywardness that infirm and choleric years bring with them.

The evil daughters accuse him of the approach of senility, but not of madness.

Lear is driven insane by a series of shocks. First, there is the attack by Goneril (I, iv). This makes him angrily pretend not to know her, or to know himself, but at this point it is still pretence:

> Doth any here know me? This is not Lear:
> Doth Lear walk thus? speak thus? Where are his eyes?
> Either his notion weakens, or his discernings
> Are lethargied.—Ha! waking? 'Tis not so.—
> Who is it that can tell me who I am?

Later in the same scene he begins to realize that he has wronged Cordelia:

> O most small fault,
> How ugly didst thou in Cordelia show!...
> O Lear, Lear, Lear!
> Beat at this gate, that let thy folly in,
> And thy dear judgement out!

In the next scene he comes to a full recognition of his folly: 'I did her wrong.' All the Fool's remarks in both scenes are designed, not to distract Lear's attention from Goneril's ingratitude, but to remind him of his foolishness in dividing his kingdom and banishing Cordelia. It is arguable that the Fool's loyalty to Cordelia helps to drive his master mad. At the end of the Act Lear has his first serious premonition of insanity:

> O, let me not be mad, not mad, sweet heaven!
> Keep me in temper: I would not be mad!

The second great shock comes in the second act when Lear finds Kent in the stocks. This causes the first physical symptoms of hysteria, which were probably borrowed by Shakespeare from Harsnett's pamphlet on demoniacs or from Edward Jorden's *Brief Discourse of a Disease Called the Suffocation of the Mother* (1603), which shows 'that divers strange actions and passions of the body of man, which in the common opinion, are imputed to the devil, have their true naturall causes, and do accompanie this Disease'. But the symptoms would now be described as 'racing heart' and 'rising blood pressure':

> O, how this mother swells up toward my heart!
> Hysterica passio, down, thou climbing sorrow,
> Thy element's below....
> O me, my heart, my rising heart! but, down!

The third shock, the rejection by Regan, follows immediately. Lear prays for patience; he threatens revenges—the terrors of the earth—on the two daughters; his refusal to ease his heart by weeping is accompanied by the first rumblings of the storm which is a projecting on the macrocosm of the tempest in the microcosm; and he knows from the thunder that what he most feared will come to pass: 'O fool, I shall go mad!' Exposure to the storm completes what ingratitude began.

Lear's identification with the storm is both a means of presenting it on the stage and a sign that his passions have overthrown his reason. He contends 'with the fretful elements';

> tears his white hair,
> Which the impetuous blasts, with eyeless rage,
> Catch in their fury, and make nothing of;
> Strives in his little world of man to out-storm
> The to-and-fro-conflicting wind and rain.

But when Lear makes his next appearance, invoking the storm to destroy the seeds of matter, urging the gods to find out their hidden enemies, or addressing the poor naked wretches, he is not yet wholly mad, though he admits that his wits are beginning to turn. What finally pushes him over the borderline is the sudden appearance of Poor Tom who is both a living embodiment of naked poverty and one who is apparently what Lear had feared to become. Edgar, in acting madness, precipitates Lear's.

> What! have his daughters brought him to this pass?
> Could'st thou save nothing? Didst thou give 'em all?...
> Is it the fashion, that discarded fathers
> Should have thus little mercy on their flesh?
> Judicious punishment! 'twas this flesh begot
> Those pelican daughters.

The Fool comments:

> This cold night will turn us all to fools and madmen.

It is in fact the exposure and the physical exhaustion which prevents Lear's recovery from the shocks he has received. He is soon trying to identify himself with unaccommodated man by tearing off his clothes.

The madness of the elements, the professional 'madness' of the Fool, the feigned madness of Edgar, and the madness of the King himself together exemplify the break-up of society and the threat to the universe itself under the impact of ingratitude and treachery. When

Gloucester appears, confessing that he is almost mad and that grief for his son's treachery has crazed his wits, only Kent is left wholly sane.

Poor Tom compares himself with emblematic animals—hog, fox, wolf, dog and lion— and Lear contrasts the naked Bedlam, who does not borrow from worm, beast, sheep and cat, with the sophisticated people who do. Man without the refinements of civilization is 'a poor, bare, forked animal', as man without reason is no more than a beast. But Lear, who has lost his reason, is anxious to discuss philosophical questions with the man he takes for a learned Theban. His first question, 'What is the cause of thunder?', had been a stock one ever since the days of Pythagoras, who had taught, Ovid tells us,

> The first foundation of the world: the cause of every thing:
> What nature was: and what was God: whence snow and lyghtning spring:
> And whether *Jove* or else the wynds in breaking clowdes doo thunder.[19]

The storm suggests the question to Lear.

Just as the cuckolded madman in *The Honest Whore* is obsessed by his wife's unfaithfulness, and just as Ophelia is obsessed by her father's death and by the warnings given by her father and brother about preserving her virginity, so Lear returns again and again to the thing which had driven him mad—his daughters' ingratitude. He asks if Poor Tom's daughters have brought him to this pass; he exclaims:

> Now, all the plagues that in the pendulous air
> Hang fated o'er men's faults light on thy daughters!—

declares that nothing but his unkind daughters 'could have subdu'd nature / To such a lowness'; and inveighs against the flesh which 'begot / Those pelican daughters'.

Just before he was driven out into the storm Lear had declared that he would avenge himself on his daughters:

> I will have such revenges on you both,
> That all the world shall—I will do such things,—
> What they are, yet I know not; but they shall be
> The terrors of the earth.

In the refuge provided by Gloucester Lear begins to brood on his revenge. But the echo from Harsnett[20] in the lines—

> To have a thousand with red burning spits
> Come hissing in upon 'em—

suggests that Lear may be thinking of his daughters being punished by devils in hell. If he is indulging in the fantasy of punishing them in this world, he suddenly decides to bring them to trial first. Poor Tom in his blanket, and the Fool in his motley, suggest to his disordered mind two robed men of justice, and he imagines—this is his first actual illusion—that he sees Goneril and Regan. When we remember Lear's later attacks on the operations of justice because the judges are as guilty as the criminals they try, the justices in the mock trial of Goneril and Regan—a Bedlam beggar, a Fool, and a serving-man—are at least as likely to deal justly as a properly constituted bench, even though Lear accuses them of corruption in allowing the criminals to escape.

Shakespeare hits on two characteristics of certain kinds of mental derangement—the substitution of a symbolic offence for a real one ('she kick'd the poor King her father') and the obsession with a visual image. Lear thinks of the 'warped looks' of Regan, though in an earlier scene he had spoken of her 'tender-hefted nature' and of her eyes which, unlike Goneril's, 'do comfort and not burn'. It was the contrast between her beauty and her behaviour when she, like Goneril, put on a frowning countenance, that impressed Lear with her warped looks; and the same contrast makes Lear ask:

> Is there any cause in nature that makes these hard hearts?

The question is an appropriate introduction to the next scene in which we see the tender-hearted Regan assisting at the blinding of Gloucester.

When the imaginary curtains are drawn on the sleeping Lear[21] we do not see him again for nearly 500 lines—about half-an-hour's playing time—but we are prepared for the development of his lunacy by the two short scenes in the middle of the fourth Act. In one of these Kent reveals that Lear refuses to see Cordelia:

> A sovereign shame so elbows him: his own unkindness,
> That stripp'd her from his benediction, turn'd her
> To foreign casualties, gave her dear rights
> To his dog-hearted daughters, these things sting
> His mind so venomously, that burning shame
> Detains him from Cordelia.

It is significant—though I do not remember that anyone has called attention to it—that after the admission at the end of Act I 'I did her wrong', Lear makes no further reference to Cordelia until he recovers his wits at the end of Act IV. The reason for this is partly, no doubt, that the ingratitude of Goneril and Regan drives everything else from his mind; but we may suspect, too, that Lear's sovereign shame prevents him from facing his own guilt. In the other scene (IV, iv) Cordelia describes her mad father,   singing aloud;

> Crown'd with rank fumiter and furrow weeds,
> With burdocks, hemlock, nettles, cuckoo-flowers,
> Darnel, and all the idle weeds that grow
> In our sustaining corn.

The significance of this picture is that Lear has reverted to his childhood. The Doctor, like the Court physicians attending both Henry VIII for his *mal d'esprit* and Elizabeth for her 'stupor', prescribes rest for the lunatic king:[22]

> Our foster-nurse of nature is repose,
> The which he lacks; that to provoke in him,
> Are many simples operative, whose power
> Will close the eye of anguish.

His colleague at Dunsinane holds out no such hopes for Lady Macbeth. The perilous stuff which weighs upon her heart cannot be cleansed from her bosom. The doctor cannot minister to a diseased mind. 'Therein the patient must minister to' herself. This is because her mental illness is caused by her mortal sin. 'More needs she the divine than the physician.' Timothy Bright, who was both physician and divine, distinguished clearly between a sense of guilt caused by neurosis and that caused by sin:

Whatsoeuer molestation riseth directly as a proper obiect of the mind, that in that respect is not melancholicke, but hath a farther ground then fancie, and riseth from conscience, condemning the guiltie soule of those ingrauen lawes of nature, which no man is voide of, be he neuer so barbarous. This is it, that hath caused the prophane poets to haue fained Hecates Eumenides, and the infernall furies; which although they be but fained persons, yet the matter which is shewed vnder their maske, is serious, true, and of wofull experience.[23]

In the scene in which the mad Lear meets the blinded Gloucester there is a wonderful blend of 'matter and impertinency'. Even the impertinency has the kind of free association which is often found in the utterances of certain types of lunatics; and precisely because he is mad Lear is freed from the conventional attitudes of society. He is able, at moments, to see more clearly and piercingly than the sane, because the sane buy their peace of mind by adjusting themselves to the received ideas of society. Lear recognizes the way he has been shielded from reality by flattery. He also sees the hypocritical pretensions of society with regard to sex and with regard to its treatment of criminals. And, finally, he sees that human life is inescapably tragic:

> Thou must be patient; we came crying hither;
> Thou know'st the first time that we smell the air,
> We wawl and cry...
> When we are born, we cry that we are come
> To this great stage of fools.

When we next see Lear he is awakening from a drugged sleep. The Doctor has given him the repose he needs. The second part of the cure consists of music which, as later with Pericles, was a means of winding up the untuned and jarring senses. The third part of the cure is Cordelia's love. It is characteristic of her that she is eloquent so long as Lear is asleep, and that she falls back into her natural reticence when he awakens. The cure is completed when he kneels to the daughter he has wronged and begs her forgiveness.

It has often been observed by doctors of widely differing views that Shakespeare is clinically accurate in his presentation of the symptoms of madness. The difference between Lear's madness and Ophelia's illustrates his extraordinary insight into different kinds of mental illness; and, moreover, the feigned madness of Edgar (suitable to the scenes in which it appears) is quite different from the feigned madness of Hamlet, suitable both to the character and to the situation, though neither would be mistaken by a competent alienist for real insanity. One has only to compare Webster's madmen in *The Duchess of Malfi* and *The White Devil,* or the more extended treatment of madness by Fletcher in *The Two Noble Kinsmen* or by Otway in *Venice Preserved* with Shakespeare's to see how immeasurably superior he is to his rivals in this respect. The mad speeches of Fletcher and Otway are irremediably 'literary', and they hardly need the parody of Sheridan's Tilburina to show up their unreality.

Many of Shakespeare's contemporaries believed that madness was often, if not always, the result of possession; but he himself treated only mistaken or feigned madness in this way. Antipholus is thought to be possessed; Malvolio, though known to be sane, is treated by Feste as though he were possessed; and Edgar pretends that he has been possessed.[24] It is significant that for Edgar's feigned lunacy Shakespeare drew on *A Declaration of Egregious Popish Impostures* in which Harsnett analysed the confessions of bogus demoniacs. It has been suggested[25] that Shakespeare shared the sceptical views of Reginald Scott and Samuel Harsnett on demonology and witchcraft. At least it may be said that the mental illness of Lear has nothing supernatural about it.

NOTES

1. *Tempest*, v, i, 60.
2. Bucknill's views are accessible in the New Variorum edition.
3. Somerville professes to diagnose the mental illnesses of a number of Shakespeare's characters—Macbeth, for example, being paranoiac, Timon a megalomaniac, and Othello impotent.
4. Cf. K. Muir, 'Freudian Interpretations of Shakespeare' (*Proceedings of the Leeds Philosophical and Literary Society*, 1952). Sharpe, *op. cit.* p. 218, says that the storm 'is an imaginative suggestion of an actual storm representing the psychical one raging in the mind of the poet'. The significance of the whole play is implicit in the opening dialogue between Gloucester and Kent (pp. 222 ff.): 'Gloucester recalls certain events in his past life, the happy intercourse with his wife and later the birth of his second son'. 'The poet, through Lear, reveals emotional reactions to the mother of his childhood and, more hidden and complicated, those experienced towards his father.' She goes on to suggest that 'mother-Goneril's pregnancy is the cause of child Lear's "storm"' in the play; that Lear's knights represent faeces; that during one of his mother's pregnancies Shakespeare became incontinent, and that during the next he ran away from home and was found decked with the flowers of late summer. Apart from any scepticism we may have of this biographical fantasy, it should be pointed out that as Joan Shakespeare was christened on April 15, 1569, her mother's pregnancy would not have been visible in the late summer of 1568. There are many other dubious interpretations in Sharpe's essay. Lear's decision to stay with each daughter a month in turn is ascribed, not to Shakespeare's sources, but to fantasies concerning Mrs John Shakespeare's menstruation. 'Goneril with a white beard' tells 'of repressed knowledge of menstruation, bandage, and pubic hair'. Oddest of all is the comment on Lear's death-scene: 'The symbolic surrender to the father is complete in his last request to the father-figure, "Pray you, undo this button". Kent replies: "Oh let him pass..." Father's heart is melted, he does not hate him. In that button undone, and the symbolic "passing" is clear enough the psychical homosexual retreat from the Œdipus conflict.'
5. D. G. James, *The Life of Reason* (1949), p. 149.
6. Cf. G. M. Young, *Shakespeare and the Termers* (1948).
7. M. Maeterlinck, *Life and Flowers* (1907), p. 200.
8. G. Orwell, *Selected Essays* (1957), p. 116.
9. Cf. *Hamlet*, III, iii, 11–23; *All's Well*, II, iii, 124 ff.
10. Cf. Ophelia's mad songs.
11. *Lear*, II, iv, 131–4.
12. *Lear*, III, ii, 49 ff.
13. *Lear*, III, iv, 28.
14. L. Schücking, *Character Problems in Shakespeare Plays* (1922), pp. 186–9.
15. K. Muir, ed. *Lear*, p. lx.
16. Cf. E. Welsford, *The Fool* (1935), *passim*; W. Empson, *The Structure of Complex Words* (1951), pp. 125–57; R. H. Goldsmith, *Wise Fools in Shakespeare* (1935), *passim*.
17. *The Honest Whore*, Part I, v, ii.
18. Cited in New Variorum edition.
19. *Metamorphoses* (trans. Golding), xv, 74 ff.

20. Cf. K. Muir, *Review of English Studies* (1951), pp. 11–21.

21. It has been suggested to me that when Lear falls asleep after his exposure to the storm he is incubating a cold, and that in the mad scene in Act IV he may display toxic delirium in addition to his mania; but, one would imagine, too long a time is supposed to have elapsed between the two scenes.

22. All physicians, however, were not so humane, and neither Henry VIII nor Elizabeth I were mad. George III, when he was insane, was beaten.

23. *A Treatise of Melancholy* (1586), sig. N1^r.

24. Possibly Shakespeare intended us to think, or was willing to let us think, that Lady Macbeth was possessed.

25. Henry N. Paul, *The Royal Play of 'Macbeth'* (1950), p. 130.

THE INFLUENCE OF *GORBODUC* ON *KING LEAR*

BY

BARBARA HELIODORA CARNEIRO DE MENDONÇA

The fact that Shakespeare rarely composed original plots is as universally known as the fact that it is his treatment of old plots that sets his work so far above his sources. One cannot but wonder, however, at the reasons which may have led him to the choice of each particular story, or avoid pondering on the influence which may have weighed on the decision about the dramatic tone of the play at hand. Obviously, most themes carry in themselves the seed of their own dramatic category, but a certain element of personal conception is always present: *Richard II* and *Richard III*, for example, contain dramatic tendencies which are absent in *Henry VI*, *Henry IV* and *Henry V*, and yet Shakespeare went to the same sources for all of them; and there is an indisputable element of personal approach in Shakespeare's use of Roman historic material in the tragic or quasi-tragic *Julius Caesar* and *Antony and Cleopatra*.

For *King Lear* there is a large number of plot-sources, but the tragic tone used by Shakespeare is alien to all of them. In spite of his rash decision about the division of the kingdom and of the grave injustice done to Cordelia, the earlier Lear is eventually restored to the throne, and in some versions of the story he continues on his throne for several years before he dies of old age, the crown being handed to Cordelia, who, in some of the stories, dies in prison after a struggle with her nephews. Shakespeare's tragic treatment of the Lear theme cannot, therefore, be directly attributed to similar treatment in his plot-sources; true, the ballad on this subject shows father and daughter dying without enjoying a happy period together at the end, but in all probability the ballad is based on, and does not come before, the play. Perhaps the confused accounts of their fates is due to a mingling of the earlier version with Shakespeare's:

> Where she, true-hearted noble queen,
>> Was in the battel slain;
> Yet he good king, in his old days,
>> Possesst his crown again.
>
> But when he heard Cordelia's death,
>> Who died indeed for love
> Of her dear father, in whose cause
>> She did this battle move;
> He swooning fell upon her breast,
>> From whence he never parted.[1]

The fact is that in the definitely pre-Shakespearian treatments of the story—*The True Chronicle History of King Leir*, Holinshed, Geoffrey of Monmouth, the *Gesta Romanorum*, John Higgins' *Queen Cordila*, Spenser's *Faerie Queene*—the theme has what may be classified as a happy ending, with the victory of the armies led by Cordelia and the restoration of Lear to the throne. Even the story of the Paphlagonian King in Sidney's *Arcadia*, source of the Gloucester plot, although it has a pathetic death for the old king, is conceived in a definitely 'chronicle' manner, the latter part of the story being almost pure medieval romance; thus it is difficult to agree with Hardin Craig in his opinion that the tragic tone of *King Lear* was suggested by this source.[2]

The essentially episodic nature of the early versions is the most limiting factor in the level of treatment which the Lear theme had received up to the time of Shakespeare's play. To give his story the heightened tone required by the tragic form, the decisive change introduced by Shakespeare was the establishment of a relationship between the story and the world in general, both through a profound study of the very nature of man, and through the political implications of the division of a kingdom and of the disregard for hierarchy and the law of primogeniture. The study of the nature of man in *King Lear* has been amply discussed in several works,[3] and is, no doubt, the most important aspect of the play; but the political inferences of the work cannot be overlooked.

The very absence of these important aspects in any of the plot-sources of *King Lear* brings to mind another play—*Gorboduc*, which, while it does not deal with the Lear story, yet treats a theme closely akin to it. *Gorboduc*, praised by Sir Philip Sidney, almost certainly must have been known to Shakespeare, and there seems every reason for inquiring whether indeed this tragic drama did not operate to direct his imagination when he turned to write his own tragedy, based directly on elements non-tragic.

The similarity between the stories of *Gorboduc* and *King Lear* is close in many respects. In both plays there is an old king who wants to rest and thinks it is time for his children to bear the burden of responsibility:

> Their age nowe asketh other place and trade
> And myne also doth aske an-other chaunge:
> Their to more trauaile, myne to greater ease,[4]

and

> 'tis our fast intent
> To shake all cares and business from our age;
> Conferring them to younger strengths, while we
> Unburthen'd crawl toward death.[5]

In both, the division of the kingdom has already been planned when the plays open and, before the court scenes, it is discussed, in *Gorboduc* by Videna and Ferrex, in *King Lear* by Kent and Gloucester. In both plays, too, the country to be divided is Britain and the two kings act against the ponderous advice from wise counsellors.

Since the two plays follow different stories, one cannot expect exact parallels, but, in both, the initial actions drive the monarchs to extreme suffering and death, bringing evil to their nations; human feelings grow abnormal, there is a pervasive 'unnatural' atmosphere, good and evil are bared and placed in mortal combat, just as they had been in the old morality plays. This morality quality of *King Lear*, including a relationship with *Gorboduc* in that very restricted sense, has been discussed by Theodore Spencer,[6] but neither he, nor, apparently, any other critic has suggested any closer relationship between the two plays.

Yet this relationship seems patent. *Gorboduc* deals fundamentally with the kind of topic, concerning the political structure of society, which Shakespeare explored in his histories and which he trenchantly discussed in *Troilus and Cressida*:

> But nowe the head to stoupe beneth them bothe
> Ne kind, ne reason, ne good order beares.
> And oft it hath ben seene, whene Natures course
> Hath bene peruerted in disordered wise,
> When fathers cease to know that they should rule
> The children cease to know they should obey...[7]
>
> Eche chaunge of course vnioynts the whole estate
> And yeldes it thrall to ruyne by debate...[8]
>
> One kinsman shall bereaue an-others life;
> The father shall vnwitting slay the sonne;
> The sonne shall slay the sire, and know it not
>
> . . . .
>
> These mischiefs spring when rebells will arise
> To work reuenge and iudge their princes fact.
> This, this ensues when noble-men do faile
> In noble trouth and subiected will be kings.[9]

King Lear, written within a very few years of *Troilus and Cressida*, is a living example of these ideas, and even though they are manifest only in very short passages and broken phrases, particularly about 'unnaturalness', the entire play speaks of the dread consequences of the disruption of the appointed order of the universe, both political and natural. A rash decision by the king involves, in *Gorboduc*, the death of all concerned with the event, including that of the 'giltlesse king, without desert at all',[10] his lack of guilt originating, we presume, from the absence of evil intentions in the division of his kingdom, which proves to be, none the less, an 'unnatural' act. Could not this unsparing massacre of all concerned, including those with no evil intent, have pointed the way to the so widely disputed death of Cordelia, whose loving (but unbending) nature involuntarily contributed to the creation of an irreparable unnatural conflict?

The very setting of *King Lear* and *Gorboduc* puts them apart from the plot-sources. The 'God of Abraham' of *King Leir*[11] and the suggested Christian God of the other sources are replaced in Shakespeare's tragedy by the mythical atmosphere of *Gorboduc*. References to classical mythology abound in *King Lear*, with its Jupiter, Apollo and Phoebus, while in *Gorboduc* Phoebus is referred to, and Jove dominates the scene. Apart from these specific references to classical deities, both plays have a large number of references to 'gods', in glaring contrast with the incidence of the word in the plot-sources. There are twenty-eight such references in *King Lear* and thirty-one in *Gorboduc*, and it is worth mentioning that while in Shakespeare's play the word 'God' appears only once, in the older tragedy it appears only twice. A glance at the chart will show that there is a marked difference in usage between the two tragedies and the *Lear* sources.

What, of course, is of special importance is the significance of the use of the words themselves. Preoccupation with the establishment of a higher—moral or religious—meaning through

CHART OF WORD INCIDENCE

	Gorboduc	King Lear	King Leir	Holin-shed	Geoffrey of Mon-mouth	Gesta Roma-norum	Faerie Queene	John Higgins	Lament-able Song	Paphla-gonian King
Mythological gods	12	6	—	—	—	—	—	—	—	—
Gods	33	28	8	—	I	I	—	I	—	2
Death	43	20	4	I	2	I	I	I	2	5
State, realm, kingdom, war, govern	142	34	5	12	14	17	6	6	3	3
Treacherous, traitor	23	15	—	—	—	—	—	—	—	—
Treachery, treason	8	9	—	—	—	—	—	—	—	—
Flattery	6	7	9	—	I	2	3	3	I	—
Nature, natural, kind	37	42	I	—	—	—	—	I	I	3
Unnatural, unkindly	10	9	2	3	—	—	—	I	—	4
Foul, monster, monstrous, heinous	10	25	—	—	—	—	—	—	—	3
Animal imagery	5	approx. 40	I	—	—	—	—	2	—	I

NOTE. *A New and Complete Concordance in Dramatic Works of Shakespeare* (1927), by John Bartlett, was amply used in the organization of this chart. The other works referred to, except for *King Lear* and *Gorboduc*, were consulted in Arthur E. Baker, *op. cit.* and in *King Lear* (Arden edition). The figures given for *King Leir* refer only to the three relevant scenes, as in the Arden edition, appendix I.

frequent reference or invocation to the gods aids in the creation of a tragic atmosphere. The same effect is created by the use of 'death', which appears no more than five times in any of the plot-sources but is used twenty times in *King Lear* and no less than forty-three times in the much bloodier *Gorboduc*; the climate of doom is everywhere present in both plays. The political significance of both works, too, is reflected in the employment of such words as 'state', 'realm', 'rule', 'war', 'kingdom', 'govern' and 'governance'; there are no less than 142 words of the kind in *Gorboduc*, and although *King Lear* presents a mere thirty-four, even then the plot-source with the greatest number is Geoffrey of Monmouth's *Histories of the Kings of Britain*, with seventeen, of which only twelve are used in the story up to the point of Lear's death. It may be added that in *Gorboduc* and *King Lear* the words 'realm' and 'kingdom' are often used in connection with the idea of government, while in the plot-sources practically all examples have the meaning of nation.

Closely connected with this political sense are the words 'traitor' or 'treacherous' and 'treason' or 'treachery'; they are not used in the plot-sources at all, but appear, respectively, fifteen and nine times in *King Lear* and twenty-three and eight times in *Gorboduc*; once again the two plays are set apart from the other related works, again in a sense that suggests an identification of approach. It is interesting to note that the only theme used in all the works we are considering with similar incidence—the only one common to all, in fact—is the pettiest, most personal and least tragic: 'flattery' and its derivatives appear most often in the three relevant scenes of *King Leir* (nine times); all the other sources have at least one reference, and there are seven examples in *Lear* and six in *Gorboduc*. The idea is approached in *Gorboduc* in the Senecan dumb-show preceding Act II, in which the king will rather drink the poison in the golden cup offered by a 'brave and lusty young gentleman' than the healthy drink presented by aged and wise counsellors in a plain cup.

A further close and important relationship between *Lear* and *Gorboduc* is revealed when we turn to the subject of nature. By placing his action against a background of the study of the nature of man, Shakespeare gave his story a meaning that, hitherto, it did not have—at least not in such vast and metaphysical proportions. It is true that the words 'nature', 'natural', 'kind' (in the sense of nature), as well as 'unnatural' and 'unkindly' do appear sporadically in the old plot-sources; one 'nature', one 'unnatural' and one 'unkind' are included in the *Leir* scenes, two 'unnatural' and one 'natural' in Holinshed, one 'nature' and one 'unkind' in John Higgins, one 'nature' in the *Lamentable Song*, and, finally, three 'nature' and four 'unnatural' in Sidney. That these usages show an understanding of the story as an 'exemplum' is certain, but again the numbers show that *Gorboduc* and *King Lear* have something more in common than is to be found in the plot-sources; in *Gorboduc* are thirty-seven instances of the words 'nature', 'kind' and 'kindly', while in *Lear* the word 'nature' is used more often than in any other Shakespearian play, with a total of forty examples, to which we may add two instances of 'natural'. To balance these, 'unnatural' or 'unkind' appear nine times in *Lear*, ten in *Gorboduc*.

Two other groups of words are logical consequences of this preoccupation with the nature of man and with the tragic consequences of 'unnatural' actions. The first is composed by the words 'foul', 'monster' or 'monstrous' and 'heinous'; among the plot-sources these occur—and then only thrice—in the 'Paphlagonian King'; there are sixteen instances of 'foul', eight of 'monster' or 'monstrous' and one of 'heinous' in *Lear*, with a corresponding six, two and four in *Gorboduc*. This emphasis on what is malevolent in the nature of man is specifically characteristic of both plays, and can hardly be accidental. The second group is that which is based on animal imagery, examined by Bradley in his *Shakespearean Tragedy* and by Caroline Spurgeon in her *Shakespeare's Imagery*. The scales weighed heavily in the direction of *Gorboduc* in the question of political imagery; now they are overwhelmingly tipped towards *King Lear*. The few instances in *Gorboduc* are expanded into nearly one hundred such images in *Lear*, nearly one half of which can be classified along with *Gorboduc*'s five, used in a derogatory sense, comparing man with animals which suggest the most obnoxious qualities. It is perhaps interesting to note that three of the instances of such animal imagery in *Gorboduc* are used in a parent-child relationship,[12] which happens to be one of the common forms of its use in *King Lear*.[13]

More important than the actual numbers of these words is the general tone that they create in the different works. In *King Lear* and in *Gorboduc* the patent intention of the authors is to give their stories a meaning beyond the action. A moral significance is to be drawn not only from the individual story of Lear and his daughters, which is to be found in all the earlier stories at a fairy-tale moral level, but from a much larger picture of the far-reaching consequences of 'unnatural' actions. Nature unleashed, the expression so often used in respect of *King Lear*, is equally true as a description of *Gorboduc*, and the main difference between these two and the plot-sources is that in both of them there is an actual use of nature as such.

This use of nature, which is all-encompassing in *King Lear*, appears in *Gorboduc* in the symbolic dumb-show preceding the first act. The mad Lear does not exist in the plot-sources (except for *A Lamentable Song*, in which he

> Grew frantick mad; for in his mind
> He bore the wounds of woe),

and yet in *King Lear* he appears 'tearing off his clothes'[14] and later 'fantastically dressed with wild flowers'.[15] Is it not likely that the fantastic figure 'dressed in leaves' played upon Shakespeare's imagination when the time came to set upon the stage a king driven mad by grief? In both instances the scenes are symbolic of the central themes of the plays in which they appear.

One more incident, absent in all the plot-sources, appears in both tragedies and establishes further the possibility of a direct influence of *Gorboduc* on Shakespeare's entire conception of the Lear theme: in both plays there are trials of evil children by their fathers. In *Gorboduc* the trial is an actual one, but this may well have suggested the weird, phantasmagorical trial of the absent Goneril and Regan by the distraught Lear.[16] Again, this does not appear to be a chance similarity.

One other peculiarity in the two tragedies may be pointed out. In all the sources, the chronicle or romance tone has set a rather leisurely pace to the development of the story. In Holinshed we read of 'a process of time' and then of two years of reign after Lear's restoration to the throne; in Geoffrey of Monmouth Lear spends two years with Goneril, one year with Regan, and has three years of reign; in the *Gesta Romanorum* there is a stay of almost a year with Goneril, 'scarcely a year' with Regan, one month in France and, again, three years of reign; in the *Faerie Queene* the stay with Goneril was 'long', and a similar stay with Regan is suggested, and although no mention of the length of his reign after Lear's restoration is made, he dies of old age. Even in John Higgins, who has the shortest stay with Goneril (six months), there is one year with Regan and a three-year reign; and even in *A Lamentable Song*, sole among the analogues to have both Lear and Cordelia die without proper enjoyment of their victory, the time is slow-moving, just as in the others: we read of 'a while', and Lear has two stays with each daughter (or at least two attempted stays).

This leisurely pace is unknown either to *King Lear* or to *Gorboduc*. There is a quality of urgency in both, and in both (particularly in the older play) action is precipitous, event falling hard upon event, in a mounting tension that leads inexorably to a tragic ending. In *Lear*, if the division of the kingdom comes in I, i, in scene ii Edmund states his plan, convinces his father of Edgar's guilt and gets rid of Edgar in exactly 200 lines, and by the time scene iii opens a crisis has already arisen in the relationship between Lear and Goneril which ends his stay with her. By the end of Act II Lear has already been rejected by both his elder daughters and the avalanche keeps growing in overwhelming proportions, and at tremendous pace, until the death of Lear and Cordelia.[17] The same urgency exists in *Gorboduc*: in I, i, we hear of the king's plan; in scene ii the king divides his kingdom; the two scenes of Act II already show the planning of civil war and the single scene of Act III ends with the news of Ferrex's death; the fourth act is taken up by Videna's speech (sc. i), followed in scene ii by Porrex's trial and immediate death at his mother's hands. In the next scene (v, i) the king and queen have already been murdered, an entire country is in upheaval and the last scene of the play (v, ii) shows complete devastation, the utter destruction of the state.

The tragic ending is not similar in the two plays we are considering because the problem is posed on different bases in each. In Shakespeare's work the issue is completely centred on the figure of Lear—who is presented both as a man and as the symbol of state—and it is his final destruction (and purification) that must needs bring the action to an end; in *Gorboduc* the state is itself the main issue, Gorboduc himself becoming merely instrumental to the final tragic solution, which is the destruction of the entire state (and its foreshadowed purification). Both plays develop against a sort of timeless background; actions and their consequences are of such moment that their actual duration in chronological time has no importance. Each particular event leads inevitably to the next, and from an initial rash decision to divide their kingdoms during their lifetime, two kings are driven to extreme grief and death, and their respective states suffer the horrors of civil war, manifest in *Gorboduc*, hinted at in *King Lear*.[18]

The consequences of the division of the kingdom, so amply analysed in the concluding scene of *Gorboduc*, are echoed, at the end of the last act of *King Lear*, by the Duke of Albany's doleful lines

> For us, we will resign,
> During the life of this old majesty,
> To him our absolute power;[19]

and

> Our present business
> Is general woe. Friends of my soul, you twain
> Rule in this realm, and the gor'd state sustain.[20]

All of these things happen to certain individuals and to certain states; their impact on the lives of these individuals and of these states is the impression that is left with us at the end of each of these two tragedies—when they happened, or how long it was necessary for these events to reach their full development, is completely irrelevant. At the end of both *King Lear* and *Gorboduc*, after a whole series of cruel and mortal events, the nation is restored, through a painful process of purification, to hierarchic rule.

Such is not, except on the most primary level, the significance of the acknowledged plot-sources of *King Lear*. There are altogether too many points of contact between *King Lear* and *Gorboduc* in tone, general conception and language, for a close relationship between them not to be admitted. The older play indeed seems to provide the stimulus which aroused Shakespeare's poetic vision, leading him to see in the Lear story the material for one of his greatest tragedies.

NOTES

1. A. E. Baker, *A Shakespeare Commentary* (New York, 1957); *A Lamentable Song of the Death of King Lear and his Three Daughters*, quoted from Percy's *Reliques of Ancient English Poetry*.
2. Hardin Craig, 'Motivation in Shakespeare's Choice of Materials', *Shakespeare Survey*, 4 (1951), 32–4.
3. The main sources used were: J. F. Danby, *Shakespeare's Doctrine of Nature* (1951). Theodore Spencer, *Shakespeare and the Nature of Man* (New York, 1949).

4. *Gorboduc*, I, ii, 55-7 (quotations are from the text in J. Q. Adams, *Chief Pre-Shakespearean Drama*, Boston, 1924).

5. *King Lear,* I. i, 39-42.

6. T. Spencer, *op. cit.* pp. 60-2.

7. *Gorboduc*, I, ii, 203-8.

8. *Ibid.*, final Chorus of Act I, 5-6.

9. *Ibid.*, v, ii, 212-14 and 242-5.

10. *Ibid.*, v, i, 15.

11. *The True Chronicle History of King Leir*, in *King Lear* (Arden edition, Appendix I), p. 233.

12. *Gorboduc*, IV, i, entirely taken up by Videna's monologue on the murder of Ferrex by Porrex.

13. 'Women will all turn monsters', III, vii, 102, is but one such instance, 'Tigers, not daughters', IV, ii, 40, another.

14. III, iv, 114.

15. *Ibid.*, IV, vi, 80.

16. The scenes are, respectively, *Gorboduc*, IV, ii and *King Lear*, III, vi.

17. Oliphant Smeaton, in his *The Life and Works of William Shakespeare* (Everyman's Library, 1937), quotes the following time-scheme for *King Lear* from P. A. Daniel, *Transactions of the New Shakespeare Society*, 1877-9:

Day I	I, i
Day II	I, ii, an interval of about a fortnight or less.
Day III	I, iii–iv.
Day IV	II, i–ii.
Day V	II, iii–iv, III, i–vi.
Day VI	III, vii, IV, i.
Day VII	IV, ii, perhaps an interval of a day or two.
Day VIII	IV, iii.
Day IX	IV, iv–vi.
Day X	IV, vii, v, i–iii.

This scheme indicates clearly the precipitous quality of the play.

18. *King Lear*: 'Have you heard of no likely wars toward?' (II, i, 11). 'I hold you but a subject of this war, Not as a brother' (v, iii, 60).

19. *Ibid.*, v, iii, 297-9.

20. *Ibid.*, v, iii, 318-20.

SOME ASPECTS OF THE STYLE OF
KING LEAR

BY

WINIFRED M. T. NOWOTTNY

Perhaps one reason why *King Lear* has been mistaken for an unactable play is that it is so nearly an unreadable play: taken passage by passage, it is so flat and grey that the better one knows it the more one feels on reopening its pages that this is almost (as Byron said of *Caractacus*) 'a tragedy complete in all but words'; the style alone might lead one to suppose that what happens in *King Lear* happens in some realm of the imagination beyond ear and eye. This cannot be true, but how is the difficulty of the language to be resolved? The apocalyptic sublime in Lear's defiance of the storm, however much it sticks in the memory, is not the play's climax, nor does this style continue. What of the rest? The 'simplicity' of the closing scenes has been remarked, as has the effective contrast with Lear's former pretensions, but in remarking this we tend to look through the language to what it is 'about', commending it only for transparency and truth to nature, and though we know that such scenes are not to be had by taking a tape-recorder to a deathbed, the terms in which to discuss this style have eluded us. It has been suggested that its art is to be discerned by tracing thematic patterns that give density or bite, but this explanation is vitiated by the fact that other plays by Shakespeare are said to have it too; the case has not been argued that the absence from *Lear* of resplendent imagery, idiosyncrasy of mind expressed in mannered style, indeed of poetry that survives quotation out of context, is deliberately compensated for by an unusually high charge of thematic power. Moreover the suggestion that the play's language draws its power from a sustained thematic undercurrent conflicts with one's obscure sense that what is really peculiar about the language is the freedom and unexpectedness of its melodic line; Lear himself is unfailingly astonishing, and this property of his words is resistant to explanation in terms of the recurrence of patterns, though, perhaps, in order to maintain this astonishment without having the play fall to bits, Shakespeare might find himself compelled to labour in the vocabulary towards the minimum number and maximum generality of moral and philosophical concepts. For, indeed, the first peculiarity of the style is that its originality is not discernible from its vocabulary, which lays a ground of permanent moral values either instantly identifiable or else so wide as to take their specific colour only from the usage of each speaker; the cultural diversity reflected in the vocabulary of *Hamlet* would be, by the standards of *Lear*, as 'finical' as Oswald seems to Kent; the deeply emotive vocabulary of *Macbeth* or the iridescence of physical and affective experience in *Othello* could have done nothing but obscure, in *Lear*, the terror of a universe whose few simple pillars fall ruining. In this respect *Lear* is at the opposite extreme from that play with which its subject has closest connection, *Timon*; the particularity of detail there, the supple periodicity of syntax sustaining a diction far removed from stereotypes of evaluation, is so much unlike the language of *Lear* that to study the rampant inventiveness of the *Timon* style opens one's eyes wider to the magnitude of the stylistic mystery in *King Lear*. What Timon says of his changed fortunes,

Shakespeare might have said of the change that came over his language between the writing of these two plays:

> myself,
> Who had the world as my confectionary,
> The mouths, the tongues, the eyes and hearts of men
> At duty, more than I could frame employment,
> That numberless upon me stuck as leaves
> Do on the oak, have with one winter's brush
> Fell from their boughs and left me open, bare
> For every storm that blows: I, to bear this,
> That never knew but better, is some burden.

What then in the language of *Lear* compensates for its apparent limitations?

First, there is less need for imagery than in other Shakespearian tragedies. Evaluating imagery that projects the conflict or quality of the hero (such as the Pontic sea and the perfect chrysolite images in *Othello*, or the cosmic, heraldic and mythological imagery used for Antony) is unnecessary where the hero is physically the image of his own tragedy. Coleridge observed that Lear has no character and does not need one because old age is itself a character and this peculiarity in the play's subject is repeated at the level of imagery. Lear is visibly old and helpless and later is visibly destitute and mad. The play, to concentrate large issues, need only advert to what the stage has given: 'a head so old and white as this'...'these white flakes'... 'Was this a face / To be opposed against the warring winds...to watch—poor perdu! — / With this thin helm?' On these terms, even a stage direction is tragic language: '*Enter Lear with Cordelia in his armes.*' The consciousness of this art may be judged by the frequency with which the play resorts to sights recognized as eloquent by the characters who see them, and by Shakespeare's care to point out their significance. There are, however, two very remarkable images of Lear's sufferings: the vulture at the heart and the wheel of fire. Both are aimed at conveying intensity rather than the structure of an experience or the quality of a man; both speak of what cannot be seen, yet is powerfully asserted to be going on here and now in the body: 'she hath tied Sharp-tooth'd unkindness, like a vulture, *here*'; 'Thou art a soul in bliss; but I am bound / Upon a wheel of fire, *that mine own tears / Do scald* like molten lead'. In both, as also in the less vivid image of 'the tempest in my mind', the body is tied to what tortures (in the tempest image, the 'greater malady' is 'fix'd'). The quality of this writing can best be discussed by way of comparisons. If we put beside it Hamlet's 'I have that within which passeth show', it becomes clear that Lear's language makes the same point whilst avoiding any appearance of concern with the 'show'. If we put beside it Gloucester's 'I am tied to the stake and I must stand the course' it becomes clear that Lear's language is not merely analogical; Lear's images of torture are embedded in sentences that bind the suffering body of the speaker to the instrument of his torture and so manage the two terms (what tortures, and what feels) as to achieve maximum impact of the cruelty of the one on the sensitivity of the other: consider simply the placing of the terms in 'a vulture, here' and the contrast between 'a wheel of fire' and 'mine own tears' (again syntactically contiguous); consider too the reality of a wheel that is brought in to explain why the tears are hot (the word 'that' is used here to mean 'and that is why' or 'in that'). If we put beside these the image used by Kent, 'he hates him much / That would upon the rack of this tough world / Stretch him out longer', it is clear that the common idea of the incommensurateness of the suffering body to what it has to endure is conveyed not so much by citing the vulture, the wheel or the rack as by making the incommensurateness a reality (rather than an analogical way of speaking). Moreover Kent's image is deployed in a sentence shaped for no other purpose than to support the analogy, whereas Lear's images of wheel and vulture seem to erupt from sentences that did not foreknow their ferocity. I labour here under the heavy difficulty of seeking to retrace in language those swift judgements that our common linguistic habits lead us to make without conscious reflection, and I would not attempt so peculiar a task were it not that I think the power of Lear's language is to be located at a level as hard to see, and as inevitably operative, as this. Since it is not to be believed that the play's power operates independently of the art of dramatic language, and since none the less this language is resistant to familiar critical tools, one must examine the possibility that its impact is due not to its displayed deviations from the language of common life but to its exploitation of the common responses we cannot avoid making when confronted by expressively ordered language. One way of breaking through to this level of power in language is to find methods for seeing the apparently simple and inevitable locution as a willed structure of functioning parts. Comparison is one method. Another is substitution for, or disordering of, the parts; when the light of the original language goes out, one knows one has broken the circuit, and where. I am encouraged to believe that so far I am on the right track because comparison has thrown up results that relate themselves to my impression that what is effective in Lear's language is its free line, the apparent absence of contrivance in the sudden blazes that illuminate the prosy syntax and commonplace vocabulary of Lear's utterances. I am the more encouraged in that these comparisons, though drawn from the main stratum of the play (the presentation of what it is to suffer), show a difference between the language of Lear and that of other characters treating the same topic. Lear's domination of the play is a linguistic domination; his is the most powerful of the voices that speak out of sufferings. Shakespeare concentrates upon Lear the style that gives a felt experience of the incommensurateness of human nature to what it must endure. In the encounter with Poor Tom, as in the poetic images, the contrasted terms are again in contiguity: '. . . to answer with thy *uncovered body this extremity* of the skies.' The syntactical manipulation does not obtrude its art but the art can be judged of by setting alongside this a passage from *Timon* which handles the same topic with a fuller battery of terms but without Lear's 'simple' force: Call the creatures

> Whose naked natures live in all the spite
> Of wreakful heaven, whose bare unhoused trunks,
> To the conflicting elements exposed,
> Answer mere nature.

Moreover, this passage, when put alongside that other passage in *Lear* to which its subject closely relates it—

> Poor naked wretches, wheresoe'er you are,
> That bide the pelting of this pitiless storm,
> How shall your houseless heads and unfed sides,
> Your loop'd and window'd raggedness, defend you
> From seasons such as these?

—is equally inferior in the placing of its terms. In Lear's way of saying these things, what sounds like a natural prose order is in fact more effective than the periodic syntax of Apemantus and though one might have expected the latter to afford more scope for telling juxtaposition of contrasted terms, in fact it is in the 'natural' syntax that the more powerful effect is engineered. (If a man who had already written 'bide the pelting' and 'how shall...raggedness defend you' and 'answer with thy uncovered body this extremity', *afterwards* set to and wrote 'unhoused trunks, / To the conflicting elements exposed, / Answer...', then we should all go away and eat our critical hats or beat them into coxcombs.)

It is of importance in Shakespeare's design that Lear's language though carrying all this power should appear to be uncontrived and matter-of-fact. Gloucester may strain language to express what he conceives—

> thy fierce sister
> In his anointed flesh stick boarish fangs.
> The sea, with such a storm as his bare head
> In hell-black night endured, would have buoy'd up,
> And quench'd the stelled fires

—or Albany call Goneril fiend, devil and monster, or Lear himself use even more violent language in the cursing episodes, but for Lear's actual prolonged bearing of a suffering to which he is tied, vociferation is useless. A similar contrast obtains between Gloucester's language in the blinding scene and the style in which he speaks in his blind wanderings; a simplicity is invented for Gloucester which does not trench upon the simple mode of Lear, but is compatible enough with it to make their encounter linguistically possible. The play is deeply concerned with the inadequacy of language to do justice to feeling or to afford any handhold against abysses of iniquity and suffering. Gloucester's denunciation, 'I shall see / The winged vengeance overtake such children' is savagely nullified by 'See't shalt thou never...Upon these eyes of thine I'll set my foot'. *Lear* begins where *Timon* ends, that is with a vision of the futility of language to encompass or direct reality: 'Lips, let sour words go by and language end.' And fittingly, when Lear enters with the body of Cordelia, his demand for lamentation is not a demand for words—'Howl, howl, howl.' One of the things this play has to say about feeling and suffering is that they are beyond words. This poses the basic problem of the play's dramatic language.

The first steps towards dealing with this problem are taken in the action, characterization and substance of the dialogue rather than in the language itself. The opening scene makes it abundantly clear that the deepest feelings do not run out into words. Next, the glib and free-thinking Bastard expresses in soliloquy his rejection of the meanings others attach to words and public forms, and goes on to show how he can manipulate them to betray. In the third scene Goneril is displayed rigging the showdown with Lear; the fourth shows Kent planning to 'defuse' his speech, but reiterates the characterization of him as 'blunt' and 'plain'; we then meet the Fool, giving a pyrotechnic display of the half-riddling form of expression peculiarly his own. Lear is now surrounded by a collection of characters in whom the relation of meaning to verbal expression is in some way defective, oblique or trumped-up. The master-stroke of the quarrel scene with Regan and Goneril is their indifference to all the verbal forms Lear grasps at to fix the chaos of his emotions or to appeal to their supposed better natures. The master-stroke of Lear as outcast was to surround him with characters whose meanings are overlaid by or filtered through some mesh that makes communication indirect—and then to make Lear seek among the utterances of these and among the burning recollections of his experiences of the false Regan and Goneril and the misunderstood Cordelia for clues in the effort to understand the nature of things and find a form of response. At the heart of Lear's tragedy there lies the great problem of traditional symbolic forms. These are the only language for love and reverence; they have, however, to be maintained against attack, and the function of authority is to enforce observance of form on those who repudiate it. The play begins by breaking from above and from below the cultural pattern that gives shape to the flux of life. From above, Authority takes the tragic step of asking for a token of love, beyond that reverence for the forms of duty it knows itself able to enforce, whilst at the same time abrogating its power: 'Since now we will divest us, both of rule, / Interest of territory, cares of state—/ Which of you shall we say doth love us most?' From below, the Bastard, following in Gloucester's footsteps ('she...had, indeed, sir, a son for her cradle ere she had a husband for her bed') rejects reverence for forms ('Wherefore should I / Stand in the plague of custom...') and acts on his rejection. This double break opens the play's central action: the anatomy of uncontrolled evil and the anatomy of formless feeling. It is, I believe, from some such point of view that one can best appreciate the linguistic art of the play, and the way in which the minor characters are used to support the language of its hero, who must use language not as the adequate register of his experience, but as evidence that his experience is beyond language's scope.

If the problem is seen in these terms, a technique of *montage* seems the obvious solution. Shakespeare 'mounts' (and of course places) a passage in such a way that its depth of meaningfulness is *inferred* from something not strictly contained within that passage itself. This technique is sustained variously: by contrasts, by preparatory passages (especially those indicating a turmoil of feeling vaster than any one expression of any one of its forms), and by surprise. Some instances of it have already had their due in criticism, as for instance the way in which Lear's 'I did her wrong', striking through the Fool's prattle, indicates feeling running deep under the surface of the dialogue; again, the use of the Fool, harping on the prudent course, to suggest the larger dimensions of Lear's concerns. The technique, however, is continuous throughout. The Fool fills in the pauses in which Lear casts about for suitable reaction to what confronts him; what Lear finally says then comes as almost an epigram for the unspoken turmoil, as in

> *Goneril.*   ...do you that offence,
> Which else were shame, that then necessity
> Will call discreet proceeding.
> *Fool.*   For, you know, nuncle,
> The hedge-sparrow fed the cuckoo so long,
> That it had it head bit off by it young.
> So, out went the candle, and we were left darkling.
> *Lear.* Are you our daughter?

The bluntness of Kent, if it had no other function in the play, would have been worth inventing for the sake of Lear's reactions to it in the scene of the stocks; Kent's reiteration of the brutal truth fights stubbornly with Lear's refusal to admit and face what it must mean, and the tension of the contradictions tells us that Lear's incredulity is a dam over which the chaotic flood of feeling will have to break:

> *Lear.* What's he that hath so much thy place mistook
>   To set thee here?
> *Kent.*   It is both he and she;
>   Your son and daughter.
> *Lear.* No.
> *Kent.* Yes.
> *Lear.* No, I say.
> *Kent.* I say, yea.
> *Lear.* No, no, they would not.
> *Kent.* Yes, they have.

When the dam breaks, it is with 'They durst not do't; / They could not, would not do't; 'tis worse than murder'. It is because so much is at stake that Lear has pitted himself against Kent's bluntness so long, and these exchanges intensify the meaning of the naturalistic speech in which Lear's turmoil of discrete responses breaks out, showing that the attitudes he brings to Regan's behaviour are compounded of the remnants of autocracy ('durst not'), of an appalled sense of what it implies ('could not'), and a pathetic need for and belief in Regan ('would not'), which itself is part self-deception, as the long struggle to force a fair construction upon Regan's demeanour in the ensuing scene so clearly shows. This turmoil is followed by characteristic overstatement, ''tis worse than murder', and then, as soon as the outrage has been faced, by a characteristic attempt to deal with it by the assumption of kingly dignity, reflected in the sudden recovery of the regularity of the rhythm, in the antithetical 'which way / Thou mightst deserve, or they impose', and in the climax 'Coming from us'. Upon the basis of this preparation is mounted the quarrel scene, which is great not by virtue of projecting into heightened language some one strain of emotion, but by tracing through shifts of diction and rhythm the Protean forms Lear's hurt casts up and the tragic failure of all of them to stay fixed or to make any difference to those he tries to reach through them. Is there anywhere in literature a comparable attempt to make us understand from within the one unadmitted compulsion, the need for love, that makes its victim box the compass of attitudes with such rapidity and apparent inconsistency? The language that carries this depends, for effect, on our responding as we do to language heard in ordinary life but—because it is after all the language of art—the cues for response are writ large. And further, we are in advance put upon interpreting it properly by the 'naturalistic' dialogue between Lear and Gloucester that precedes Regan's entry. Upon Gloucester's 'You know the fiery quality of the duke', Lear bursts out 'Vengeance! plague! death! confusion! Fiery? what quality?' He is not disputing the fact of the Duke's temper (as in the Quarto's botch, 'what fierie quality'); he is dismissing his right to have any temper at all that could concern a King, let alone a fiery one, and his next words are meant to call Gloucester to his senses ('Why, Gloucester, Gloucester') and to stress what is due to Lear by using titles sarcastically, 'I'ld speak with the *Duke* of Cornwall and *his wife*'. Gloucester's unhappy reply so incenses Lear (by its implication that he must wait the pleasure of his betters) that he flies at its terms—'Inform'd them! Dost thou understand me, man?' and then with

icy displeasure anatomizes the situation: 'The king would speak with Cornwall; the dear father /
Would with his daughter speak', and uses (in the Folio text) for each bond of duty the appropriate verb: 'commands, tends service' (commands it from a subject, expects it of a daughter)
and he goes on to substitute for 'fiery' the contemptuous 'hot': 'the fiery duke? Tell the hot
duke that—'. In these exchanges Lear reacts to and uses language as it is used in common life;
his attitudes are expressed not in an overtly heightened theatrical language but through the
implications, expressive choices, and significant usages available in the common tongue. But
Shakespeare writes into this common speech pointers to what prompts it. For instance, the
abrupt shift to a resolutely different attitude is cued by the unfinished state of 'Tell the hot
duke that—' and by the explicit 'No, but not yet'; the forced nature of this attempted tolerance
is brought out by the contrast between its suddenly regular rhythm and syntax, and the exclama-
tory irregularity of the preceding lines. Then this forced calm breaks in the middle of a line,
to the accompaniment of wrenched accent: 'To take the indisposed and sickly fit / For the sound
man. Death on my state! wherefore / Should he sit here?' This style exploits the expressive
ranges of common language (cueing it where necessary) and supports the expressiveness by
metrical mimesis; it is a style far removed from 'poetic' blank verse that uses the conventional
licence of poetry to elaborate a literary equivalent of the state of feeling supposed in the speaker,
yet we must admit this style to be, in its own way, far removed from the 'naturalism' that
seems merely to transcribe common speech. And though this is by no means the only style
used in the play, it is one that makes it easy to overlook the art, and to suppose the play to be
deficient in heightened language. Upon these exchanges with Kent and Gloucester Shakespeare
mounts the great quarrel scene that follows, where Lear's turmoil of conflicting attitudes is
conveyed through the obliquities, the expressive choices and nuances and even the extravagances
and transparent pretences of language as used by the common man making a scene. But we
should not forget how much is done to support this language; especially, that the very shifts
of tone illuminate one another by contrast, and that the whole scene would have been impossible
if Lear's hopes of Regan, set off against his despair of Goneril, did not so clearly annotate his
ambivalence to both; it was not for nothing that Shakespeare contrived in the plot to get
Goneril to Regan's house.

This 'mounting' of great passages on verbal encounters that prepare for them (and even,
ultimately, on characterization and plot) is a continuous technique, and to bear it in mind may
make some apparent miracles of style less impregnable to commentary. When Lear wakens in
the presence of Cordelia and says, 'You do me wrong to take me out of the grave', though no
critical words are needed to draw attention to the astonishing effect of this, it would need a spate
of words to trace the cause, but leaving aside considerations of diction, prosody and syllabity,
one may observe that what matters very much is that this is precisely the most unexpected
thing Lear could have said; it is mounted on the immediate background of Cordelia's prayerful
concern and pity, her anxiety for 'restoration' and 'medicine', her sense of the wrong others
have done him. This is why Lear astonishes us—but astonishment is as swiftly subsumed into
understanding when these words are revealed to be Lear's interpretation of what he sees, an
interpretation at once morally true and factually 'still, still, far wide': 'Thou art a soul in bliss;
but I am bound / Upon a wheel of fire, that mine own tears / Do scald.' Indeed, throughout this
scene, the language taken line by line or speech by speech resists attempts to trace effect to

cause, for each reverberates against the others, whilst at the same time being itself epigrammatic of vast issues in the antecedent action; the language, despite its simplicity of diction, is sculptural and lapidary in effect. Yet this is none the less a linguistic feat: what moves us is written into the language. One cause of our responses I cannot particularize except by some such term as 'contrast in dimension' (as between, for instance, 'wheel of fire' and 'tears'). A contrast of dimension has already characterized the language in which Lear explored man's bondage to sufferings of infinite depth, and this contrast now re-enters the language with augmented force. Just before the reunion scene opens, Gloucester makes explicit the tragic triad of sensitivity, vast sorrows, and protracted endurance: 'how stiff is my vile sense, / That I stand up, and have ingenious feeling / Of my huge sorrows!' The language of the reunion scene reiterates the contrast (as in 'this great breach in his abused nature', in 'those violent harms' and in the speech 'Was this a face / To be opposed?') but the scene goes beyond the play's earlier point of view by adding a further dimension, that of the holiness of the human being. 'Abused nature' is commended to the cure of kind gods and then, by a further rapid contrast, to the cure of little human pieties; 'let this kiss / Repair those violent harms'. In Cordelia's great speech of retrospect and pity the diction charges the poor human body with dignity ('these white flakes') as it charges the elements with majesty ('the deep dread-bolted thunder') yet at the same time, it reiterates, now under the aegis of pity, the diminutiveness of man's warfare ('this thin helm'...'fain, poor father, to hovel thee'). In this very element of holy compassion, Lear, wakening, burns anew.

A test of the relevance of such suggestions as I have made, is whether they throw light on the language which in the last scene conveys that truth to nature all recognize it to have. '*Enter Lear with Cordelia in his armes*': visual language reaches sublimity here, putting all the play has said into one visible word and bringing the whole plot to its point. Along the receding planes keyed into this tableau we see in an instant of time Lear's sin and its retribution, the wider evil that has struck both, the full fatherhood of Lear bearing his child in his arms whilst at the same time the natural course of life is seen reversed (Lear senile, so lately cared for by Cordelia), the world's destruction of the love and forgiveness that had transcended it—for the reverberation of the reunion is still strong and the language of that scene has opened the way to those suggestions of a saviour's death which now make it inescapable that Cordelia dead in her father's arms and displayed by him to the world, should strike deeply into responses that lie midway between religion and art. 'Howl, howl, howl': there is to be no language for meanings such as these; the point is reiterated in '*Had* I your tongues and eyes, I'ld use them so / That heaven's vault should crack' and with the descent to 'She's gone for ever!' it is as though Shakespeare announced that the language to come is not heaven-shattering uproar, but the terms of common grief. And perhaps the greatest single reason why such terms become uncommon language is the prosody. Its function is obvious, once one looks; but who does, at such moments? Yet we shall not estimate this language rightly if we ignore it. This almost miraculous prosodic art defeats conjecture as to how far it was consciously contrived or how far it sprang with the certainty of long expertise subserving the fury of creation. Lear's 'Howl', iterated (according to the Folio) thrice, rises clear above the metrical pattern into a diapason that leaves the prosodic norm, as it leaves vocabulary, far below, obliterated. Yet still the ear, never losing the expectation of the iambic pentameter, hears this diapason as cut short, abandoned (contrast 'No, no, no, *no*! Come, let's away to prison'); the missing arsis of the second foot is so palpable that the Globe editors filled it in. Shakespeare has managed the apparently impossible feat of making a dumb ululation of terrible length seem inadequate. In the next line the norm is restated with perfect regularity. In the following line the extrametrical final syllable of 'ever' exemplifies the fitness with which in this play Shakespeare uses this licence. It is used in general, as is the frequent mid-line ending of Lear's speeches, to make Lear's own rhythm swing free of conformity to expected pattern, but in the execution of this general effect there is a notably successful placing of these freedoms so that they support the sense of the words. Such prosody adds decisively to the expressiveness of the diction; indeed it is as though Shakespeare filled up the blank verse pattern not from what our mere vocabulary offers but from the intonation patterns of expressive English speech. In the line 'Corde | lia, | Corde | lia! Stay | a litt | le. Ha!' the name is pronounced differently the second time. This is exactly what we all do in calling a name again after getting no answer. One can hear the increasing urgency expressing itself in changed intonation and stress. How Shakespeare came to do all this does not matter, but by doing it he wrote the interpretation of the words into the blank verse structure. Lear's 'Never, never, never, never, never!', a recognized stroke of prosodic art, is not isolated; it is the master-stroke of a prosodic brilliance that helps to make the play's language transcend that natural language of human feeling which it so convincingly simulates.

And, as to my final suggestion that a 'contrast of dimension' is a characteristic of the play's tragic vision: surely it hardly needs saying that the heartbreak of the very last scene is in the contrast between infinite concern and the finiteness of its object; put into words, it is all hope and all despair divided by the down of a feather: 'This feather stirs: she lives! if it be so, / It is a chance which does redeem all sorrows / That ever I have felt.'

KEATS AND *KING LEAR*

BY

D. G. JAMES

I

The first reference to Shakespeare of notable import in Keats' letters is a reference to *King Lear*. It occurs in a letter written to Reynolds from Carisbrooke on 17 April 1817. Keats had crossed from Southampton to the Isle of Wight on the 15th, and at his inn at Southampton earlier that day he had (he says in a letter of the 15th to his brothers), felt lonely at breakfast and went and 'unbox'd a Shakespeare'. The Shakespeare he unboxed was, no doubt, as Miss Spurgeon has said, the seven-volume edition of the Dramatic Works which we know he had bought in London in 1817. He was going to the Isle of Wight for a short period of recreation and study, and he had no doubt made his purchase with these ends in view. Miss Spurgeon thought that he probably got out the first volume of the set. The first play in the first volume was *The Tempest*; and certainly, after saying 'I went and unbox'd a Shakespeare' he adds, quoting Stephano, 'Here's my Comfort'. *King Lear* was in the last volume, along with *Pericles*, *Romeo*, *Hamlet* and *Othello*. After breakfast he went down to Southampton Water to inquire about his ferry. He found it would leave at 3 o'clock. No doubt, during the day and on the crossing, he read his Shakespeare.

He slept at Newport that night and went on to Shanklin. He was delighted by Shanklin, and there was some debate in his mind whether he should settle there or in Carisbrooke. 'Shanklin is a most beautiful place' he wrote in his letter of 17 April to Reynolds,

sloping wood and meadow ground reaches round the Chine, which is a cleft between the Cliffs of the depth of nearly 300 feet at least. This cleft is filled with trees and bushes in the narrow parts; and as it widens becomes bare, if it were not for primroses on one side, which spread to the very verge of the Sea, and some fishermen's huts on the other, perched midway in the Ballustrades of beautiful green Hedges along their steps down to the sands.—But the sea, Jack, the sea—the little waterfall—then the white cliff—then St Catherine's Hill.

But he decided in favour of Carisbrooke, and arranged a lodging in Castle Road. He spent the morning of the 17th settling into his room and unpacking his books. He had found a picture of Shakespeare hanging in the passage of the house; he took it into his room and hung it above his books. Amongst other pictures was one of Milton with his daughters. Later in the letter from which I have just quoted, he wrote: 'From want of regular rest I have been rather *narvus*—and the passage in *Lear*—'Do you not hear the sea?'—has haunted me intensely.' He goes on at once to write out the sonnet *On the Sea*. I give it here exactly as he wrote it out in his letter:

> It keeps eternal Whisperings around
> Desolate shores, and with its mighty swell
> Gluts twice ten thousand Caverns; till the spell

Of Hecate leaves them their old shadowy sound.
Often 'tis in such gentle temper found
    That scarcely will the very smallest shell
    Be moved for days from whence it sometime fell
When last the winds of Heaven were unbound.
O ye who have your eyeballs vext and tir'd
    Feast them upon the wideness of the Sea
O ye whose Ears are dinned with uproar rude
    Or fed too much with cloying melody—
Sit ye near some old Cavern's Mouth and brood
    Until ye start as if the Sea Nymphs quired—

It is certain that he was in a state of great and creative excitement, and that his mind was 'heap'd to the full' with Shakespeare. 'I find', he says later in the same letter, 'that I cannot exist without poetry—without eternal poetry—half the day will not do—the whole of it—I began with a little, but habit has made me a Leviathan—I had become all in a Tremble from not having written any thing of late—the Sonnet over leaf did me some good. I slept the better last night for it—this Morning, however, I am nearly as bad again.' This state of excitement continued; he could not sleep at night; 'I was too much in Solitude, and consequently was obliged to be in a continual burning of thought as an only resource.' Within a week he fairly fled from the strain to join Tom at Margate. 'I became not over capable in my upper Stories and set off pell mell for Margate.'[1]

Keats then was in a state of great excitement, which amounted to a state of nervousness. We must recall that *Poems 1817* had appeared in March; *Endymion* was now much in his mind—he probably embarked on it at Carisbrooke; and we may suppose that part, or much, of his excitement came from his growing sense of poetry as his great vocation and his knowledge that he was at a decisive time in his life. When, on 10 May, he wrote to Hunt from Margate, he recounted something of his visit to the Isle of Wight, and said, 'I have asked myself so often why I should be a Poet more than other Men,—seeing how great a thing it is,—how great things are to be gained by it—What a thing to be in the Mouth of Fame—that at last the Idea has grown so monstrously beyond my seeming Power of attainment that the other day I nearly consented with myself to drop into a Phæton—yet 'tis a disgrace to fail even in a huge attempt, and at this moment I drive the thought from me.' No doubt such thoughts were distressing and exciting his mind at Carisbrooke; these sentences help to build up vividly our picture of him during the week or so he spent on the Island.

The vocation of poetry then, and Shakespeare, filled his mind; and on the 17th, his first full day at Carisbrooke, he wrote that the passage in *Lear*—'Do you not hear the sea?' had been haunting him intensely. He had been coming down from London to the Island and the sea on the 14th and 15th. Whether he read *King Lear* at Southampton, on the ferry, or after he landed on the Island, we do not know. Probably he read *The Tempest*, Shakespeare's island play; but however that may be, Edgar's words to Gloucester were beating in his mind; and it was these words which moved him to write, on the evening of the 16th, his sonnet *On the Sea*.

I give now the passage from *King Lear*:

> *Edgar.* Hark, do you hear the sea?
> *Gloucester.* No, truly.
> *Edgar.* Why, then, your other senses grow imperfect
> By your eyes' anguish.
> *Gloucester.* So it may be, indeed....
> *Edgar.* Come on, sir; here's the place: stand still. How fearful
> And dizzy 'tis, to cast one's eyes so low!
> The crows and choughs that wing the midway air
> Show scarce so gross as beetles: halfway down
> Hangs one that gathers samphire, dreadful trade!
> Methinks he seems no bigger than his head:
> The fishermen, that walk upon the beach,
> Appear like mice; and yond tall anchoring bark,
> Diminish'd to her cock; her cock, a buoy
> Almost too small for sight: the murmuring surge,
> That on the unnumber'd idle pebbles chafes,
> Cannot be heard so high. I'll look no more;
> Lest my brain turn, and the deficient sight
> Topple down headlong.

Now when Keats says that 'the passage in *Lear*—"Do you not hear the sea?"—has haunted me intensely', we take him as referring not only to the words, 'Do you not hear the sea?', but to the passage in which the words are set. Still, Keats picked out these words; these especially haunted him. Why should they? He thinks of Edgar and Gloucester making their way to Dover: stricken and perplexed humanity making its way to the sea, until at last it comes within sound of it. No doubt the sea carries a huge symbolical power; and we may think (as Keats in a later letter[2] suggested we might) of—

> Though inland far we be,
> Our souls have sight of that immortal sea
> Which brought us hither...

to illustrate this. Then Keats composes his sonnet. It is not indeed a great sonnet; but we are moved to read it in the light of the passage he quotes from *King Lear*; and if we do so, one thing appears plainly. The whispering sea of Keats is, in the passage in *Lear*, 'the murmuring surge' which, from the supposed height at which Edgar and Gloucester stood, cannot be heard; and then if we look to the lines of the sonnet—

> Often 'tis in such gentle temper found
> That scarcely will the very smallest shell
> Be moved for days from whence it sometime fell
> When last the winds of Heaven were unbound—

we look also to

> The murmuring surge,
> That on th'unnumber'd idle pebbles chafes—

the gentle sea *chafes* the pebbles, but does not stir them. (We think of

But where the dead leaf fell, there did it rest.

The image of a thing, a leaf, a shell, coming to rest, the stillness of things, or their coming to stillness, was dear to Keats' imagination.) For the rest (if we leave aside the reference to Hecate, which recalls 'The mysteries of Hecate and the night'), I do not see any further debt to the passage in *Lear* or to the play as a whole. (There are words and phrases which show *The Tempest*: 'desolate shores' recalls 'this most desolate isle' of Ariel (III, iii, 80); and 'eyeballs' and 'Sea Nymphs' come from I, ii, 301–4.)

But the sonnet did not work off the excitement in Keats' mind which was connected with the passage in *Lear*. I quoted from the letter of 17 April to Reynolds the passage about Shanklin Chine, 'a cleft between the cliffs of the depth of nearly 300 feet at least'. It was probably the Chine at Shanklin that brought the passage from *Lear* vividly to his mind, or at least, it sharply reinforced it if it was already working in him; 'But the sea, Jack, the sea—the little waterfall—then the white cliff—then St Catherine's Hill'; the sea, the cliff and the hill with the deep chine may well have precipitated the passage into his consciousness. Besides, the passage remained in his mind; it came to play a vivid part in his envisagement of his present and future fortunes. In a letter written to Haydon on 10–11 May from Margate, with the first book of *Endymion* giving him trouble, he refers to Haydon's having told him not to give way to his forebodings, and goes on: 'I am "one that gathers samphire, dreadful trade" the Cliff of Poesy Towers above me—yet when Tom who meets with some of Pope's Homer in Plutarch's Lives reads some of those to me they seem like Mice to mine.' It is clear then that Edgar's lines in *Lear* became closely associated, in a way I cannot pretend to be able to analyse clearly, with Keats' thoughts on his progress in poetry.

A little later in the same letter, he writes: 'I remember your saying that you had notions of a good Genius presiding over you. I have of late had the same thought. Is it too daring to Fancy Shakespeare this Presidor? When in the Isle of Wight I met with a Shakespeare in the Passage of the House at which I lodged—it came nearer to my idea of him than any I have seen—I was but there a Week yet the old Woman made me take it with me.' In view of what I have recounted, it seems certain that the lines in *Lear* contributed a good deal to the notion of Shakespeare as his 'Presidor'.

II

We think of 1819 as Keats' wonderful year. But 1817 was wonderful too: it was the year chiefly of *Endymion*. I pass by the months intervening between his leaving Carisbrooke and Christmas. He was now in Hampstead, and on 21 December he wrote a letter to his brothers in the course of which he said, speaking of West's picture 'Death on the Pale Horse', 'The excellence of every art is its intensity, capable of making all disagreeables evaporate, from their being in close relationship with Beauty and Truth. Examine "King Lear", and you will find this exemplified throughout; but in this picture we have unpleasantness without any momentous depth of speculation excited, in which to bury its repulsiveness.' Now, we know that *King Lear* contains, more than any play of Shakespeare, extreme and revolting wickedness; and no doubt it was for this reason that Keats singled out *King Lear* as his example of the power of great art.

Still, we must ask, what is meant by saying that the wickedness of Goneril, Regan, Edmund and Cornwall 'evaporates' in the context of the play? In this, Keats says, consists the play's 'excellence', and it is this that proves its 'intensity'. But we must also notice what he says in the last sentence of the quotation. He says that West's picture does not, as *Lear* does, excite a 'momentous depth of speculation' in which its repulsiveness may be 'buried'. Later in the same letter he speaks of 'negative capability' as the quality which Shakespeare possessed 'so enormously'—'*Negative Capability*, that is, when a man is capable of being in uncertainties, mysteries, doubts, without any irritable reaching after fact and reason—Coleridge, for instance, would let go by a fine isolated verisimilitude caught from the Penetralium of mystery, from being incapable of remaining content with half-knowledge'; then he says, apparently repeating his previous thought about the 'evaporation' of 'repulsiveness', 'This pursued through volumes would perhaps take us no further than this, that with a great poet the sense of Beauty overcomes every other consideration, or rather obliterates all consideration'.

It is clear then that the subject of my essay carries us to the heart of Keats' 'speculations' about poetry. Just a month earlier he had written his famous letter to Bailey[3] in which he said things that lie very near to the sentences about *King Lear* which I am now discussing. They are too well known to require quoting here; they speak of the poet as not having 'any individuality and determined character', of what the imagination seizes as beauty being also truth, and of the imagination being comparable to Adam's dream in *Paradise Lost*. It seems clear that he saw *King Lear* as the point of departure for, or an illustration of, his deepest speculations about poetry.

This essay is not the place in which to try to explore fully Keats' thoughts about poetry and all their implications. 'I am running my head into a Subject which I am certain I could not do justice to under five years Study and three vols octavo', Keats himself said in the letter to Bailey. I shall in what follows only 'speculate', so far as I can, in the spirit of Keats' own 'speculations', on what he says in these sentences.

III

The disagreeableness and repulsiveness in *King Lear*, which is 'evaporated', 'buried', 'obliterated', is concentrated in Goneril, Regan, Cornwall and Edmund, and their actions. But over against them are set characters of transcendent beauty, above all, Cordelia and Edgar; there are also Kent and the changed Lear we see at the end of the play. Now I take Keats as saying, when he speaks of the disappearance of what is disagreeable in the play, that, as the play advances and comes to its end, it is upon the great spiritual beauty of some of the characters, upon the scene in which Lear and Cordelia are reconciled, and again upon the scene in which Lear dies over Cordelia's dead body, that our minds are concentrated. Evil and the evil characters are finally seen only as evoking and proving the great spiritual beauty of Cordelia and Edgar. We may say, in a certain abstract point of view, as Keats himself said, that the poet 'delights as much in conceiving' a Regan as a Cordelia: but also, the repulsiveness of Regan is overcome by the beauty of Cordelia and falls away from our minds. The beauty that we behold in Cordelia, Edgar, Kent, Lear, is tragic and sorrowful; but it is the greater for that; it is this beauty, intensified indeed by sorrow, which obliterates every other consideration; it draws to itself all our attention and 'speculation'.

I think that this is what Keats intended in the sentences I am discussing, and it is, I think, a just rendering of our experience in reading the play. Now Keats speaks of the 'momentous depth of speculation' excited by the play, and says that what is repulsive in the play is 'buried' in this 'depth of speculation'. The word 'speculation' plays a great part in Keats' letters when he is reflecting on the nature of poetry; and it is very important to catch accurately the sense in which he employs it. He does not mean by it any ideas or pieces of doctrine which are applied by the poet to life in his poetry, as required by Matthew Arnold in his exposition of the nature of poetry. Matthew Arnold's notion that poetry should have or supply 'a thorough interpretation of the world' would have been abhorrent to Keats. Keats' view of the poet required that he neither bring to his poetry, nor distil from his poetry, any body of doctrine, set of ideas, or interpretation of the world. So far from the poet's 'speculations' being a doctrine or a set of doctrines affirmed by the poet, they are, instead, no more than 'uncertainties, mysteries, doubts' which go along with no 'irritable reaching after fact and reason'; the 'speculative' mind of the poet 'remains content with half-knowledge'. Coleridge could not, he says, be content with this; and in speaking of Wordsworth once, he said, 'For the sake of a few fine imaginative or domestic passages, are we to be bullied into a certain Philosophy engendered in the whims of an Egotist?...Many a man can travel to the very bourne of Heaven and yet want confidence to put down his half-seeing'.[4] Here it is 'half-seeing'; earlier it was 'half-knowledge'. Now this 'half-seeing' or 'half-knowledge' are what Keats means by 'speculations'. They are not doctrines or formulations; they are a properly poetic thing (we think of 'Thou hast no speculation in those eyes'), and may not be resolved into theory and philosophy; they are all that a poet can properly lay claim to. They belong to 'sensation', not to thought; they may not be clarified, brought to certainty, reduced to fact and reason. The poet proceeds by imagination; he does not lapse into the intellect. His imagination may, indeed, only go so far; it provides a half-seeing only; but with that the poet is, and must be, content, or he is less a poet. Now this is the heart of Keats' thought about poetry.[5]

I ask, What did Keats mean when he spoke of 'a momentous depth of speculation' being excited by *King Lear*, in which all repulsiveness is 'buried'? What are Shakespeare's 'speculations' in *King Lear*, and what emerges in the play as a 'half-seeing', or a 'half-knowledge', which 'buries' repulsiveness? Now we must understand that to this question, from its nature, there can be no clear explicit answer; there can only be uncertainties, mysteries, doubts; and a man may travel to the very bourne of Heaven and yet want confidence to put down his half-seeing. It is a part of the greatness of the play that its half-seeing is not 'put down'.

Still, perhaps we are required to try, to the best of our power, to provide some sort of answer; or perhaps to try to do so is folly. How can one render the half-seeing in which the play and the speculation consist? The answer in the end is the play, and it is poetry; it cannot be turned into prose. But if we persist in asking, What does Shakespeare see, in the form of his play, which is at best a half-seeing? we must reply by asking whether it is not true that in the 'momentous depth of speculation' which gathers about the spectacle of the innocence, suffering and death of Cordelia, all repulsiveness is 'buried' and lost to view, except in so far as it makes beauty, at its farthest human reaches, full of sorrow and all the greater on that account? And is not this power of beauty, thus proven and impregnable, and bearing, in serenity, the world's evil, the only point from which we can comprehend, so far as may be, human experience? This is 'speculation' only, though it is indeed momentous speculation and carries us far. But it is not *in* the play or stated by it. It is 'excited' by it, and an integral part of its power, and the proof of its excellence.

IV

On 23 January 1818, Keats wrote to Bailey and said, 'My brother Tom is getting stronger, but his Spitting of blood continues. I sat down to read King Lear yesterday, and felt the greatness of the thing up to the writing of a Sonnet preparatory thereto—in my next you shall have it.' On the same day he wrote to his two brothers, and said, 'Nothing is finer for the purposes of great productions than a very gradual ripening of the intellectual powers. As an instance of this—observe—I sat down yesterday to read "King Lear" once again [*sic*] the thing appeared to demand the prologue of a Sonnet, I wrote it and began to read....' He then writes out the sonnet.

I give the sonnet as he transcribed it in his Folio edition of Shakespeare, on the end leaf of *Hamlet* and facing the first page of *Lear*:

> O Golden-tongued Romance, with serene Lute!
>   Fair plumed Syren, Queen of far-away!
>   Leave melodizing on this wintry day
> Shut up thine olden Pages, and be mute.
> Adieu! for, once again, the fierce dispute
>   Betwixt Damnation and impassion'd clay
>   Must I burn through; once more humbly assay
> The bitter-sweet of this Shakesperean fruit.
> Chief Poet! and ye Clouds of Albion,
>   Begetters of our deep eternal theme!
> When through the old oak forest I am gone,
>   Let me not wander in a barren dream:
> But when I am consumed in the fire,
> Give me new Phoenix Wings to fly to my desire.

He then adds: 'So you see I am getting at it, with a sort of determination and strength.'

I call attention first to the sentences, 'Nothing is finer for the purpose of great productions than a very gradual ripening of the intellectual powers. As an instance of this...I sat down yesterday to read "King Lear" once again.' Their meaning is not clear. But Keats has said, in the sentences immediately preceding them, that he had been for a long time 'addicted to passiveness'; but, now, he said, he could not bear to be 'uninterested or unemployed'. In this state of renewed energy he sets about reading *King Lear* again, and speaks of 'a gradual ripening of the intellectual powers'. By this I take him to mean that his periods of apparent laziness played their part in the ripening of his powers and helped to prepare him for periods of creative energy. Now, in one such period, he sets himself to 'burn through' *King Lear*. Then, having written out the sonnet, he says, 'So you see I am getting at it, with a sort of determination and strength'; and by 'getting at it' I take him to mean that he is now addressing himself with renewed determination to what he judges to be the highest task of poetry, namely meditation upon and treatment of the tragic quality of human life; and in doing so, he sees *King Lear* as the supreme gift to him of his presiding genius in the gradual ripening of his intellectual powers. It was in this condition of mind that he was moved to compose his sonnet. His doing so was like a prayer.

We do not know (at least, I do not know) whether in the apostrophe to Romance he has in mind a book of Romance he may previously have been reading. I do not think he can have had in mind his own *Endymion*: *Endymion* was not a Romance of the kind he has in mind in the sonnet. I therefore take the reference as a general one: he wishes to turn from Romance to Tragedy: and we may call to mind what he says in one of his notes on Milton: Milton 'had an exquisite passion for what is properly, in the sense of ease and pleasure, poetical luxury... but there was working in him as it were that same sort of thing as operates in the great world to the end of a Prophecy's being accomplish'd: therefore he devoted himself rather to the ardours than the pleasures of Song'; and he goes on to say that Milton broke 'through the clouds which envelope so deliciously the Elysian field of verse, and committed himself to the Extreme'. This is the thought, without relation to Milton, which animates the opening of the sonnet. It is indeed possible that in

> Adieu! for, once again, the fierce dispute,
> Betwixt Damnation and impassion'd clay
> Must I burn through

there is an echo of his reading of *Paradise Lost*—'Betwixt Hell torment ["Damnation" is "Hell torment" in the version he gives in the letter] and impassion'd clay' may make us think so; and when we read

> once more humbly assay
> The bitter-sweet of this Shakesperean fruit

our surmise has some confirmation: Eve, addressing the Forbidden Tree, says of it that its taste

> too long forborn, at first assay
> Gave elocution to the mute.

But however that may be, I remark that he speaks of 'burning' his way through this dispute as it is rendered in *King Lear*; and we recall him saying in his letter to Leigh Hunt about his stay in Carisbrooke: 'I was too much in Solitude, and consequently was obliged to be in a continual *burning of thought*.' It seems clear that we can hardly exaggerate the power of the impact of *King Lear* upon him, and its importance to him in his growth as a poet. Of the phrase 'bitter-sweet' I shall speak a little later on. I go on to the sestet of the sonnet. Keats apostrophizes Shakespeare and the clouds of Albion (Albion is the name for Britain in the text of *Lear*— 'The realm of Albion', III, ii, 91) as begetting the eternal theme which is no doubt the 'dispute' of the earlier lines; and he speaks of himself as going through 'the old oak forest', which I can only take to mean prehistoric Britain, the setting of the play, covered by forests of oak. He asks that the reading of the play leave his life no barren dream, but instead be a consuming, and then a creative, 'Fire' from which he will emerge with a new life.

I remark now the phrase 'bitter-sweet' in the line

> The bitter-sweet of this Shakesperean fruit.

It has often been truly said that Keats' own poetry exhibits frequently a poignant fusion of joy and sorrow, and of life and death: *To Autumn* most perfectly exhibits it. And in *King Lear*, what Keats has chiefly in mind, we may suppose, is what is shown in these famous lines of the Gentleman describing Cordelia:

> patience and sorrow strove
> Who should express her goodliest. You have seen
> Sunshine and rain at once: her smiles and tears
> Were like a better way: those happy smilets,
> That play'd on her ripe lip, seem'd not to know
> What guests were in her eyes; which parted thence,
> As pearls from diamonds dropp'd. In brief,
> Sorrow would be a rarity most belov'd,
> If all could so become it.

This takes us back to what I spoke of earlier: the beauty which overcomes what is disagreeable and repulsive is one suffused with sorrow; and we may think of the affliction which, Leontes said—*King Lear* and the last plays may be seen as commentaries on one another—'has a taste as sweet as any cordial comfort'.

V

There are a number of other references, direct or oblique, to *King Lear* in Keats' letters. But I have spoken of those places in the letters where *Lear* engaged his most creative attention.

It remains for me to add that it seems clear that Keats read *King Lear* chiefly in a copy of the 1808 reprint of the Folio of 1623. He read it also in the last volume of the seven in the Princeton copy; but he did not mark it. The Folio reprint shows it heavily underlined. Miss Spurgeon did not have very much to say about these markings. But one thing she said which is of great interest. 'It is clear', she said, 'from the marking throughout how strongly Keats felt the truth which he expressed more than once in various forms, and with special reference to this play in the letter to his brothers of the 28th of December 1817',[6] and she then quoted the sentence about the excellence of every art being the intensity which makes all disagreeables evaporate through being in close relationship with beauty and truth. Miss Spurgeon did not however explain in what ways Keats' markings of the Folio reprint show this. I have myself studied these markings in Keats' reprint; and I can only, and regretfully, say that I fail to see that they throw any special light on what Keats intended by his sentence. But it is possible that a more detailed study of Keats' markings might bring to light significances which I have not discerned.

Keats' copy of the Folio reprint makes clear that, early in 1818, he was reading *King Lear*. Tom Keats' health was sinking fast, and Keats underlined 'Poor Tom!' in III, iv, 38, and wrote alongside 'Sunday evening, Oct. 4. 1818'. On 1 December Tom died. Now it seems clear that Keats had begun to compose *Hyperion* in September; we cannot be sure, but we may assume, that early in October he was composing the poem's first book. It is of great interest to us that at this time he took himself again to the reading of *King Lear*. His brother was dying; and he wrote to Dilke on 21 September: 'I wish I could say that Tom was any better. His identity presses upon one so all day that I am obliged to go out—and although I had intended to have given some time to study alone, I am obliged to write, and plunge into abstract images to ease myself of his countenance his voice and feebleness—so that I live now in a continual fever.' This gives us a picture of Keats' state of mind in the autumn and early winter—looking after his brother, writing *Hyperion*—and reading *Lear*. He was in 'a continual burning of thought'.

Hyperion was Keats' most ambitious poem. It was his epic. This is certainly how he saw it. It was no 'cup of old wine'; he was 'committing himself to the Extreme'. He accompanied its composition by reading *Lear*; and we must consider briefly this important fact. I shall confine myself to a single 'speculation'.

Early in the first book, Keats describes the face of Thea:

> But oh! how unlike marble was that face:
> How beautiful, if sorrow had not made
> Sorrow more beautiful than Beauty's self.

We think of

> patience and sorrow strove
> Who should express her goodliest...
> In brief,
> Sorrow would be a rarity most belov'd
> If all could so become it.

Then, when Apollo, in Book III, sees the face of Mnemosyne, he exclaims:

> Goddess! I have beheld those eyes before,
> And their eternal calm, and all that face,

it is that face, at once serene and filled with tragic suffering—

> Names, deeds, gray legends, dire events, rebellions
> Majesties, sovran voices, agonies

—which makes him into a God.

I think it most probable that, in describing Thea and then Mnemosyne (and indeed in describing the face of Moneta in the revised *Hyperion*) Keats' imagination was moved by the description of Cordelia given to Kent:

> it seem'd she was a queen
> Over her passion; who, most rebel-like,
> Sought to be king o'er her....
> patience and sorrow strove
> Who should express her goodliest. You have seen
> Sunshine and rain at once; her smile and tears
> Were like a better way; those happy smilets,
> That play'd on her ripe lip, seem'd not to know
> What guests were in her eyes; which parted thence,
> As pearls from diamonds dropp'd. In brief,
> Sorrow would be a rarity most belov'd
> If all could so become it.

Keats translates into the countenances of his Goddesses what is shown in Cordelia's face; and Shakespeare with his

> There she shook
> The holy water from her heavenly eyes,
> And clamour moisten'd: then away she started
> To deal with grief alone,

appears to give to Cordelia a more than mortal nature.

Matthew Arnold put Keats with Shakespeare, and general assent has been given to this. They had the same order of imagination, and Keats said that he believed he understood Shakespeare to his depths. Both reached the limits of the imagination's power in their beholdment of sorrow as heightening beauty and of serenity as containing suffering. In their writings we see the world's pain and evil, in the end, in the form of the sorrow of the innocent, and, as borne, encompassed, and overcome by beauty. Then comes death. We can only add that it then becomes clear that the end of poetry is not in itself: it excites 'speculations' which it may not itself treat or adjudicate upon; and Keats and Shakespeare were above all alike in seeing that this is so.

NOTES

1. To Leigh Hunt, 10 May 1817.
2. To Jane Reynolds, 14 September 1817.
3. 22 November 1817.
4. To Reynolds, 3 February 1818.
5. On 29 January 1818, in the week following that in which he wrote to his brothers and copied out for them the sonnet on *King Lear*, Keats wrote a letter to Haydon. This letter is, alas, lost. We owe it to Cecil Price, of Aberystwyth, that we know of it (*Neuphilologische Mitteilungen*, 3, LIX, Helsinki, 1958). He has shown that in Sotheby and Wilkinson's sale catalogue 12–17 May 1851, there is listed a letter from Keats to Haydon. The catalogue describes the letter as 'full of philosophical feeling' and quotes from it these sentences: 'Some people believe everything, some believe nothing, and some will give credit to anything. I am none of those. I can only say that I do not disbelieve anything.' Would we had this letter!
6. *Keats's Shakespeare* (Oxford, 1928).

KING LEAR ON THE STAGE:
A PRODUCER'S REFLECTIONS

BY

ARNOLD SZYFMAN

More than once it has been said that *King Lear* is unsuited for the stage. Most of those who have expressed this opinion were not connected with the theatre and consequently we might perhaps be prepared to set their opinions aside; but recently the same judgement on the play has been passed by one whose words deserve very careful consideration. Miss Margaret Webster, descended from a well-known stage family, is an actress herself and a director responsible for numerous Shakespeare productions in England and the United States, and when, after an acute examination of the text, in her *Shakespeare Today* she questions the theatrical value of *King Lear*, obviously her words must be duly weighed.

For myself I am at variance with her, and perhaps the fact that, as director of the Teatr Polski in Warsaw, during the course of forty years (of which ten war years were theatrically wasted) I have had the opportunity of directing twenty-one productions of Shakespeare's dramas, including *King Lear*, justifies my entry into this long-continuing debate—a debate which presumably will not be closed either by Miss Webster's remarks or my own.

I

Miss Webster writes:

Macbeth, whatever the spiritual or abstract significance with which it has been variously endowed, has always been played for its tremendous dramatic impact. The structural basis of *Othello* ensures a sweep of movement which, in the theatre, overwhelms all theoretical debate as to the motivation of its principal characters. And it is the lack of this fundamental theatre economy, rather than any insuperable difficulty in the playing of the leading part, that makes *King Lear*, for me, the least actable of the four plays—

the fourth, of course, being *Hamlet*.

Now, I doubt whether comparisons of this kind are really valid or profitable. What we must look for is the truly essential quality of any given play, and this quality can be found only by a consideration of its own text. We might argue that *King Lear* displays no greater psychological *naïveté* than *Othello*, that its pessimistic strain is no deeper than that of *Macbeth*; but what we are concerned with basically is this tragedy in and for itself.

We may, of course, choose to deny its greatness. I remember how, after a production of the play at the Teatr Polski in 1935, the Polish critic Tadeusz Boy Żeleński dismissed Shakespeare's wretched monarch as 'an old fool' and a 'moron'. Rarely, however, are the arguments which are used to deny *King Lear*'s theatrical worth based on a rejection of its artistic value. Rather, these arguments are founded on a deep appreciation of its fiery quality and passionate impact, and more than once they have been associated with a complete approval of Bradley's assessment of the play as a work to be deemed one of the greatest artistic creations of all time, a masterpiece worthy of being ranked with *Prometheus Bound* and *La Divina Commedia*, Beethoven's symphonies and the statues in the Medici Chapel.

II

In approaching this question, we certainly should not permit ourselves to aver that because we may not have seen a thoroughly satisfying production of *King Lear* therefore no satisfying production can ever prove possible. I recall vividly the Stratford Memorial Theatre performance of *Titus Andronicus* in 1955. This was unforgettable, in which Peter Brook's direction gave the play a completely fresh structural quality, and in which an excellent cast headed by Sir Laurence Olivier, Vivien Leigh and Anthony Quayle created a convincing and deeply moving interpretation. Everything here—the performers, the settings, the costumes and the music— was in harmony.

If, before seeing this production, I had been asked whether *Titus Andronicus* was suited for effective revival, I confess, somewhat reluctantly, that I should have said 'No'; and I expect that most people would have said the same. Yet Peter Brook's achievement demonstrated effectively that this early work of Shakespeare's, admittedly not one of his masterpieces, could be made on the stage to produce an overwhelming impression.

In *King Lear* we have a play much more deeply poetic, much closer to the human heart, much finer in its structure; and we must be cautious, thinking of this production of *Titus Andronicus*, not to dismiss it from the theatre so lightly.

III

The storm scenes are, of course, those which are most commonly adduced by those who believe that *King Lear* cannot effectively be presented in the playhouse. Basing their views on productions which they have seen, the writers who hold to such an opinion come to the double conclusion (1) that the storm scenes, central to the tragedy, can never be adequately shown in the theatre, and (2) that therefore *King Lear* should be read and not seen.

But these conclusions are not truly valid. It is true, of course, that the storm may be shown in such a way as to destroy the quality of the text. Two years ago I saw another production by Peter Brook, that of *The Tempest*, and it must be admitted that this failed to capture the spirit of the idyllic scenes, of the supernatural elements, or of the clowns. The storm was certainly impressive—as a storm; but unfortunately this led to a drowning of the actors' words, and thus it interfered with the exposition of the text.

This does not, however, imply that a storm must always have such an effect. For myself, I should endeavour, in *King Lear*, not to introduce the elements of a real storm, with lashing rain and leaves shivering in the wind, but rather to suggest a storm by means merely of light and music. Unquestionably, the theatre possesses the power of thus arousing the impression of a tempest without in any way removing emphasis from the text itself.

IV

It has, however, been further argued that, despite its grandeur, *King Lear* exhibits many weaknesses. This tragedy, it is said, abounds in strange situations and irritating conventions, in inhuman atrocities and unbearable melodramatics which can make little appeal to modern audiences; its structure is weakened by the introduction of too many plot threads; its characters are treated over-schematically; it exhibits, as often in Shakespeare, weak scene endings. Thus, the argument goes, the true effect of the tragedy may be gained more by reading than by seeing it on the stage. My own view is that these weaknesses are quite as apparent in the study as in the theatre, and that in a *good* theatre production an imaginative director and sensitive actors may, in combination, clarify many of the difficulties apparent in the text and may so humanize the characters as to draw our attention away from what otherwise might seem puzzling, distasteful or foolish.

Here the theatre's peculiar magic can be of greater force than the imagination of the average reader, who has only his own perception and fantasy to aid him. By their skill the director and the actors (and here, of course, I repeat that what I have in mind are creative interpreters of more than ordinary ability) can achieve so much that even structural faults become hardly noticeable, while the characters, invested with the individualities of the actors who take these parts, are wrought from rough symbols into human personalities. We may readily admit that an unimaginative director can easily ruin the play by losing a sense of proportion and imposing on it a tempo false to its inner being; but such directors should not take from us our willingness to recognize what can be achieved in truly great productions.

One thing has to be recognized. The realism, and particularly the naturalism, which reigned in the theatre at the end of the nineteenth century and still persists on many stages today, can, and indeed must, ruin every production of *King Lear* to which it is applied. From beginning to end this tragedy comes before us as a *legend*, bearing with it all the elements of the folk-tale of past ages. To treat it in any sense realistically is to destroy its quality, but, provided its scenes are treated imaginatively and without elaboration in the spirit in which Shakespeare conceived them, it stands alongside *Œdipus Rex*, as one of the finest of all tragedies. *King Lear* is a popular drama, in the highest and noblest sense of the word 'popular', and consequently it possesses a peculiar directness and simplicity. Even if it is acted without a storm at all, without a drop of rain or a single dishevelled hair on Lear's head, so long as it is played in the spirit of a folk-tale by performers who know how to make a distinction between legendary and realistic truth, it must move and stir us in the theatre.

This comes to saying: Let the director and his actors not think of the tragedy as a 'gigantic attack upon humanity itself', or as a 'bitter and terrible cry against the overwhelming power of the Gods', or as an expression of 'the cosmic forces beyond mortal knowledge'; let them play it humanly as a simple tragic legend of an unfortunate King and his three daughters and of an easily-misled father and his two sons.

COSTUME IN *KING LEAR*

BY

W. MOELWYN MERCHANT

The greater number of the illustrations to *King Lear*, whether in frontispieces and other published engravings or in easel pictures, are set on the heath during the storm. Rarely in Shakespeare has costume played so full a part either in direct stage business or in symbolic action as in these scenes on the heath. The argument sways uncertainly in Lear's mind through a complete circle to revulsion; in compassionate prudence he counsels Edgar:

Why, thou wert better in thy grave, than to answer with thy uncovered body, this extremity of the skies. (III, iv, 105–6)

and this momentary insight into dereliction, in its pity for Edgar's nakedness, is pointed by the contrast with the 'courtly' costumes of the Fool, Kent and Lear himself, who are all indebted to the worm and the beast for their 'lendings'. Edgar's previous speech to Lear had approved in advance his rejection of a garment's 'sophistication', and with precisely Lear's choice of hide and silk:

Let not the creaking of shoes nor the rustling of silks, betray thy poor heart to woman. (III, iv, 97–9)

Edgar and Lear take up the same theme in the fourth act. Edgar obliquely declares his constancy to his father in the ambiguous words:

> You're much deceived: in nothing am I changed
> But in my garments (IV, vi, 9–10)

and in the same scene (IV, vi) Lear returns to his former argument:

> Through tatter'd clothes small vices do appear;
> Robes and furr'd gowns hide all. Plate sin with gold,
> And the strong lance of justice hurtless breaks;
> Arm it in rags, a pigmy's straw does pierce it. (IV, vi, 168–71)

Yet vesture has its positive significance; at the reunion of Cordelia with Kent and then with her father, her first request to Kent is that he Be better suited,

> These weeds are memories of those worser hours:
> I prithee, put them off. (IV, vii, 6–8)

Her immediate concern for her father's condition, 'Is he array'd?', is answered by the Gentleman's assurance: in the heaviness of his sleep

> We put fresh garments on him (IV, vii, 21–2)

and Lear himself, in his continued mental chaos, directs attention to these new regal garments, to which he is not yet suited: all the skill I have

> Remembers not these garments. (IV, vii, 66–7)

To the end of the tragedy Lear is not to resume the 'Rule' of which he had shown such anxiety to 'divest' himself.

If any coherent conclusions are to be drawn from the multitude of paintings and engravings which attempt to realize in theatrical costume this aspect of the interior tragedy, there must be sharp selection. With few exceptions, it is profitable to consider mainly the costumes of Lear, Cordelia, Edgar and the Fool. There are one or two drawings of Lear in full regal costume and this survives in varying degrees into the storm scenes; Cordelia will be found throughout the eighteenth century in tolerably modish costume until Regency fashions introduced a new 'Classical' approach. No trace of the sixteenth- and seventeenth-century engravings of Bedlam Beggars appears to survive in the presentation of Edgar; as we shall find, the early illustrated Shakespeares in the eighteenth century establish his costume in strict conformity with the descriptions in the text. The Fool is the most complex figure. In the course of the eighteenth century we shall find many different survivals: the 'motley' described by Leslie Hotson;[1] the young and helpless figure which is implied in Lear's words, 'In Boy; go first, you houseless poverty'; a *commedia dell'arte* figure mediated for the eighteenth-century stage by the paintings of Watteau; and, finally, persisting through all these variants on Shakespeare's Fool, the traditional figure in coxcomb and bells, found, among Shakespeare's immediate predecessors and contemporaries, in Greene's *Friar Bacon and Friar Bungay* ('Naturall Idiots and Fooles...weare in their Cappes, cockes feathers or a hat with a necke and heade of a cocke on the top, and a bell theron') and in Whitney's *Choice of Emblemes*, where the costume is cited complete: 'A motley coate, a cockescombe, or a bell.'[2]

Three frontispieces, the engravings for Rowe's editions of 1709 and 1714, and Hayman's drawing engraved by Gravelot for Hanmer's edition of 1744, establish the manner of presentation for the first half of the eighteenth century. There is an unusually sharp distinction between 'literary' and 'theatrical' comment in the two Rowe engravings. In the frontispiece for the 1709 edition (Pl. I*a*), Kent and Gloucester urge the distracted Lear towards the thatched hovel which was to reappear in this form throughout the century; all three are in the 'modern dress' of current theatre usage. Edgar as Poor Tom is, however, unusually elaborately costumed (most subsequent engravings suggest only the Fool's comment, 'Nay, he reserved a blanket, else we had been all shamed') but there are two details, the wisps of straw bound in at the calves and the stout staff, which become established for almost all his later appearances. Du Guernier's crude engraving for the 1714 edition (Pl. I*b*) has a more elaborate group based on Shakespeare's text rather than on Nahum Tate's, from which the Fool was excluded. The gestures and attitudes ingeniously suggest fragments of speeches from a considerable part of III, iv. Lear plucks at his garments at 'Off, off you Lendings', while the Fool admonishes him, 'Prithee, nuncle, be contented, 'tis a naughty night to swim in'; the stage direction, '*Enter Gloucester, with a Torch*', is therefore anticipated, with his gesture to the hovel, 'Go in with me'. Kent is an indeterminate figure, and Edgar, bonneted as in the 1709 engraving, is distinguished by little more than his staff. There is not much to be said about the costume in this undistinguished little drawing; the Fool, Lear and Gloucester have suggestions of ruffs at the neck, perhaps an antique gesture. Hayman's frontispiece (Pl. I*c*) has the distinction that we find in all the drawings for Sir

Thomas Hanmer's edition of 1744.[3] Edgar, with blanket, staff and straw, is established as the recognizable stage figure of the next century or so; Kent is a roughly dignified figure, but Lear's costume is ambiguous. It is possible that Hayman's drawing reflects Garrick's performance at Goodman's Fields in the 1741/2 season, for, as we shall see, they were in friendly correspondence about the role at this time; certainly the drawing anticipates Garrick's Lear of twelve years later and in general the costume resembles his. But the simple strap-work decoration where Garrick was to use ermine, and the odd suggestion of smocking on the vest, tone down the regality (though Lear's hose and shoes have an elegance greater than Garrick's; cf. Pl. I*d*). The Fool again sends us back beyond Tate; he wears a rather poverty-stricken version of the garb shown in Du Guernier's engraving in 1714.

We have very full indications of Garrick's costuming for his *Lear* productions. There are many versions of Benjamin Wilson's painting (which has some of Zoffany's authority[4]) and a portion of the McArdell mezzotint is reproduced here at Pl. I*d*. A. C. Sprague comments on 'something of a novelty', that Garrick 'and the other actors in his production were "judiciously habited", not in contemporary, but in old English dresses'.[5] This is not readily apparent in the engraving, and Garrick as Lear preserves something of the tradition, found also in productions of *Henry the Eighth*, that contemporary coronation dress was worn. We have further evidence of Garrick's practice in Hayman's drawing for Charles Jennens' edition of 1770/4 (of which only five plays, including *Lear*, were published).[5] This drawing was almost certainly made within a few months of the Hayman frontispiece for Hanmer, for at the Folger Shakespeare Library there is a letter from Garrick to Hayman, written probably in the summer of 1745, giving precise indications of Garrick's reading of the scene, which Hayman followed exactly in his drawing (reproduced at Pl. II*b*, *Shakespeare Quarterly*, vol. IX, 2, Spring 1958).[6] Garrick writes:

If you intend to alter the scene in Lear [from the design used in Hanmer]...what think you of the following one. Suppose Lear mad, upon the ground, with Edgar by him; his attitude should be leaning upon one hand & pointing wildly towards the Heavens with the other. Kent & Footman attend him, & Gloster comes to him with a Torch; the real Madness of Lear, the frantick affection of Edgar, & the different looks of concern in the three other carracters, will have a fine effect.

The published drawing is a clearer indication of Garrick's intentions in the theatrical grouping than of costume and is of the greatest importance as an indication of the relations between artist and actor in the eighteenth century; but some costume details are of interest. Gloucester and Lear are roughly draped, though preserving that elegance in shoes and hose that we have found in earlier engravings; Edgar is naked to the waist, with his customary wisps of straw and his staff.

Peter van Bleeck's 'Mrs Cibber as Cordelia', painted in 1755 and now in the Memorial Theatre, Stratford-upon-Avon, gives us the heath scene as Nahum Tate rewrote it. Cordelia has returned from France and searches for her father on the heath until she and her maid, Arante, are attacked by 'two Ruffians' and rescued by Edgar, 'a wandering lunatic' (Pl. I*e*).

The brothers John and Alexander Runciman provide two most valuable complementary comments on the heath scene. John Runciman painted his 'King Lear in the Storm' (now in the National Gallery of Scotland, Edinburgh)[7] in 1767 and the costumes have many of the qualities common to the stage and to heroic painting at this period; Lear in full Van Dyck dress, regularly worn by characters of the pre-Tudor period, Kent in full Rembrandt costume, and the Fool, a young boy with little suggestion of professional motley. I am now inclined to identify the bearded man on Lear's right shoulder, in a turban, seemingly derived from a Rembrandt self-portrait, with Gloucester, and the figure to Kent's left with Edgar, though he seems rather fully clothed (Pl. I*f*). Alexander Runciman made a pen drawing of the same scene (Pl. I*g*),[8] a precise comment on the Shakespearian text at an identifiable moment, the entry of Gloucester with a torch, in a small, huddled group behind the main figures. The latter are all interesting in their independence of the stage and of contemporary critical comment. Edgar's rags and windswept blanket require no conventional addition of straw and staff from the stage representation; the Fool, with cap and bells but naked at the waist, has the most direct suggestion of this character's bawdy comments on Lear's predicament, unique, I believe, until the more indirect phallic suggestion in Robert Colquhoun's *décor* for the 1953 *King Lear* at Stratford-upon-Avon. Lear and Kent are conceived as a Passion group; both recall Dürer, Lear himself having a strong suggestion of a 'Man of Sorrows',[9] while the flying drape about his shoulders unites a frequent Renaissance form with a suggestion of a Scottish plaid, originally worn over the bare torso. The whole group is less ambitious than John Runciman's painting and carries the suggestion of an exercise in pastiche. Nevertheless by its many recollections of classical paintings and through them conveying scriptural overtones, it pursues interpretation of the scene well beyond the range of a conventional illustrator and of most theatre productions. The Runciman painting and drawing together constitute one of the highest points in visual comment in their century.

The Bell theatre editions and the plates for the British Library add little to our knowledge beyond confirming Garrick's pervasive influence over all productions of *Lear* in the latter half of the century. The drawing by Edwards, engraved by Hall for the 1773 Bell edition, illustrates unadventurously the caption, 'Thou art the thing itself'. De Loutherbourg's drawing for the 1785 edition shows Lear in a tattered ermine gown and an old and wizened Fool in a shapeless cloak. Burney's drawing, engraved by Hall in the same year, illustrates the caption, 'Ay every inch a king'; Lear is elaborately drawn, barefoot but with puffed hose, a doublet trimmed and a cloak lined with ermine, the whole engraving surmounted by the manifold emblematic suggestion of a pelican in her piety.

During the last decade of the eighteenth century and until the publication of Howard's edition by Cadell in 1832, there was a strongly classical tradition in setting and illustrating *Lear*. At its most individual this is seen in Fuseli's contributions to the Boydell Gallery and to the Rivington *Shakespeare* of 1805. The Boydell plate engraved by Richard Fenton illustrates the rejection of Cordelia in the first act; it has a characteristically febrile atmosphere, in strange contrast to the heavily draped, 'Gothic revival' hall. Lear and his courtiers have a suggestion, no more, of classically draped figures; Goneril and Regan are drawn with the elaborate head-dresses and closely-moulded, long-limbed draperies of Fuseli's courtesan figures, a manner scarcely modified when he depicts Cordelia and perpetuated in the scene from the last act, engraved by Cromek for the Rivington plate (reproduced here at Pl. II*a*). Two others of the Boydell paintings, by Benjamin West and James Barry, are in the grandly classical manner of the History paintings which the Boydells wished explicitly to foster. West's figures are all draped (even the unusually dignified and seated Edgar) and have little precision of form or period. Lear wears no regal costume, though the soft drapery of his toga-like outer garment appears flecked with a suggestion of ermine. Gloucester's torch throws a strong light on an augustly bearded and powerful Fool, in a belled hood with ass's ears. James Barry's painting is more precise in its historical suggestions. Dover is backed by a classical landscape under whose cypresses trilithons from Stonehenge are elongated to Grecian proportions and grace. Lear wears a furred gown but he is surrounded by soldiers and courtiers in an approximation to Roman costume (Pl. II *b*). A minor point of interest in these Boydell plates may be seen in Schiavonetti's engraving after Smirke, in which the Fool on the heath closely resembles the boy-fool in Runciman's painting, both in costume and bearing.

At this same period, in the last decade of the century, two frontispiece engravings appear to preserve at least some details of actual theatre scene and costume. Each shows Kent in the stocks: in the Bellamy and Robarts edition of 1790 Lear is in doublet and hose, with a cloak and feathered hat and leaning on a tall and elaborate staff; in 1798 Stothard repeated the scene for Edward Harding's edition; Lear is almost identically costumed, even to the tall staff, but the cloak is now more clearly fur-lined in a 'Tudor' fashion, perhaps recalling the Holbein portrait of Henry VIII but more probably illustrating an actual costume on the stage of Stothard's day.

At the height of this classical manner we should expect a Kemble production. Roach has an engraving which records the production at Drury Lane on 13 May 1801; Kemble as Lear wore a very simple gown; Mrs Siddons's dress was high-waisted with puffed and slashed sleeves, a Regency mode later given scholarly finality by Frank Howard's drawings, published in 1832/3 by Cadell, *The Spirit of the Plays of Shakespeare, Exhibited in a Series of Outline Plates*. Howard declares the principles by which he dated the play before embarking on the costume drawings:

The date assumed for the occurrences which form the plot of this celebrated tragedy, is after the Romans had been in Britain but before the arrival of the Saxons. The costume entails some disadvantages from want of variety and, in many instances, want of elegance; but it has been deemed right to complete the illustrations upon the principle laid down of strict antiquarian accuracy; and it is hoped that character will amply atone for casual inelegancies.

Two drawings offer marked contrast in approach: the characters on the heath are in rather undifferentiated dresses, the main interest being in the Fool's coxcomb and belled ass's ears. A later drawing shows Cordelia at her father's couch; here the furnishing, with delicate scroll-work, small amphorae and two-handled cups, shows all the fashionable conceptions of classical setting.

While these attitudes had been crystallizing out for some thirty years, other artists, the Sto-thards, Smirkes and Thurstons, had continued their pedestrian frontispiece illustrations. Two little works stand out from this uninspired mass. The fourth edition of Lamb's *Tales from Shakespeare*, published by Godwin in 1822 contains in the first volume a 'Lear and Fool' (Pl. II *c*). It is a curious scene: Lear is garlanded, wears a plain gown and a single sandal and is accompanied by the Fool in *Commedia* costume. Yet the setting is a cliff above a stormy sea. It has been assumed that the engravings for this edition were minor work by Blake, similar to his two engravings after Fuseli for the Rivington edition in 1805 but Sir Geoffrey Keynes treats the drawings for Lamb's volumes as Mulready's. The second of these more notable *Lear* illustrations during the Romantic period is the small Blake in the Tate Gallery,[10] which shows the unusual scene, not in the Shakespearian text, but regularly seen on the stage, of Lear and Cordelia in prison.

The first half of the nineteenth century saw two traditions in illustrating *Lear*, not always closely related: the acting tradition, largely perpetuated by Edmund Kean, Macready, Samuel Phelps and Charles Kean; and book illustration, characteristically seen in the work of John Gilbert, in Knight's *Pictorial Shakspere* and in the Cowden Clarke volumes.

Macready first played Lear in London in 1834 and seems to have worked on the costume himself. He writes in his Diary: 'May 6. decided on Lear's dress, etc. Looked through prints for a head but found none affording more information than I already possessed', which appears to suggest that he was more interested in his make-up than in the costume for the part.[11] His diary for 10 January 1838 shows that he was pursuing the matter for his second and better-

Fig. 1. The costumes for Macready's production of *Lear* at Covent Garden in 1838.

known production, in which Shakespeare's text was to be restored: 'Called at the Garrick Club to look at some costumes for Lear; Saw Thackeray, who promised to send me a book on the subject.' This production is well documented from notices, plates and drawings: Fig. 1, part of a drawing from George Scharf's *Recollections of the Scenic Effects of Covent Garden Theatre, 1838–9*, shows Edgar's costume surviving unchanged from the previous century; Lear wears a simple gown edged with ermine, and the Fool, played by Priscilla Horton, wears a simply formalized coxcomb and a smocked dress edged with a child's nursery frieze of animals.

Samuel Phelps produced *Lear* in 1845; it has become customary to qualify any production of his with some such phrase as 'by the scholarly Phelps', and with justice. The evidence shows a gravity and breadth of approach to Shakespeare which contrasted healthily with the growing flamboyance of the other players. The Forrest Collection in the Birmingham Public Library contains a splendid colour lithograph published in Berlin,[12] which shows Phelps as Lear, wearing an enveloping blue cloak lined with fur, over a simple red gown, panelled and orffreyed in a gold and white chequer design. His costume accords with the general impression of unostentatious dignity in his productions.

Charles Kean's *Lear* was produced in April 1858 and became the mid-century focus of an argument over the propriety of 'Scenic illustration'. The *Illustrated London News* notice for 24 April is concerned about Kean's general approach: 'There is always a danger in scenic illustration pictorially carried out and archaeologically conducted, that the spectacular will overlay the dramatic', and though the critic is reassuring ('the subordination of the mechanist and painter to the poet and actor is duly maintained throughout'), the production seems to have been excessively elaborate.[13] The costumes seem to have been more modest than the settings, though the Fool wore a motley collection from several traditions: a cap with bells, a striped tunic and a diaper-checked pair of pantaloons.

The prolific book illustrations of this period show the same elaborate tendencies as the theatre but with more precision of detail. Knight's *Pictorial Shakspere* (1830–43) must suffice as representative of this abundance. This edition is usually pedantically 'accurate' but takes a sensible critical line over *Lear*, disavowing Douce (by implication, in one note, 'a professional detector of anachronisms') who had spoken of Shakespeare's 'plentiful crop of blunders' in this play. The editor is content to regard the play as 'describing events of a purely fabulous character' in 'an age to which we cannot attach a precise notion of costume (we use the word in its large sense)'.[14] For these reasons he does not object to seeing Lear painted with a 'diadem on his head, and the knights in armour', as in Harvey's frontispiece to the play in this edition.[15]

The years immediately following Knight's *Shakspere* saw an important development in historical sense, differing greatly from the 'modern dress' tradition of the eighteenth century and the growing archaeological precision of the nineteenth. In 1844, when Delacroix produced some of his finest lithographs of *Hamlet*, Ford Madox Brown was in Paris; in his exhibition catalogue of 1865 Ford Madox Brown describes his 'Lear and Cordelia', painted in 1848 under the influence of Delacroix:

Shakespeare's King Lear is Roman-pagan-British nominally; mediaeval by external customs and habits, and again, in a marked degree, savage and remote by the moral side. With fair excuse it might be treated in Roman-British costume, but then clashing with the mediaeval institutions and habits introduced; or as purely mediaeval. But I have rather chosen to be in harmony with the mental characteristics of Shakespeare's work and have therefore adopted the costume prevalent in Europe about the sixth century, when paganism was still rife, and deeds were at their darkest. The piece of Bayeux tapestry introduced behind King Lear is strictly an anachronism but the costume applies in this instance.

Madox Brown has here seen the ambiguities which Shakespeare introduces into any historical presentation and particularly into *Lear*. 'Roman-British' carries with it the implications of decayed grandeur and authority, a civilization poised between empire and barbarity. Most of the artists who have concerned themselves with scenery have been content with a rough magnificence in the interiors and an evocation of Stonehenge in exterior setting. But costumes set a further problem, hitherto not wholly faced, though Madox Brown has set out its terms. Shakespeare implies a remote period, latent in the characters and their mode of thought, while 'The Vines of France, and Milke of Burgundie' argue a later polity of Europe; the Fool and Edmund introduce still later overtones of courtliness, the Tudor court fools and their antecedents, and, in Edmund, the 'machiavel', still nearer Shakespeare's own day. Madox Brown's confident phrase, 'strictly an anachronism but the costume applies in this instance' justifies the still more far-reaching confidence of his claim, 'I have rather chosen to be in harmony with the mental characteristics of Shakespeare's work'; Cordelia's elaborate gown with the *fleurs de lis* of France preserves this temper, in the portion of his painting here reproduced at Pl. II*d*.

When, in November 1892, Irving produced *King Lear* at the Lyceum, he wrote in the preface to his acting version: 'As the period of King Lear, I have chosen, at the suggestion of Mr Ford Madox Brown...a time shortly after the departure of the Romans, when the Britons would naturally inhabit the towns left vacant.' The Black and White Souvenir of the production, illustrated by Bernard Partridge and Hawes Craven, shows Irving to have employed his usual team of designers, Hawes Craven and Harker, but the 'Synopsis of Scenery' carries the note: '*The Scenes of Lear's Palace and Gloster's and Albany's Castles are from designs by* Ford Madox Brown' (Irving says specifically that Madox Brown 'designed three scenes in the first and second acts'). Examination of the plates in the Souvenir shows that the 'Tent in the French Camp' owes nothing to Madox Brown's painting, either in temper or design, and any creative ambiguity in the period suggested has been removed. A short way has been taken with any 'anachronism' in costume. Courtiers are dressed with a suggestion of Roman armour but the helmets are frequently horned in the 'Saxon' manner. The women are elaborately gowned with a vague suggestion of early mediaeval detail in girdles, fillets, flowing head-dresses and pieces of jewellery. The Fool wears a conventional court jester's dress but his sandals have extended thongs carried over the calves, appearing to have been but recently promoted from villeinage. Lear's costume, 'of barbaric splendour', may be seen in Partridge's drawing from the Souvenir (Pl. II*e*).

Irving's production established the main lines of elaborate spectacle and of dating the play until almost our own day. Designs for *Lear* since the late war sufficiently demonstrate contemporary eclecticism in *décor* and costume. In 1946 Roger Furse designed the Old Vic *Lear* for Sir Laurence Olivier and all the costume drawings echo the colours, patterns and designs of figures in the Winchester Bible. The 'Byzantine' distortion of curve and proportion in these drawings, imposing a suggestive Christian allusion upon the pagan setting, was a tentative return to the complexity of Madox Brown's approach. A wholly different ambiguity, justified as an isolated experiment, was found in the Stratford *Lear*, designed by Isamu Noguchi and produced by George Devine in 1956. Here the setting and costumes transferred the tragedy to an alien medium, an approximation to the conditions of the classical Japanese stage, and imposed upon the production a fundamentally different sophistication and conventionality. The producer and designer, with Sir John Gielgud who played Lear, published a brief statement in the programme:

Our object in this production has been to find a setting and costumes which would be free of historical or decorative associations, so that the timeless, universal and mythical quality of the story may be clear. We have tried to present the places and characters in a very simple and basic manner, for the play to come to life through the words and acting.

The production released interpretation from any banality but it was by its nature unrepeatable. Two previous productions in this country within this decade had brought to bear the individual vision of creative artists on the problems considered here: Leslie Hurry's designs in 1950 and Robert Colquhoun's in 1953. Hurry, with some of the most intense insights into Shakespeare's tragedies in our day, employed a less macabre range of images than those which had distinguished the two productions of *Hamlet*—play and ballet—for Robert Helpmann. Colquhoun's designs in 1953, when again the play was produced by Devine, made no attempt to particularize period, so that ambiguities based on deliberate anachronism were set aside. The costumes, however (Lear and the Fool are illustrated at Pl. II *g*), were heavy, even ponderous in impression, with leather and much quilting, and were congruous with the simple, monumental sets. Though the costumes were richly varied, they were in a small range of hues and a limited number of tones, but unity was kept by the motifs or bands of white introduced at some focal point in each costume. It was noteworthy that the Fool's obscenities in the heath scenes were now visually suggested not in costume but in the set itself.

Lamb, in common with other Romantic critics, had considered *Lear* too vast for adequate stage presentation; it is scarcely necessary to say here that there are imponderables in the play which defy theatrical production or indeed any other visual interpretation—and in this *Lear* is not unique. Yet there is no major play of Shakespeare's that has more successfully and in more varied fashion challenged the creative comment of painters, engravers and artists in theatre *décor*. Each comment is partial and inadequate, reflecting some of the distortions as well as the critical insights of their age, but they have their cumulative power and penetration, contributing another dimension to the criticism of Shakespeare's text.

NOTES

1. Leslie Hotson, *Shakespeare's Motley* (1952).

2. Hotson, *op. cit.* pp. 5 n., and 38.

3. See *Shakespeare Quarterly*, vol. IX, 2 (Spring 1958), W. M. Merchant, 'Francis Hayman's Illustrations of Shakespeare', where the Hanmer edition in the Folger Shakespeare Library, Washington, containing Hayman's own drawings bound in with Gravelot's engravings, is discussed; eight plates are reproduced.

4. Ellis Waterhouse, *Painting in Britain* (1953), pp. 228–9, suggests that Zoffany may have had a hand in Wilson's painting.

5. A. C. Sprague, *Shakespearian Players and Performances* (1953), p. 34.

6. This plate is reproduced with the Hayman drawings in *Shakespeare Quarterly*, IX, 2, 1958 (note 3 above). In the same issue of the *Quarterly* Kalman Burnim considers 'The Significance of Garrick's Letters to Hayman' and quotes in full the letter cited here.

7. This plate has been treated at length in Merchant, *Shakespeare and the Artist* (1959), chapter XII.

8. National Gallery of Scotland, Edinburgh, D. 313. I owe knowledge of this drawing to the kindness of Keith Andrews, Keeper of Prints and Drawings at the National Gallery of Scotland.

9. Mrs Eric Newton, to whom I put this suggestion, amplifies it by referring the Lear head to Tietze, *Dürer Cat.* I, 183, and suggests further that Kent recalls a Dürer drawing in the British Museum, Tietze, I, 226.

10. Reproduced in Merchant, *op. cit.* Pl. 29 *b*.

11. Macready would have found many Heads of Lear in the drawing portfolios of the preceding half-century. Reynolds has a noble drawing and there is a very fine Romney drawing in the Folger Library. Nearer his own day, Sir John Gilbert made one of his best drawings of Lear for Staunton's *Shakespeare*.

12. The lithograph, in Forrest, *King Lear*, II, 531, is headed, 'Friedrich-Wilhelmstädtisches-Theater' and published by Eduard Bloch.

13. The Victoria and Albert Museum has a full series of designs for this production; the design by Grieve for the heath scene is reproduced in Merchant, *op. cit.* Pl. 71 *c*.

14. Presumably by 'costume' the critic here means *décor* 'in its large sense'.

15. The set of Knight's *Pictorial Shakspere* in the Library of the University College, Cardiff, contains Harvey's drawings bound in with the engravings. The frontispiece for *Lear* has, in Harvey's drawing, only a slight suggestion of Roman costume which is clarified in the engraving.

THE MARRIAGE-CONTRACTS IN
MEASURE FOR MEASURE

BY

ERNEST SCHANZER

In a valuable essay on *Measure for Measure*, published in 1942, L. C. Knights, discussing Shake-speare's presentation of Claudio, expressed his belief that 'it is the slight uncertainty of attitude in Shakespeare's handling of him that explains some part, at least, of the play's disturbing effect'. The source of this uncertainty he finds in 'feelings at war with themselves' in the poet, the result of a temporary 'emotional bias' that 'seems to blur some of the natural positive values which in *Macbeth* or *Lear* are as vividly realized as the vision of evil'.[1] Apparently alone among commentators he points to 'something odd and inappropriate' in Claudio's attitude towards the offence for which he has been sentenced to death. Upon Claudio's first appearance on the stage the following conversation takes place between him and Lucio:

> *Lucio.* Why, how now, Claudio! whence comes this restraint?
> *Claudio.* From too much liberty, my Lucio, liberty:
>   As surfeit is the father of much fast,
>   So every scope by the immoderate use
>   Turns to restraint. Our natures do pursue,
>   Like rats that ravin down their proper bane,
>   A thirsty evil; and when we drink we die.
> *Lucio.* If I could speak so wisely under an arrest, I would send for certain of my creditors: and
>   yet, to say the truth, I had as lief have the foppery of freedom as the morality of imprison-
>   ment. What's thy offence, Claudio?
> *Claudio.* What but to speak of would offend again.
> *Lucio.* What, is't murder?
> *Claudio.* No.
> *Lucio.* Lechery?
> *Claudio.* Call it so.   (I, ii, 128–44)

Yet five lines later he declares,

> Thus stands it with me: upon a true contract
> I got possession of Julietta's bed:
> You know the lady; she is fast my wife,
> Save that we do the denunciation lack
> Of outward order: this we came not to,
> Only for propagation of a dower
> Remaining in the coffer of her friends,
> From whom we thought it meet to hide our love

81

Till time had made them for us. But it chances
The stealth of our most mutual entertainment
With character too gross is writ on Juliet.
Lucio. With child, perhaps?
Claudio. Unhappily, even so.
And the new deputy now for the duke—
Whether it be the fault and glimpse of newness,
Or whether that the body public be
A horse whereon the governor doth ride,
Who, newly in the seat, that it may know
He can command, lets it straight feel the spur;
Whether the tyranny be in his place,
Or in his eminence that fills it up,
I stagger in:—but this new governor
Awakes me all the enrolled penalties
Which have, like unscour'd armour, hung by the wall
So long that nineteen zodiacs have gone round
And none of them been worn; and, for a name,
Now puts the drowsy and neglected act
Freshly on me: 'tis surely for a name.

What are we to make of this young man, who is overwhelmed by a feeling of sinfulness for having cohabited with his wife and at the same time sees himself as the only nominally guilty victim of a tyrannical ruler? Most commentators escape from the perplexity by ignoring Claudio's remarks about his marriage-contract. But once they are given their due value, how are we to account for the sense of guilt and shame, not only on the part of Claudio but also that of Juliet, as is shown in her interview with the Friar-Duke?

Duke. Repent you, fair one, of the sin you carry?
Juliet. I do; and bear the shame most patiently....
Duke. 'Tis meet so, daughter: but lest you do repent,
As that the sin hath brought you to this shame,
Which sorrow is always towards ourselves, not heaven,
Showing we would not spare heaven as we love it,
But as we stand in fear,—
Juliet. I do repent me, as it is an evil,
And take the shame with joy. (II, iii, 19–36)

And, above all, if Claudio and Juliet are husband and wife, what legal right has Angelo to arrest them and to sentence Claudio to death for fornication?

An answer to all these questions is to be found in the complex and inherently contradictory nature of the contemporary laws and edicts relating to marriage, which had remained basically unchanged since the twelfth century. The contradictions sprang from two opposed and irreconcilable objectives on the part of the Church. On the one hand it wished to make the contraction of a legal marriage as easy as possible in order to encourage people to live in a state of matri-mony rather than 'in sin'. It therefore decreed that any *de praesenti* contract (i.e. one in which a man and a woman declared that henceforth they were husband and wife) constituted a legal marriage. Such a contract did not need the presence of a priest, or, indeed, of any third person to witness it, nor did it demand any deposition in writing. All that was required was the mutual consent of both parties. As Henry Swinburne puts it in his *Treatise on Spousals*, 'albeit there be no Witnesses of the Contract, yet the Parties having verily, (though secretly) Contracted Matrimony, they are very Man and Wife before God'.[2] But to counteract the obvious evils to which such laws were bound to give rise, the Church also insisted that, though valid and binding, such secret marriages were sinful and forbidden, and that, if they took place, the offenders were to be punished and forced to solemnize their marriage *in facie ecclesiae*. These inherent contradictions in the Church's attitude to clandestine marriages are well brought out by William Harrington in his *Commendacions of matrymony*:

Yf that man & woman or theyr proctours do make matrymony secretly by them selfe without any recorde or but with one wytnesse that is called matrymony clandestinat the whiche for many causes is forboden by the lawe. And they whiche done make suche matrymony are accused in that dede doynge not withstondyng that matrymony is valeable and holdeth afore God in to so much that and the one of the same forsake the other and take other they lyue in a dampnable aduoutry.[3]

If the Church denounced the contraction of clandestine marriages *per verba de praesenti*, it inveighed even more vehemently against their consummation before they had been publicly solemnized, an act which it regarded as fornication and a deadly sin. Again Harrington states it accurately:

And whan matrymony is thus lawfully made yet the man maye not possesse the woman as his wyfe nor the woman the man as her husbonde nor inhabyte nor flesshely meddle togyther as man and wyfe: afore suche tyme as that matrymony be approued and solempnysed by oure mother holy chyrche and yf they do in dede they synne deadly.[4]

We see, then, that Claudio and Juliet are guilty in the eyes of the Church of two transgressions— of having contracted a secret marriage and of having consummated it. Being technically guilty of fornication, Claudio is therefore punishable under the law which Angelo has revived. When Arthur Underhill, in his chapter on Law in *Shakespeare's England*, declares that 'Angelo's condemnation of Claudio for alleged fornication was, and was intended by Shakespeare to be, absolutely tyrannical and illegal',[5] it is only the first part of his statement which is correct. Angelo's condemnation of Claudio was, and no doubt was intended by Shakespeare to appear, absolutely tyrannical, but it is also unquestionably legal. Claudio knows this only too well, and never suggests that he could save himself by appealing to the legal circumstances of his case. It is by relying on Isabel's power to move the tyrannical ruler to mercy that he hopes to save his life.

We can now understand why it should be possible for Claudio to feel guilt and shame for having cohabited with his own wife, and at the same time to see himself as a judicial victim, condemned to die merely 'for a name'. Claudio is depicted as a deeply impressionable youth, sensuous, passionate, and—like his sister—religious. His very opening words, always important in Shakespeare's plays as an index to character, echo the *Epistle to the Romans*:

> The words of heaven: on whom it will, it will;
> On whom it will not, so; yet still 'tis just. (I, ii, 116–17)

When he therefore finds himself condemned to death for fornication, and the cause of Juliet's disgrace, it is not surprising that, in spite of his indignation at Angelo's legal tyranny, he should see himself as the Church saw him, a sinner who must suffer for his misdeeds.

It seems to me, therefore, that the contradictions in Claudio's attitude towards the action for which he has been sentenced to death are not, as L. C. Knights suggests, the result of 'feelings at war with themselves' in the poet, but rather spring from Shakespeare's exploitation, for his own purposes, of the contradictions inherent in the Church's edicts relating to the marriage-contract. What were these purposes? In order to show up in its blackest colours Angelo's legalism, his adherence to the letter rather than the spirit of the law, which is one of the main concerns of the play, Shakespeare needed a case in which the death-penalty could be lawfully imposed for an offence which would not lose for its perpetrator the sympathies of the audience and one in which a proper regard for its circumstances should have earned him the judge's pardon. Claudio's counterpart in Cinthio's story had actually committed rape, though he was willing to make amends by marriage.[6] His counterpart in Whetstone's story and play had committed no rape, as Cassandra pleads, 'but with yeelding consent of his Mistresse, *Andrugio* hath onlye sinned through Loue, and neuer ment but with Marriage to make amendes'.[7] Shakespeare exculpates Claudio still further by making him actually the husband of Juliet, and supplying him with a strong reason why the marriage has not yet been solemnized. The fact that Shakespeare should also have chosen to embody in Claudio something of the conflicting emotions which the Church's pronouncements in this matter must have aroused in many couples who had consummated an unsolemnized *de praesenti* contract, must, I think, be accounted for on dramatic grounds: apart from making him a more interesting and, to many, a more sympathetic character, it makes Claudio a more perfect foil to Angelo. The self-incriminations of the comparatively innocent and lovable Claudio form a complete contrast to the self-righteousness of the guilty and repellent Angelo.

Now let us turn to the other marriage-contract which figures importantly in this play, that between Angelo and Mariana. Here the legal position is far more complex and obscure. It has been assumed by the few commentators who have touched on these matters at all[8] that like the contract between Claudio and Juliet it was a *de praesenti* one. In favour of this view can be cited the Duke's repeated references to Angelo as Mariana's 'husband'.[9] But Elizabethan terminology in this field was notoriously vague (e.g. in its use of the word 'spousals' for *de futuro* betrothals, *de praesenti* contracts, as well as the solemnizing of marriages).[10] And the arguments against it are numerous and powerful, and they all point to the contract being a *de futuro* one (in which the parties engage themselves to become husband and wife at a future date). To begin with, had it been a *de praesenti* contract Angelo, though he could have denied that it ever took place (provided it was clandestine), could never have attempted to break it off. For, as Swinburne puts it, 'that woman, and that man, which have contracted Spousals *de praesenti*...cannot by any Agreement dissolve those Spousals, but are reputed for very Husband

and Wife in respect of the Substance, and indissoluble Knot of Matrimony'.[11] And again: 'for Spousals *de praesenti*, though not consummate, be in truth and substance very Matrimony, and therefore perpetually indissoluble, except for Adultery',[12] just like any solemnized and consummated marriage.[13] *De futuro* contracts, on the other hand, could be dissolved for a variety of reasons (Swinburne gives a long list of them, pp. 236–40). For instance, 'when as the Party doth after the Contract made, commit *Fornication*, for the Innocent Party is at liberty, and may dissolve the Contract'; or 'when as the Contract is conditional, and the Condition infringed; for the Condition being broken, the Bond is untyed, and the Parties at liberty to marry elsewhere; or when as the Party doth promise to give so much in Marriage, as afterwards he is not able to perform; In which Case the other Party is not bound to perform the Contract'.[14] As William Perkins puts it more explicitly,

Those espousals, which are made vpon condition, which is honest, possible, and belonging to Marriage, doe cease or depend: so far forth as the condition annexed ceaseth or dependeth. For example; If the one partie promiseth to marry the other vpon condition, that his or her kinsman will yeeld consent to the match; or vpon condition of a dowrie that shee shall bring vnto him, sutable to her education, and the familie whereof she cometh: these conditions being kept or not kept, the promise doth likewise stand, or not stand.[15]

Had Angelo's contract been of this kind, conditional upon the receipt of Mariana's dowry, it would have lapsed automatically when her dowry was lost at sea. But we find that the contract has in fact never been dissolved, as the present tense used by the Duke and Mariana, 'he is your husband on a pre-contract', 'I am affianced this man's wife', makes clear. And we can understand why this should be so, in spite of Angelo's claim that it was

> broke off,
> Partly for that her promised proportions
> Came short of composition, but in chief
> For that her reputation was disvalued
> In levity,   (v, i, 218–22)

when we realize that their bond was not that of a simple or conditional *de futuro* contract, which could be broken off against the wishes of one of the parties to it.[16] Theirs were *sponsalia iurata*, sworn spousals, as we are told repeatedly: 'was affianced to her by oath' (III, i, 222); 'This is the hand which, with a vow'd contract, / Was fast belock'd in thine' (v, i, 209–10); 'I am affianced this man's wife as strongly / As words could make up vows' (v, i, 227–8). Of such spousals Swinburne writes: 'It is generally concluded by all Interpreters, as well of the Civil, as of the Canon Law; That it is not in the power of either Party alone, without the Consent of the other to renounce or dissolve the Spousals confirmed with an Oath.'[17] He goes on to discuss the further problem 'whether the unwilling Party may be compelled to marry the other, willing according to their mutual promise, confirmed by Oath', and comes to the conclusion that

either there is *just Cause* of refusal, or not; if there be *just Cause* already ministred, as if the other party have committed Fornication, or be stricken with Leprosy, Palsy, or some notable deformity, or that some impediment have happened, for the which Spousals may be dissolved (whereof hereafter), In this Case the Party may be monished, but not compelled to the Observation of his Oath.... If there be not *just Cause* precedent, then the unwilling Party is to be admonished; and if he yet obstinately refuse, he is to be compelled by the Censures Ecclesiastical to Solemnize the Matrimony, by him before promised and Sworn.[18]

We see, then, that Angelo could not dissolve the contract without Mariana's consent, and that his 'pretending in her discoveries of dishonour' may be seen not only as designed to justify his promise-breach in the eyes of the world,[19] but also, perhaps, as an attempt to provide the 'just cause' without which he could have been forced to solemnize the marriage. The fact that the spousals were sworn is a further clear indication that we are dealing with a *de futuro* contract, for in *de praesenti* contracts an oath played no part, as no promise was involved.

Any *de futuro* contract, whether sworn or unsworn, simple or conditional, was turned into matrimony and acquired the same legal status as a *de praesenti* contract as soon as cohabitation between the betrothed couple took place. This is repeatedly emphasized by Swinburne among many others: 'Spousals *de futuro* do become Matrimony by carnal knowledge betwixt the Parties betrothed.'[20] It is this point of law which seems to me to be basic to the Duke's substitution-plot and appears to be alluded to by him when he declares, 'if the encounter acknowledge itself hereafter, it may compel him to her recompense' (III, i, 261-3). Here we have another strong indication that the contract was a *de futuro* one, for in the case of a *de praesenti* contract cohabitation between the parties made no difference to its legal status.[21] And a recognition of this point of law may make the so-called 'bed-trick' more acceptable to those who have been distressed by the expedient and by Isabella's immediate consent to it.

The apparent contradiction between Isabella's condemnation of her brother's offence and her ready connivance in what would appear to be an identical transgression on the part of Mariana has often worried commentators, and has even been called by D. P. Harding 'the central problem of *Measure for Measure*.'[22] His suggested solution is that her inconsistency in condemning the one and abetting the other 'exactly mirrors a national inconsistency. The Elizabethans recognized and acknowledged the ideal, but *Usus efficacissimus rerum omnium magister*, and they, a practical people, readily accepted the reality'.[23] I should prefer to account for it in other ways. Isabel appears ignorant throughout of her brother's marriage-contract. Lucio fails to mention it in his report to her of Claudio's arrest, while the words he uses, 'He hath got his friend with child', 'Your brother and his lover have embraced' (I, iv, 29, 40) would, on the contrary, give the impression that there was no matrimonial bond between them. But why did Shakespeare choose to keep Isabel ignorant of the marriage-contract? Because had she known of it her entire plea before Angelo would have had to be different, an appeal to equity rather than to mercy. And it would have much lessened her inner conflict, 'At war 'twixt will and will not' (II, ii, 33). For not even the 'enskied and sainted' Isabel would have called the consummation of a *de praesenti* contract 'a vice that most I do abhor' (II, ii, 29) and have thought of it as justly deserving the death-penalty ('O just but severe law', II, ii, 41). It is apparently the situation of the saintly novice exculpating the seeming libertine which above all kindles Angelo's lust and gives him his opening in the seduction-scene. And all this Shakespeare would have had to forego, had he made Isabel cognizant of the circumstances of Claudio's transgression.

To Isabel, therefore, her brother's 'vice' and Mariana's nocturnal encounter with Angelo, with its multiple benefits ('by this', the Duke tells her, 'is your brother saved, your honour untainted, the poor Mariana advantaged, and the corrupt deputy scaled', III, i, 263–6) would not have seemed by any means identical, or indeed to have much in common. And the fact that the scheme is put forward by the Friar-Duke as spokesman of the Church would have helped to counteract any possible scruples raised in her mind by the Church's commands in this matter.

When the Duke tells Mariana,

> Nor, gentle daughter, fear you not at all.
> He is your husband on a pre-contract:
> To bring you thus together, 'tis no sin,
> Sith that the justice of your title to him
> Doth flourish the deceit. (IV, i, 71–5)

he is, as the words make clear, not thinking of the sin of consummating an unsolemnized contract, but of the sin of deceiving Angelo by the substitution. This is an odd way of looking at the matter, but it is indisputably the Duke's way. He here merely reiterates his earlier justification of the scheme to Isabel: 'If you think well to carry this as you may, the doubleness of the benefit defends the deceit from reproof' (III, i, 267–9). It is all of a piece with his asking Angelo in his final speech to forgive the provost for having deceived him when bringing him 'The head of Ragozine for Claudio's' (V, i, 539). As Lucio says, 'the Duke had crotchets in him'. But that he is not unaware of the opprobrium attached to the consummation of an unsolemnized marriage-contract is shown by his words to Mariana at the end of the play:

> Consenting to the safeguard of your honour,
> I thought your marriage fit; else imputation,
> For that he knew you, might reproach your life
> And choke your good to come. (V, i, 424–7)

Finally, it may justly be asked how many in Shakespeare's audience possessed the requisite knowledge of these various legal points relating to the marriage-contract. The answer to this must inevitably be speculative. Certain basic facts, such as the Church's condemnation both of clandestine marriages and of the consummation of unsolemnized *de praesenti* contracts, must have been familiar to most people through the exhortations of their parish priests. For instance, among the 'Injunctions given by John Hooper, bishop of Gloucester, in his visitation in… 1551…to be observed and kept of all parsons' we find:

Item, that every minister within this diocese do diligently exhort and teach the parishioners that all privy and secret contracts be forbidden by God's laws, and not to be used among Christian people. …Item, that when any persons be contracted and faithed together in matrimony either by two or three records out of the congregation, or else openly proclaimed in the church by banns, after the godly laws of the realm, that the same persons be compelled with all convenient speed to marry openly in the face of the church, and the persons contracted cohabitate nor dwell together before the matrimony be solemnized.[24]

The point that a *de futuro* contract was transformed by cohabitation into matrimony must also have been common knowledge. Quite apart from the admonitions of the clergy, grammar-school boys, for instance, could have learnt it from one of their school texts, Erasmus's *Colloquia*, where a footnote by Cornelius Schrevelius to the *Gerontologia* explains: 'Si quis dicat puellae, *ducam te* & mox habeat rem cum illa, ratum est matrimonium, perinde, quasi dixisset, *duco te*. Hoc reti multi adolescentes capiuntur, magno suo malo discentes hoc sophisma.'[25] As for the special conditions governing sworn spousals, this may have been known only to a judicious few in the audience, but very little in the play hinges upon an understanding of this point.

But so far as the modern playgoer or reader is concerned, there can be little doubt that of all Shakespeare's plays *Measure for Measure* is the one where an ignorance of Elizabethan moral tenets and edicts is likely to lead him farthest astray.

NOTES

1. 'The Ambiguity of *Measure for Measure*', *Scrutiny*, x (1942), 225, 228.

2. Henry Swinburne, *A Treatise on Spousals*, p. 87. This treatise, published in 1686 but written *c.* 1600, is our chief source of knowledge of Elizabethan laws and legal opinions relating to the marriage-contract.

3. William Harrington, *Commendacions of matrymony* (1528), A4–A4ᵛ. See also Pollock and Maitland, *The History of English Law* (1923), II, 370.

4. *Op. cit.* A4ᵛ. It is true that many people, and perhaps Shakespeare among them, paid little heed to the Church's commands on this topic. But it is quite erroneous to say with Halliwell-Phillipps (*Outlines of the Life of Shakespeare*, I, 62) that 'no question of morals would in those days have arisen, or could have been entertained', or to claim with J. Q. Adams that if Shakespeare 'took advantage of the privileges such a contract was supposed to give, it could not have offended the moral sensibilities of the Stratford folk' (*Life of Shakespeare*, p. 69). There is no justification for endowing Stratford folk with such monolithic moral sensibilities, and the same must be said of Shakespeare's audience when W. W. Lawrence writes of them: 'it seems clear that an Elizabethan or Jacobean audience would not have been repelled by sexual intercourse after formal betrothal but before the final religious ceremony, since this was a frequent and generally accepted occurrence' ('*Measure for Measure* and Lucio', *Shakespeare Quarterly*, IX, 1958, 450). As E. I. Fripp points out, 'Puritan opinion was strong against the practice.... Stern laws were proposed on the lines of Old Testament legislation, and at Stratford, as elsewhere, clergy and churchwardens brought no light pressure to bear on erring couples' (*Shakespeare: Man and Artist*, II, 613).

5. *Shakespeare's England* (1916), I, 408.

6. Cinthio, *Hecatommithi* (1574), R2ᵛ.

7. Whetstone, *An Heptameron of Ciuill Discourses* (1582), N3ʳ.

8. Principally by D. P. Harding in 'Elizabethan Betrothals and *Measure for Measure*', *J.E.G.P.* XLIX (1950), 153 ff. This is much the most important and extensive discussion of the subject. Though in disagreement with him on many points, I owe much to his lucid treatment of several of the topics discussed in this article.

9. 'her combinate husband' (III, i, 230); 'he is your husband on a pre-contract' (IV, i, 72).

10. For a discussion of the varied use of this term see Swinburne, *op. cit.* pp. 2 ff.

11. *Op. cit.* p. 13.

12. *Op. cit.* p. 15.

13. It was, however, not quite so indissoluble. 'A spouse may free himself or herself from the unconsummated marriage by entering religion, and such a marriage is within the papal power of dispensation.' Pollock and Maitland, *op. cit.* II, 366.

14. *Op. cit.* p. 237.

15. William Perkins, *Christian Oeconomie* (1609), pp. 21–2.

16. On this, however, Canon and Civil Law took up opposed positions. See Swinburne, *op. cit.* p. 216.

17. *Op. cit.* p. 217.

18. *Op. cit.* pp. 217–18.

19. Supposing the contract to have been public. Whether Shakespeare, if he thought about it at all, meant it to have been public or secret is of little importance. But it seems fairly clear that at the opening of the play he meant the Duke to be ignorant if not of the contract at least of Angelo's treatment of Mariana after the loss of her dowry, and that he learnt this from her in his role of Friar confessor. If, with some commentators, we take the opposite view we rob his opening lines to Angelo of their dramatic irony and substitute for it conscious verbal irony:

Angelo,

There is a kind of character in thy life,
That to the observer doth thy history
Fully unfold.

(I, i, 27–30)

20. *Op. cit.* p. 224. See also pp. 73, 218.

21. It is doubtful, however, whether a court of law would have ruled that cohabitation with one's bride when taken for another person turned a *de futuro* contract into matrimony. Certainly *error personae*, i.e. marriage contracted with a person mistaken for someone else, was one of the recognized grounds for annulment. See A. Esmein, *Le Marriage en Droit Canonique* (1929), I, 346–50.

22. *Op. cit.* p. 156.

23. *Ibid.*

24. *Later Writings of Bishop Hooper*, Parker Society reprints, XXI (1852), 137–8.

25. Erasmus, *Colloquia* (1693), p. 299. Quoted by T. W. Baldwin, *William Shakespeare's Small Latine and Lesse Greeke*, I, 739.

TOM SKELTON—A SEVENTEENTH-CENTURY JESTER

BY

E. W. IVES

In the Elizabethan theatre, the stage fool, or clown, had an obvious, if somewhat complex, dramatic function. But in almost every other respect, study of this character bristles with difficulty. The connection between the fool and the Vice of the medieval drama remains obscure, and it is still doubtful how far the fool, the jester and the clown were distinct figures. Even if this problem is by-passed and all are treated as one, for the historian of the theatre the relationship of the court, or domestic, jester to the stage clown, the distinction between the stage fool and the court fool represented on the stage, and, not least of all, the costuming of the character in these various modes still remain open questions. To a large extent these problems arise from the fragmentary nature of the evidence and any further information which can be presented is of value.

Additional evidence about the fool's costume has, indeed, come to light following the purchase by the Shakespeare Institute in November 1957 of an unusual seventeenth-century oil painting, formerly part of the Haigh Hall collection of the Earl of Crawford and Balcarres.[1] It depicts Tom Skelton, the family fool, in a checked costume with various impedimenta of his trade and these are explained in a piece of doggerel on the left-hand side of the picture. At first, the work presented a puzzle. Its size—66½ by 40½ inches—and careful detail suggested an importance which was belied by the quality of the workmanship. Certain parts of the figure—the face and the upper trunk in particular—were adequately, if thinly painted, but the rest displayed a complete defiance of proportion and an ignorance of the elements of anatomy, even to the extent that the second and third phalanges of the digits of the left hand were missing. The subject of the picture was equally curious. The doggerel specifically mentioned Haigh Hall and the surrounding countryside, but gave no clue to the date of the portrait or to the name of the artist concerned—the jester was simply referred to as 'Tom fool'. The nineteenth-century label attached to the picture described it as 'Tom Skelton, fool to the Crawford and Balcarres Family', but, since the Lindsays possessed Haigh only from 1770,[2] this ascription could obviously not be relied upon. Artistic and historical difficulties about the painting were, moreover, coupled with a considerable interest for students of the theatre. Not only did the picture seem to be unique—no full-length oil painting of another English Jester is known[3]— but also to promise an answer to the riddle of the fool's stage costume. Further examination seemed justified (Pl. V B).

In the course of investigation it became clear that the Haigh Hall portrait, now at Stratford, is another version of a picture at Muncaster Castle, near Ravenglass in Cumberland, the property of Sir William Pennington-Ramsden, Bt. (Pl. V A). A photograph of this picture appeared in *Country Life* on 15 June 1940, but, presumably because of the national crisis, received no attention at the time.[4] The existence of the Muncaster picture—*Skelton I*—solved some of the problems

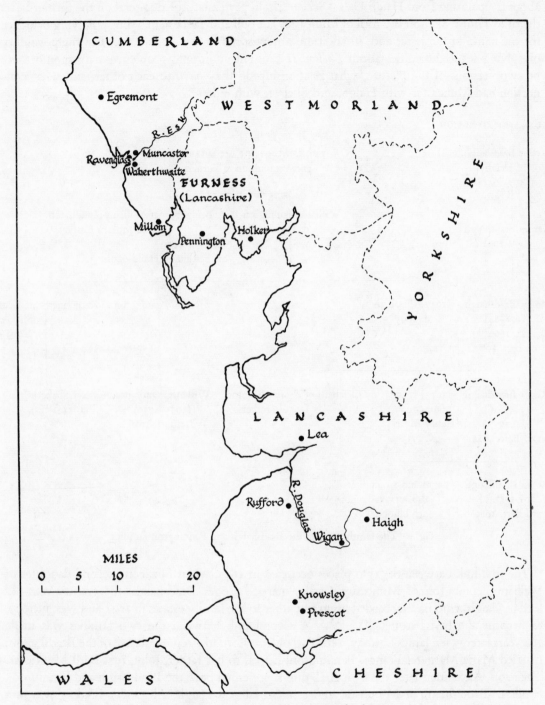

Fig. 1. Lancashire and N.W. England.

about the painting from Haigh Hall—*Skelton II*. In particular, the doggerel on the former bears the title 'Thom^s Skelton late fool of Muncaster last will and Testament', thus supplying evidence for the name of the jester and, in addition, a new scene for his operations. But the possibility of solving some difficulties about *Skelton II* brought additional problems; why should there be two versions of the picture, what relationship do they have to each other, and what connection had Muncaster with Haigh, and Skelton with either?

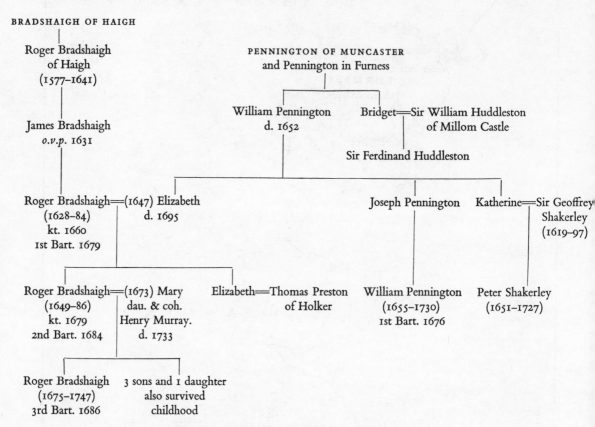

Fig. 2. The family trees of the Bradshaigh and Pennington families.

The first link between the two places occurred in 1647, when Elizabeth, second daughter of William Pennington of Muncaster Castle, married Roger Bradshaigh, the twenty-year-old lord of Haigh, who had succeeded his grandfather to the family estates in 1641 and was, in 1679, to become the first baronet (Fig. 2).[5] A second link between the two families was made 164 years later when James Lindsay, 24th Earl of Crawford, the representative of the Bradshaighs, married Maria Margaret Frances Pennington, heiress to her father, John, first Lord Muncaster. Their son, Alexander, later the 25th Earl, thus represented both the Bradshaigh and Pennington families. Brought up at Muncaster and resident later at Haigh, Alexander Lindsay was in a position to know and unite the traditions of both houses. According to the 25th Earl, Tom Skelton was originally the fool 'or privileged jester' at Muncaster Castle. He moved to Haigh with a William Pennington who had inherited Muncaster as a minor and became a ward of Sir Roger Bradshaigh of Haigh, the first baronet.[6] This William Pennington, later the first baronet, was Sir Roger's nephew, and the move from Cumberland to Lancashire took place in 1659 when Joseph Pennington, William's father and Sir Roger's brother-in-law, died.[7] The heir was only four or five years old at the time, and, assuming that he remained at Haigh during the whole of his minority, would not have returned to Muncaster until 1676.[8] The year 1659 is, thus, the earliest date for Skelton's appearance at Haigh. A *terminus ad quem* for his activities is provided by the date of his death: 'Thomas Skelton of Haigh' was buried at Wigan on 13 January 1667/8.[9] One of the Skelton portraits at least must have been painted before that date, for the doggerel refers to the fool as living, but, in fact, an earlier limit for the picture than 1668 can be set. Ralph Waite is mentioned in the verses as alive and he was buried on 9 January 1665/6.[10] Skelton, therefore, must have sat for his portrait between 1659 and the end of 1665. The earlier of the dates is preferable; the type of collar worn is characteristic of the period before, rather than after, 1660.

Very little can be discovered about Skelton apart from the doggerel testament on the portraits. The tradition of the Fool's 'Will and Testament' goes back at least to the fifteenth century,[11] but the Skelton will is more specific than most. The full text is found only in *Skelton I*; in the other version, the inscription and the authenticating formula and signatures are missing:

Thom⁵ Skelton late fool of Muncaster last will and Testament

> Be it Known to yᵉ, oh Grave & wise men all
> That I Thom' fool, am sheriffe of yᵉ Hall
> I mean yᵉ Hall of Haigh, where I Command
> What neither i nor you do Understand
> My Under sheriffe is Ralf Wayte you know
> As wise as I am and as witty to
> Of Egremond I have Burrow serjᵗ been
> Of Wiggan Bayliffe too as may be seen
> By my White staff of Office in my hand
> Being Carryed streight as yᵉ Badge of my comᵐᵃⁿᵈ
> A Low High Constable too was once my Calling
> Which I enjoy'd under kind Henry Rawling
> And when yᵉ ffates a new sheriffe send
> I'm Under sheriffe Prickt, world without end
> He who doth question my Authority
> May see yᵉ seal & Patten here Ly by
> The Dish with Luggs wᶜʰ I do Carry here
> Shews all my living is in good strong beer
> If scurvey lads to me abuse's do
> Ile Call em scurvey Rogus & Rascalls to
> Fair Dolley Copeland in my Cap is plac'd
> Monstrous fair is she & as good all the Rest
> Honest Nich Pennington honest Tho Turner ᵇᵒᵗʰ

Will bury me when I this world go forth
But let me not be Carry[d]. o're the Brigg
Least falling I in Duggas River ligg
Nor let my body by old Charnock lye
But by Will Caddy, for he'l lye quietly
And when I'm bury'd then my friends may Drin[k]—
But each man pay for his self, y[ts] best I thinke
This is my will, and this I know will be
Perform'd by them as they have promis'd me.

Sign'd Seal'd publish'd ⎫   his
& Declar'd in y[e] Presence of⎰   Thom' Skelton   T
Henry Rawling   mark
Henry Trougton   [Representation of a
Thom'[s] Turner   seal, but no markings]

     Much of the humour in this fictional will is obvious and the personal allusions, as far as they can be checked, are comic. Skelton never held such an important office as Bailiff of Wigan or Under-sheriff of Lancashire, and was almost certainly not Borough Sergeant of Egremont either. This official was responsible for the policing of Ravenglass fair which 'Tomfool', no doubt, attended.[12] Skelton's claim to the sergeanty may be no more than a jibe at authority, but it could be an attempt to pay off old scores; something similar may underlie his other two claims. Ralph Waite of Haigh, sometimes called 'gentleman', had for many years been the leading tenant of the manor[13] and in 1641 had served as an executor to the will of Roger Brads-haigh, grandfather of the first baronet.[14] He was the son of James Waite of Haigh and had been christened on 1 February 1583,[15] so that, at the time of Skelton's arrival at Haigh, he would have been seventy-six years old or more. Hence, in his old age, he was 'as wise as' Skelton the fool 'and witty'—that is, senile. 'Honest Nich. Pennington' and 'honest Tom Turner', whom Skelton expected to bury him, were two of the leading local businessmen; the implication, of course, is that they would strip his carcase without waiting for permission anyway. Pennington was born in 1616 or 1617, ranked as a gentleman[16] and was Mayor of Wigan in 1660 and 1674.[17] How honest he was, in fact, is not certain. Skelton's jibe is more clearly justified in the case of Tom Turner, who was a lawyer.[18] An alderman of Wigan in 1682 and 1683,[19] Turner had, in 1679, paid Sir Roger Bradshaigh, the High Sheriff, £750 and accepted some stiff conditions for the privilege of acting as his Under-sheriff for one year,[20] a post from which a good return could be expected. Turner was probably the Bradshaigh's man of affairs and from about 1675 he lived at Haigh.[21] Sir Roger's son, the second baronet, succeeded in 1684 but survived his father by only two years, and his widow Mary was left to bring up five young children. Turner seems to have seized the chance to feather his own nest. Lady Elizabeth Bradshaigh, widow of the first Sir Roger and a most vigorous correspondent, gave her views on the situation in a letter to Peter Shakerley, the Governor of Chester, the guardian of her grandchildren:

...Tom Tornore that contrived to make such a fellow administrator I dowe well beleve will never dowe the family of Haigh so much credit as by thatt ackshon he hath disgrast it but he is a base fellow & will never dow any thing but for his owne ends. He hath beene at the house alone alevein years and haid more his diet & washing & starching & fire & candell light which was more than I haid but what he hath paid my son I know not.... Whiles he stay at Haigh I shall never sett my foot for nevere any one did receve so base languig from a pettyfoll felow as I did from hem. Which haid anyone done the like to my doghter I would have kect him forth of my house. But he is a faveret which I wish may prove well for all hes faire words to my doghter are for his owne ends more than hir profit.[22]

Lady Elizabeth's remarks after Turner's death on 27 November 1686 reflect equally on his 'honesty'.[23]

Skelton's requests about his place of burial are not completely clear. The normal route from Haigh to Wigan, the only graveyard in the huge parish, crossed the River Douglas, so that the wish not to be carried 'o're the Brigg' would rule out the normal place of interment. 'Old Charnock' may refer to another graveyard at Charnock Richard or again to Wigan; the Charnock family were important tenants of Haigh and many were buried in the parish church.[24] Skelton wished to lie by Will Caddy, a name which suggests a connection with Muncaster where the Caddys were a large local clan; it may refer specifically to the William Caddy of Ravenglass who was buried in Muncaster churchyard in 1643.[25] If this solution to the riddle is correct, Skelton was asking to be taken home to Muncaster for burial. The lines '...I Thom' fool, am sheriffe of ye Hall, I mean ye Hall of Haigh' also conceal a local joke. The Rector of Wigan was also the local squire and, consequently, his residence has always been known simply as 'The Hall'. Other references have not been traced, but they were clearly of the same sort.

The comic effect of the painting, however, does not depend only on the verse, it is supported by the whole composition of the work. This parodies the formal state portrait of a great minister of the crown. Like Leicester, Burghley, and others,[26] Skelton grasps a wand of office—not the 'white stave' of the Lord Steward or Lord Treasurer, but the 'White staff' of a fictitious Wigan bailiff. Instead of an inscription giving details of the rank and the title of the subject, Skelton has beside him a scroll bearing a mock will. Some Chancellors had the pouch containing the Great Seal included in their portraits,[27] some Knights of the Garter had the George.[28] Skelton's picture neatly parodies both. The patent of his office should bear the Great Seal which, until the Restoration at least, bore on one side a figure of the monarch on horseback with a dog running by his side. Instead, while Skelton's seal appears at first sight to be the George, in place of the expected dragon the saint is piercing the royal greyhound.

Comparison of the Skelton portraits indicates quite clearly that the Muncaster picture was the earlier of the two, and that the Haigh Hall painting was dependent on it. This explains many of the artistic deficiencies of *Skelton II*. The fingers of the left hand were truncated because of the difficulty in coping with the brim of the hat in *Skelton I*, and the curious treatment of the waist is explicable as a failure to depict the belt correctly. The misunderstanding of the costume at the collar and skirt are other faults typical of the copyist. But it is doubtful whether the term 'copy' is not too strong a description of *Skelton II*. The omission from the will of several vital lines, the loss of the wispy beard, the odd downward curve in the pattern of the skirt on the right of the figure, the rearrangement of the will and seal and the change from a label on the seal, with only the suggestion of writing, to the bold 'A Pattent for my Offices'—a phrase obviously derived from the text of the will—make it by no means certain that the painter of *Skelton II* was working with the earlier picture before him, or had even seen it. At least one sketch—probably by another artist—may separate the two pictures.

As has been shown, the first Skelton portrait was produced between 1659 and 1665. It seems certain that it was actually painted at Haigh. There is no reason to suppose that Skelton ever returned to Muncaster after 1659 while his master was away. In the will he calls himself 'Thom⁵ Skelton late fool of Muncaster', an obvious joke on the expected 'Thomas Skelton late of Muncaster, fool'. The wealth of reference to Wigan and Wigan people, as well as the opening lines of the will, also suggest that the picture was painted at Haigh and removed to Muncaster at some later date. As far as can be discovered, *Skelton II* had always been at Haigh. All reference to Muncaster is missing from this portrait. A Skelton portrait was part of the collection at Haigh which was inherited by the Lindsays in 1770 and was cleaned between 1826 and 1829.[29] There is no possibility that the pictures were changed over after the heiress of Muncaster had married the 24th Earl of Crawford in 1811. Many of the Pennington pictures were brought down from Cumberland to Haigh in 1822 but there was no Skelton picture among them.

Several hypotheses might account for the two Skelton portraits, but it seems most likely that *Skelton I* was painted for the young heir of Muncaster while he was at Haigh, and then taken back to Muncaster with him at the end of his minority. The portrait of a notable jester was, perhaps, a prized possession in many houses.[30] While the heir to the Penningtons lived with Sir Roger Bradshaigh at Haigh, a single picture of Skelton there would have served both families, but on his return home about 1676, a gap would have been left in the Bradshaigh collection. Moreover, to Sir Roger's wife, Elizabeth, the painting was a reminder of her home at Muncaster, and Sir Roger's heir would have played with Skelton as a boy. The Bradshaighs were great collectors of pictures, particularly portraits, and it would be natural for them either to send a local travelling painter to Muncaster to sketch the picture, or more likely, to instruct him to work up a sketch made from the picture by a third person before the transfer to Cumberland. No evidence can be put forward to support this theory, but it seems to fit what facts there are. This hypothesis would, therefore, date *Skelton II* after, or more probably about, the time of Pennington's departure for Muncaster. A date after 1686 would be most unlikely. The death of the second baronet in that year removed the last member of the family at Haigh who had known Skelton. His mother Elizabeth, the Dowager Lady Bradshaigh, it is true, survived him, but she lived with her daughter at Holker and had no power over the furnishings at Haigh after her husband's death in 1684.[31] Furthermore, the Bradshaighs do not seem to have had any close association with the Penningtons after that date. Skelton's patron, Sir William, had maintained friendly relations with his former guardian[32] but was, perhaps, not very intimate with the second baronet, and certainly played no part in the affairs of the family after the death of the second Sir Roger.[33] Thus, *Skelton II* was in all probability painted at Haigh about 1676, but not later than 1686, from sketches made at the time of the transfer of *Skelton I* to Muncaster.

Despite the fact that the portraits of Skelton associate him so closely with the Wigan area, his memory persists today in Muncaster and the neighbourhood—even at a considerable distance from the castle.[34] In several cases, of course, the stories of 'Tomfool' have become confused with other traditions or with folklore, but the more gruesome elements in the Skelton legends—

he is supposed to have acted as the bully and unofficial hangman for the lord of the manor—may also derive from memories of the notorious lawlessness of the area. Rough justice shades into folklore in some stories. According to one tale Tom was given three shillings by Sir Ferdinand Huddleston of Millom Castle and he hid them in a secret place. Each time the jester examined them he found that they were thinner and he accused the carpenter of tampering with his hoard. Finding him asleep one day, Skelton cut off the carpenter's head with an axe and afterwards said to the other servants, 'There, I've hid Dick's head under a heap of shavings, and he will not find that so easily when he awakes as he did my shillings'. In another version of the same incident, the circumstantial details which have been added only accentuate the obvious folk element. Heloise Pennington, presumably one of the daughters of the squire of Muncaster, was affianced to Sir Ferdinand Huddleston, but was in love with Dick the carpenter on her father's estate. She had met Dick and danced with him at the maypole in Eskdale. 'Wild Will of Whitbeck' decided that what was allowed to a carpenter should be allowed to him, and he claimed a kiss from Heloise. Dick knocked him down. Will then went to Millom Castle and informed Sir Ferdinand of the affection between Dick and the future Lady Huddleston. Her betrothed swore to be revenged on Dick and offered a reward to anyone who would punish him. This was overheard by Tom Skelton, who already had a grudge against the carpenter who teased him constantly. The fool stole quietly upon Dick as he was asleep during the dinner hour in his shop, cut off his head with the craftsman's own axe and came into the castle roaring with laughter and saying that he had hid Dick's head in the shavings and he would have a job to find it when he awoke. Heloise never married Sir Ferdinand but retired to a convent. Tomfool escaped punishment under the cloak of idiocy through the protection of the Penningtons whom he had thus saved from an unfortunate mesalliance.[35] The decapitation motif occurs again in a legend about the crossing of the River Esk below the castle. Tom Skelton is supposed to have encouraged travellers to ford the river on their way to Waberthwaite so that they would be trapped in the quicksands. The most obvious motive for this would be robbery, but when Tom recovered the bodies he is supposed to have cut off the heads and buried them under tree trunks.

Other stories about Skelton have more in common with the crude practical jokes characteristic of other fools and found in the Jest Books. He is supposed to have outwitted a condescending servant, who asked if the Esk was fordable at a particular spot, by saying that 'Nine of our family have just gone over'. The footman thereupon stepped into a very deep pool and was saved from drowning only by being helped out by his tormentor. The fool explained afterwards that the members of his family who had crossed the river were geese. On one occasion, he secretly smeared the banisters of the great stairs of the castle with grease, to the extreme annoyance of the guests. When asked if he knew anything about the matter, Skelton said that, in his opinion, everyone had had a hand in it. Another tale gives Tom the character of a public entertainer. He would sometimes climb up on to the branch of a tree and after amusing the crowd with his antics would make his exit by sawing through the branch between himself and the trunk. The spot where he performed this trick, together with 'Tomfool's Hill', 'Tomfool's Tree' and 'Tomfool's Walk' are still pointed out at Muncaster, but as the gardens have been remodelled since the seventeenth century, the existence of such labels is no proof of authenticity.

As Leslie Hotson has taught us to expect, Skelton is attired in the petticoat adopted by so many of the Elizabethan fools.[36] The colours are white, blue and yellow—bands of white and blue alternate with bands of white and yellow in a pattern of checks which, so far as can be determined from a painting, was produced on the loom and not by later patching or dyeing. The coat buttons can be seen to a little below the waist, the buttonholes coinciding with the lines of the pattern. Whether the coat buttoned to the ground, was closed from the last visible button downwards or fell open thereafter is not clear. The apparent end to the fastenings two buttonholes below the belt and the way in which the skirt hangs make the last most likely. A white shirt pokes out above the leather belt and the collar is worn outside the coat; the two points of the neckband which hang down below the collar are red. The shoes are laced, one with blue and the other with pink cord, and two knots of the same colours are on the hat. In the hatband, in the fashion of the gallant, is the name of Skelton's lady. None of the traditional accessories of the jester appear in the picture. There is no sign or mention of coxcomb, hood, ears, bauble or bells; the hat is typical of normal headgear common at the period.

Any theory connecting this costume with the stage-wear of the early seventeenth century must be advanced with caution. Hotson has demonstrated that one meaning of the word 'motley' is 'a cloth of mixed colour'. He suggests that the fabric resembled homespun or tweed, and was woven from a number of different coloured threads. The predominant colour—frequently green—fixed the description, 'green motley', 'blue motley' and so forth. Motley, however, when used for fools, certainly made them conspicuous. How a 'homespun' cloth could have achieved this, except at very close quarters, is difficult to imagine. If one colour predominated, motley cloth would have been indistinguishable, at more than a few yards' distance, from ordinary fabrics of the same colour. It is, moreover, difficult to see how the blended shade Hotson describes can properly be defined as a 'mixed colour'.[37] Skelton's costume provides an alternative interpretation of motley cloth. If the different coloured threads were not mixed together but were kept separate and woven into patterns—in this case checks—the difficulties are overcome. The fool is distinguished by a cloth whose patterns proclaim his condition as soon as it becomes visible, colour is determined not by an overall tinge but by the dominant hue in the design—in Skelton's case by the blue checks—and motley appears as a true mixture of colours and not as a blend.

The discussion of a Restoration family fool and his costume in a volume devoted to the drama of the Shakespearian period might be considered a major anachronism. Indeed, since the taste for fools in drama did not revive when the theatres reopened, it could be argued, that as well as having little relevance to Shakespeare, Skelton has little to do with the drama either. Even if the period had been much earlier, the location of his doings would have been enough to discredit any deduction made from the picture if applied to the London stage. The North of England, including Cumberland and parts of Lancashire, was one of the wildest and least accessible areas of England before the Industrial Revolution; it was the last region to succumb to the influence of the capital. Skelton's costume could, therefore, very well be an example of an obscure local tradition. Nevertheless, the fact that Tomfool was closely associated with Haigh must not be forgotten (Fig. 2). The Bradshaighs lived only ten miles from the playhouse at Prescot[38] and the same distance from Knowsley, the seat of the Earl of Derby, once the headquarters of a company of professional actors and a frequent stopping place on the itineraries of London players. Sir Roger Bradshaigh was, in fact, an intimate friend of the Earl. Less than seven miles from Haigh was Rufford, once the base for another company of professionals.[39] Thus Tom Skelton was far from being isolated from the influence of the theatre, and his uniform cannot summarily be dismissed as parochial.

The link between Skelton and the London theatres does not, however, depend only upon the accidents of topography. A line of illustrations can be drawn which connects Skelton's costume to the fool's dress of Shakespeare's day. In 1634 Thomas Heywood's *A Maidenhead Well Lost* was printed by Nicholas Okes.[40] On the title-page and, slightly cropped on sig. H3, is a woodcut illustrating the play (Fig. 3). On the right of the larger section of the block is

Fig. 3. The title-page of *A Maidenhead Well Lost*, by T. Heywood (1634).

a figure who is quite obviously the fool and who is attired in a cap with a coxcomb, a cape and a long check gown with guarded sleeves. The connection with Skelton's coat is clear. While the maker of the woodcut has not illustrated any particular scene in the play but seems rather to have produced an amalgam of three of its outstanding features—the baby in a box, the antics of the jester and a love-episode in the forest—it would seem certain that he followed what he had seen on the stage. Thus the kinship between this fool's dress and Skelton's has prime significance.

Patterned motley is found as the wear of the jester in another book from the same printing house, *A Pleasant History of the Life and Death of Will Summers* (1637). This contains eight illustrations, possibly by the same artist who illustrated the Heywood play,[41] depicting the career of Will Summers; five show him in normal Caroline dress, but in three he wears his fool's costume and in two of these he is accompanied by Patch, Cardinal Wolsey's fool. The link with the fool's costume in *A Maidenhead Well Lost* is seen most clearly in the block showing Summer's welcome to Patch after the Cardinal had handed him over to the King (Fig. 4).

Fig. 4. Will Summers and Patch: *A Pleasant History of Will Summers* (1637), sig. C5ᵛ.

Patch, on the right, has exactly the same kind of head-dress as the Heywood clown except for the bell which the latter has hanging from the beak of the coxcomb.[42] Instead of this, Patch has bells at each elbow. The cape sleeves are again guarded, but the undersleeves are striped and the design of the coat is different. The armholes, the waist and the edge of the skirt are outlined in scallops; the tunic of the coat is divided down the middle, and the skirt is divided into segments. The other figure represents Will Summers, and the costume he wears is seen at a different angle in another illustration earlier in the book (Fig. 5).[43] The skirt has four rows of decoration instead of the scalloping; the sleeves are apparently striped and are decorated with bells. The upper part of the coat has a central panel which is striped horizontally and is flanked by panels of guarded material which pass over the shoulder and down the back. A cape is worn with this dress—in both pictures it is striped horizontally and has four rows of decoration at the edge.[44]

Fig. 5. Henry VIII and Will Summers: *A Pleasant History*, sig. B8.

Will Summers' costume in the *Pleasant History* is clearly related to his well-known portrait engraved by Delaram some time between about 1615 and 1624 (Fig. 6). The connection is seen most clearly in the hat, in each case a low bonnet with an ornamental band and a large curling feather, and each figure has a 'muckender' with tassels tucked into his belt. The block is, however, not a copy of the engraving—the cape seems to be handled differently, a ruff is worn instead of a collar, four rows of decoration instead of two adorn the hem of the coat, the chain and royal cypher are omitted and bells included. The engraving shows yet another pattern

Fig. 6. Will Summers: engraving by Francis Delaram, *c.* 1615–24.

of cloth for the jester's coat; this time the motley is speckled. With the evidence of striped and scalloped cloth in the *Pleasant History* and checked cloth both in the Heywood play and in the Skelton portraits it serves to demonstrate that the fool's costume was, in the early and middle seventeenth century, distinguished by its patterns.

The identification of 'motley cloth' with a patterned material is consistent with various uses of the word 'motley'—for example, to describe Joseph's coat of many colours or a field covered with flowers. In Jonson's *Every Man out of his Humour*, a coat of arms is described as 'of as many colours as e'er you saw any fooles coat in your life' (III, ii, 29); the 'aud motley jacket' of the Scots peasant must have been tartan, and the checkered apron of the barber was described by Beaumont as a 'motley garment'.[45] The use of motley in this sense leads to the word 'mottled' and from there it is only a short step to 'pied' or 'parti-coloured'—expressions which are almost as commonly used of Elizabethan and Jacobean jesters as the term motley. For example, in *Laugh and Lie Downe* (1605), the following passage occurs (sig. F2ᵛ): 'But, when this Maske had once gone aboute the Roome, comes out a Foole in a pied coat, and tels them, they must make an ende quickly.' Indeed, if the essence of motley was a strongly contrasting pattern the difficulty of resolving 'motley', 'pied', 'parti-coloured' or similar expressions for the fool's coat disappears; 'pied' and 'parti-coloured' may indicate particular types of pattern but both lie within the generic 'motley'. Sidney Thomas has already pointed out that in *The Three Ladies of London* (1584)[46] 'painted motley' is synonymous with 'parti-coloured'. Another expression which was used for the fool's coat, 'patched', also fits into the picture. Dekker equated motley with patches,[47] while in R. Copland's *The Highway to the Spital-House* (1535)[48] the Porter included among the inmates

> They that will not suffer their clothes whole
> But jag and cut them with many a hole
> And payeth more for making than it cost,
> And when it is made the garment is but lost,
> Patching them with colours like a fool;
> At last they be ruled after our school.

This passage, indeed, would suggest that the fool's coat could be made of patchwork rather than a patterned cloth, but the way that the effect was achieved is immaterial. The essential thing was that the fool's coat should be patterned in an unusual fashion. Motley thus had no regular form, variations could be made to please each individual. Checked, striped, speckled, pied, patched or parti-coloured coats were all admissible.[49]

NOTES

1. The portrait was purchased by the Rev. A. R. Allen, the Vicar of St John's, Lytham, Lancashire, at the sale of effects at Haigh Hall in 1947. In 1957 it was purchased by George Higgins of Blackpool and later was transferred to the Shakespeare Institute, through the kind agency of Mrs Constance Thomson.

2. Except where otherwise stated, biographical details are taken from A. J. Hawkes, 'Sir Roger Bradshaigh of Haigh, 1628–1684', *Chetham Miscellanies, VIII*, Chetham Society, New Series, CIX (1945).

3. Cf. the picture known as '1st Viscount Stormont', Scottish National Portrait Gallery, Edinburgh.

4. A third Skelton portrait—of a smaller size—also exists at Muncaster. It is a copy of '*Skelton I*', probably from the eighteenth century. For the purposes of this article it has been disregarded.

5. Hawkes *op. cit.*; W. Dugdale, 'Visitation of Lancaster 1664–5', part 3, *Chetham Society, Old Series*, LXXXIII (1873), 231.

6. Crawford Muniments, Notebook of Pictures, p. 117.

7. Dugdale, *op. cit.* p. 231.

8. He was born 16 March 1655. His marriage, after which he would certainly have had a separate establishment, took place *c.* 1677. G. E. Cokayne, *Complete Baronetage*, IV (1904), 78.

9. Wigan Parish Registers, II, 26.

10. *Ibid.* II, 13.

11. E. Welsford, *The Fool* (1935), p. 122.

12. W. Hutchinson, *The History of the County of Cumberland* (Carlisle, 1794), I, 567–8.

13. Crawford Muniments, Haigh Manorial Records—Court Baron 26 January, Aº 5 Chas. I; Manorial Present-ments, *c.* 1639; Court Book, 5 November 1649 to 20 November 1650; List of tenants, 9 September 1651.

14. Crawford Muniments, Will of Roger Bradshaigh of Haigh, *ob.* 1641.

15. *Parish Registers of Wigan 1580–1625*, ed. J. Arrowsmith. Lancashire Parish Register Society (1899), p. 8.

16. Dugdale, *op. cit.* p. 232.

17. *Wigan Almanac*, Municipal Officers of Wigan, 1627–1834.

18. Crawford Muniments, Transcription of Shakerley Papers, p. 29.

19. *Wigan Almanac*, Municipal Officers.

20. Crawford Muniments, Accounts of Sir Roger Bradshaigh as High Sheriff of Lancashire, 1679–81.

21. *Ibid.* Shakerley Papers, p. 24.

22. *Ibid.* Shakerley Papers, p. 24.

23. *Ibid.* Shakerley Papers, p. 29.

24. *Parish Register of Wigan*, pp. 5, 9, 33 and *passim.* A Ralph Charnock seems the most likely person to be 'old Charnock'. He was a leading tenant at Haigh *temp.* Elizabeth I and James I: Crawford Muniments, Haigh Manorial Records—Manor Book, Philip and Mary *sqq.*, 'List of tenants lysenced to take canell, Rauffe Charnocke xxx lodes', no date; presented at Court Baron 16 August 4 James I. His son Roger is a possible alternative; he was baptized 1 February 1594 (*Parish Register of Wigan*, p. 33) and died between 1646 and 1651 (*Calendar of Committee for Compounding with Delinquents*, IV (1892), 2798; V (1893), 3257).

25. Muncaster Parish Registers.

26. Robert Dudley, Earl of Leicester, Lord Steward. Nicholas Hilliard—Collection of the Duke of Buccleuch and Queensberry; William Cecil, Lord Burghley, Lord Treasurer. M. Gheeraedts—National Portrait Gallery, no. 362.

27. Sir Nicholas Bacon, Keeper of the Great Seal. National Portrait Gallery—no. 164; John Williams, Arch-bishop of York, Keeper of the Great Seal. Collection of the Marquis of Bath, Longleat, no. 158.

28. Sir Christopher Hatton. National Portrait Gallery, no. 1518; William Cecil, Lord Burghley. Collection of the Duke of Bedford, Woburn, no. 49.

29. Crawford Muniments, Catalogue of Pictures, etc., at Haigh Hall—section headed 'Family Portraits of yᵉ Bradshaighs'.

30. G. Holles, *Memorials of the Holles Family, 1493–1656*, ed. A. C. Wood, Camden Society 3rd Series, LV (1937), 42–3.

31. Crawford Muniments, Shakerley Papers *passim.*

32. *Ibid.* Accounts of Sir Roger Bradshaigh as High Sheriff—List of liveries 17 March 1678/9.

33. *Ibid.* Shakerley Papers *passim.* It is significant that Peter Shakerley and not Sir William was the guardian of his young cousins.

34. I am indebted for the stories of Tom Skelton to Sir William Pennington-Ramsden, the Rev. M. K. Hodges, the late Ernest Baker, and *The Verge of Western Lakeland* by the late W. T. Palmer (London, 1941), pp. 108–11. Skelton stories from Haigh must exist but it has not been possible to collect them. A notebook of the 25th Earl of Crawford containing Skelton legends is known to exist among the unsorted Crawford Muniments at the John Rylands Library, but I was unable to examine it.

35. The story may have been confused with the real marriage of Bridget Pennington to Sir William Huddleston (Fig. 2). Sir William's father and son were both called Ferdinand.

36. *Shakespeare's Motley* (1952).

37. The term 'homespun' is really an indication of texture and not of colour. It applies to a coarse cloth woven from yarn spun on the domestic spinning wheel; true homespun is extremely rare today. 'Tweed' is now almost always made up from machine-spun yarn, and the complex blend of colours in the thread now characteristic of the cloth would have been difficult to produce in the seventeenth century.

38. F. A. Bailey, 'The Elizabethan Playhouse at Prescot', *Transactions of the Historic Society of Lancashire and Cheshire*, CIII (1952), 69–81.

39. Lancashire County Record Office, W.C.W. 1581. Will of Alexander Houghton of Lea.

40. The illustration was seen by Douce, *Illustrations of Shakespeare* (2nd ed. 1839), p. 516, but was wrongly described as belonging to Heywood's *Fair Maid of the Exchange*.

41. The illustration of a table, sig. D2ᵛ, in *The Pleasant History*, has a clear connection with Fig. 3.

42. Since the Skelton portraits give no information about the fool's head-dress, consideration of this part of the attire in the other illustrations has been reduced to a minimum. However, the accessories in Figs. 3–5 merit close examination.

43. Summers wears dark glasses in this illustration to shade his eyes from the splendour of Henry VIII.

44. The third block, sig. C6ᵛ, not reproduced here, shows Patch and Summers discovering Wolsey's gold. The costumes are almost identical with those in Fig. 4.

45. Hotson, *op. cit.* pp. 35, 42.

46. S. Thomas, 'A Note on Shakespeare's Motley', *Shakespeare Quarterly*, x (1959), 255.

47. *Henry VIII*, ed. Foakes, p. 5, n. 16; cf. Milton's 'The motley incoherence of a patch'd missall' (*N.E.D.* 'Motley', A.2, 1641).

48. *The Elizabethan Underworld* (ed. A. V. Judges, 1930), p. 16.

49. The extent to which motley could be woven was restricted by the capacity of the hand-loom which, in the seventeenth century, could not produce complicated designs. Large square or rectangular patches of colour can, however, be woven on the simplest hand-loom. The structure of the fabric is very simple, but the large blocks of colour make the cloth look elaborate.

The emphasis on pattern persists in the use of the term 'motley' in the modern textile industry. Today, motley is normally woven from several different colours which are arranged in some form of decoration—a floral design of spots or a geometrical pattern is most usual. Less commonly the same effect is produced by sewing vari-coloured patches together, or on to a base. If desired, an irregular mottled effect all over the cloth can be achieved if groups of differently coloured fibres are mixed together when the yarn is spun. This method is akin to that suggested by Leslie Hotson, but the fabric produced is not a mixture, such as tweed, but a cloth which has a blotched appearance. This also results accidentally when patches which are 'off shade' appear in a worsted or woollen; the defective cloth is then described as 'mottled'.

I am indebted for their kind assistance in the preparation of this article to the Rt Hon. the Earl of Crawford and Balcarres who allowed me to consult the Crawford Muniments and to the Librarian and staff of the John Rylands Library where they are deposited—to Sir William Pennington-Ramsden, Bt., for permission to reproduce the Muncaster Skelton and to examine the picture and the Pennington manuscripts at Muncaster Castle—to Canon Arthur Finch, Rector of Wigan, for permission to consult the registers of the parish—to the Rev. M. K. Hodges, Vicar of Muncaster, for very kindly searching the parish registers there—to the Dean, and to the staff of the Radiography Unit of the Medical School of the University of Birmingham and to S. Rees-Jones and the staff of the Courtauld Institute of the University of London for a technical examination of the Haigh Hall picture—to David Piper of the National Portrait Gallery, Robin Hutchison of the Scottish National Portrait Gallery, the Rev. A. R. Allen, Vicar of St John's, Lytham, H. Hornyold-Strickland of Sizergh, and H. H. G. Arthur, Librarian of the Wigan Public Libraries—to the Folger Library and to the British Museum for permission to reproduce Figs. 3–5 and Fig. 6 respectively—and to the proprietors of *Country Life* for the use of their photograph of *Skelton I*. I also thank N. C. Gee, head of the textile department of Dewsbury and Batley Technical and Art College for information incorporated in footnotes 37 and 49.

ILLUSTRATIONS OF SOCIAL LIFE III:
STREET-CRIES

BY

F. P. WILSON

Englishmen began to advertise their wares by word of mouth as soon as Englishmen began to live together in towns. This we may presume; but the earliest literary reference I know of is in the Prologue to *Piers Plowman* where cooks and their servants outside their shops cry 'Hot pies hot! Good gris [little pigs] and geese. Go we dine, go we!' The fifteenth-century *London Lickpenny* describes the misfortunes of a poor Kentishman in London and Westminster in sixteen eight-line stanzas with the refrain 'For lack of money I may not speed!' The lawyers in Westminster gave him nothing for nothing, and the shopkeepers of London with their 'Strawberry ripe and cherry in the rise [on the branch, fresh]', 'Hot sheeps' feet', 'Rishes [rushes] fair and green' were not more generous. From the sixteenth century onwards hundreds of these cries have come down to us.

We may distinguish between the cries of shopkeepers and those sung by itinerant traders. Shopkeepers and their apprentices assailed passers-by with such comments as 'What is't ye lack?', 'Buy a very fair cloak, sir', 'See here, Madam, fine cobweb lawn, good cambric', 'Will ye buy any starch or clear complexion, Mistress?' There were complaints of 'scoffing girds' from the apprentices if man or woman departed without buying.[1] But most of the cries are to be assigned not to shopkeepers but to itinerant vendors who carried their shops about with them and advertised their goods in word and tune. We learn much about them from ballad, poem, pamphlet, play, musical composition, and of course from the series of woodcuts and engravings considered below. Good examples of two Jacobean ballads are in the Pepys Library at Magdalene College, Cambridge: the one of *c.* 1612 sung by 'a handsome Wench' in Coleman Street with the refrain 'I have fresh Cheese and Cream', and of about the same date the more satirical 'Dish of Lenten Stuff' by William Turner,[2] an antidote to the sentimental view of the engravers and the poets. As for the latter we have but to think of the variations made by Campion and Herrick on the theme of 'Cherry Ripe' or Drayton using the formula of the town-crier to advertise for a lost heart. Add that the old cries will not wholly disappear from the modern world so long as mothers and their children value 'Old Chairs to mend' and the deflationary 'One a penny, two a penny, Hot cross buns!'

Of the kind of information supplied by the pamphleteers take an example from Donald Lupton's *London and the Country Carbonadoed* (1636, p. 91). He tells us of those 'Crying, Wandring, and Trauailing Creatures' the fishwives, whose storehouse was Billingsgate or the foot of London Bridge and whose residence Turnagain Lane:

Fiue shillings a Basket, and a good cry, is a large stocke for one of them...their Shoppe's but little, some two yards compasse, yet it holds all sorts of Fish, or Hearbs, or Roots, Strawberries, Apples, or Plums, Cowcumbers, and such like ware: Nay, it is not destitute some times of Nutts, and Orenges, and Lemmons....If they drinke out their whole Stocke, it's but pawning a Petticoate in *Long-lane*, or themselues in *Turnebull-streete* for to set vp againe. They change euery day almost, for Shee that was this day for Fish, may be to morrow for Fruit; next day for Hearbs, another for Roots.

Among their many cries were 'Buy my poor John'—salted hake, which had a very ancient and fish-like smell when 'not of the newest', as we learn from Trinculo on Caliban.

The cries of shopkeepers and itinerants add to the gaiety of many a play. In Robert Wilson's *Three Ladies of London*, Conscience in her affliction has to take to selling brooms and is given a cry and a song. The plays of Thomas Dekker abound with shopkeepers and apprentices recommending their wares, and many a 'What do ye lack?' adds to the fun and bustle of *Bartholomew Fair*. Thomas Heywood brings the cries of London into his *Rape of Lucrece. A True Roman Tragedy*, each cry bearing the burden 'Thus go the cries in *Romes* faire towne, First they go up street and then they go downe'. There is a pedlar's song in Chettle and Munday's *Downfall of Robert Earl of Huntingdon*, and Autolycus's 'Lawn as white as driven snow...' is an example of how Shakespeare leaves things better than he finds them. In *his* plays we shall not look for much information of this kind, but he refers to the orange-wife, to the raucous shouts of the town-crier, and twice to his 'Oyes!'; and into *King Lear* of all plays he brings a cry to be heard in English town and country: 'Poor naked Bedlam, Tom's a cold, a small cut of thy bacon or a piece of thy sow's side, good Bess, God Almighty bless thy wits.'[3] Another cry this play may remind us of is 'Buy a barrel of samphire', a herb used for pickling which grew (as every schoolboy knows) on Dover Cliff.

Even more informative are the musicians, who used the cries in their compositions. Thomas Ravenscroft in his *Pammelia* and *Deuteromelia* of 1609 and his *Melismata* of 1611 gave us our earliest texts of many a round, catch and freeman's song, including 'Three Blind Mice' and 'A frog he would a wooing go'; he also included 'canons in unison' on such themes as 'Have you any wood to cleave?', 'What kitchen stuff have you, maids?', and 'Wall fleet oysters at a groat a peck'. Whoever wrote these lines[4] was taking a romantic view of a street-trader's life:

> Who liueth so merry in all this land
> as doth the poore widdow that selleth the sand?
> *Chorus* And euer shee singeth as I can guesse,
> will you buy any sand, any sand Mistris?
>
> The Broom-man maketh his liuing most sweet
> with carrying of broomes from street to street:
> *Chorus* Who could desire a pleasanter thing,
> than all the day long to doe nothing but sing?

More fruitful still are the remarkable series of 'Fancies' for voices and instruments arranged by Orlando Gibbons, Richard Deering, Thomas Weelkes and other composers, some of them written down by Thomas Myriell in 1616 and preserved in the British Museum. The fact that they often use the same notes for the same cries suggests that they retain the actual tunes sung in Shakespeare's London. Among the most attractive are the sweep's: 'Soope Chimny soope: soope Chimny Mistris with a hay derrie derrie derrie soope from the bottom to the tope soope Chymny sope there shall noe sutt fal into your porrege pott with a hay derrie derrie derrie soope'; the rat-catcher's: 'Rats or myce, ha ye any rats, mise, polcats, or weesils, or ha ye any old sowes sick of the measels, I can kill them, and I can kill mouls, and I can kill vermin that creepeth vp & creepeth downe, & peepeth into holes'; and the toothdrawer's with its boastful reticence: 'Touch and goe Ha ye work for kindheart the toothdrawer touch & goe'.[5]

I turn finally to the representations of street-criers in woodcut or engraving. Woodcuts of these are found occasionally in ballad or pamphlet—the town-crier, the bellman, the rat-catcher—but he who searches for early *series* of cries and criers meets with disappointment. He will be disappointed at the crudity of most of the representations, especially if he comes to them with memories of such notable craftsmen as Paul Sandby, Francis Wheatley and Thomas Rowlandson. And he will be disappointed that so few examples have survived, and those often in fragments, of the many which must have been published before 1660. Issued most of them in broadsheet form, they were stuck upon walls and perished accordingly, as did many a ballad for the same reason. They did not recommend themselves to the early collectors of works of art, and to preserve such ephemera would occur only to a few antiquaries like Samuel Pepys. Yet if we come to these scanty remains as social historians we may not be disappointed, for they tell us something of manners and costume and of the sights and sounds in the streets of seventeenth-century London. In rough chronological order, in so far as that can be ascertained, I set out below a summary account of all the series published before 1660 which I have been able to consult, and I do so in the hope that other early examples may be brought to light. Unfortunately space can be spared only for a few specimen illustrations. I am most grateful to the authorities who have given permission to reproduce the prints under their care.

(1) Of Jacobean date are two companion sheets of engravings now in the British Museum Department of Prints and Drawings. One of these is reproduced in Pl. III. The sheets measure some $12\frac{3}{16} \times 10\frac{3}{16}$ in., the engravings some $10 \times 7\frac{3}{16}$ in. Each has four rows with ten figures in each full row. In the centre of the second and third rows, however, a trader and his cry take up a double space. In the one sheet, beneath the large figure of a bellman and his dog, is the cry: 'Mayds in your smocks. Loocke Wel to your lock Your fire And your light And god Giue you good night. At One a Clock !; for the town-crier on the other sheet and his facetious cry (a standing joke)[6] see the reproduction.[7]

(2) In the same collection and also Jacobean in date is a fragment of a relevant woodcut. Two columns supporting an arch divide one trader from another (as in (1)), men and women alternate, there are six in a row, and rhymed verses are supplied beneath each cry. Two rows only survive in the Museum copy. These and two other rows are preserved in a copy in the Pepys Library, but unfortunately the verses have disappeared, borders have been inked in, and the cries are supplied in a hand later than the woodcuts. The set was probably issued as a broadsheet. The Museum copy measures $14\frac{1}{2} \times 9\frac{1}{8}$ in. The figures closely resemble those in (1), but which is the earlier I do not know. The cries in the two rows missing from the Museum copy are: 'The Cryer', 'Kitchin-Stuff', 'The Fidler's Goodmorrow', 'Waintfleet-Oysters', 'Chimney-Sweep', 'Rosemary & Bays'; and in the other row, 'Bread & Meat for ye poor Prisoners', 'My Rope of Onyons white S^t. Thom^s. Onyons', 'Ends of Gold or Silver', 'Hott Pudding-Pyes hott', 'Buy a Matt for a Bed', 'Hott Codlings'.

(3) The most attractive of all the series of cries before 1660 is that from which two samples are shown in Pl. IV A and B, from the copy in the Huntington (formerly in the Bridgewater)

Library. This is a series of thirty-two unnumbered copper plates, each measuring $3\frac{1}{10} \times 3\frac{7}{8}$ in., printed on thirty-two leaves with versos blank: it is the only early series here described which could have been stitched and sold as a pamphlet. It survives in two states and three copies. State (i) is represented by the Huntington copy, one of the seven small books of engravings mentioned in *Shakespeare Survey*, 12, p. 107: state (ii) by copies in the Museum and the Pepys Library. (Two plates only are in the Douce Collection mentioned under (5): 'I haue Screenes if you Desier' (see Pl. IV) and 'I haue fresh Cheese and Creame'.) The chief difference, apart from the greater freshness and sharpness of state (i), is that the cry 'Quicke parauin kells quicke quick' (i.e. 'Periwinkles all alive-o') gives place to 'New wall fleete Oysters', the figure of the woman-trader remaining unaltered. Here again men and women alternate. Above the first plate in the Huntington copy—that of a bellman with the cry 'Lanthorne and a whole Candell light, hange out your lights heare'—the second Earl of Bridgewater wrote 'The Manner of Crying Things in London'. The *Short-Title Catalogue* (no. 16761) is certainly wrong in identifying this series with the entry to John Wolfe on 16 May 1599 of 'The Crye of London together with the song...vj^d'.[8] A likely date for it is *c.* 1640.

(4) A curious survival, of which two specimens are shown in Pl. IV, is a series of silver counters, 1 in. in diameter, twenty-four in all but originally thirty-six, twenty-two of which are now in the London Museum and two (nos. 15 and 19) in the Department of Coins and Medals in the Museum. Designed for use in some game, each coin has a number and floral design on one side and on the other the figure of a trader with some word or words of his or her cry. The figures are copied from the plates described in (3) (state (ii)) with only such changes as were required by the smaller size and different shape. The counters are said to resemble a half-length set of counters of the sovereigns, considered to have been made about the year 1636.[9]

(5) Later than (1) and (2), and probably later than (3) and (4), is a sheet, again in the Museum collection, which resembles (1) in that there are four rows with ten small figures in a row except in the second and third rows where the figure is of double size. But here the figures are in oval frames. The central figure is of two rat-catchers. Above it is the title 'Parte of the Criers of London' and beneath are these verses: 'Hee that will haue neither Ratte nor Mowsse Lett him plucke of the tilles And sett fier of his hows.' The sheet measures $11\frac{5}{8} \times 10\frac{3}{8}$ in., the engraving $10\frac{5}{8} \times 7\frac{3}{16}$ in. In the same collection is a recutting of this engraving, perhaps of the reign of Charles II, which retains the same single figures and their cries but in the centre gives the title 'The Common Cryes of London' and beneath the figure of a newsvendor; above this figure are the words 'The Weekly inteligenc.', and beneath 'Buy a new Booke'. The name and address of the printseller John Overton are added.[10]

(6) The earliest dated series that I know is that sold by R. Pricke at the Flowerpot in Fleet Street in 1655. See Pl. IV from the copy in the Bodleian Library (Douce Prints, Portfolio 139, no. 44). The original measures $3\frac{3}{16} \times 5\frac{1}{2}$ in. The series, originally issued no doubt in sheet form and possibly in two companion sheets, has been much cut up, but sixty-two figures of single size and four of double size survive. These four are: 'The Common Cryer' as in Pl. IV, and immediately beneath it 'Ha y' any Knives to Grinde', 'A Couple of Dray Men', and 'The Siddan Carriers'. The Museum copy is still more imperfect and fills none of the gaps in the Bodleian copy. It lacks one figure of double size (the two draymen) and thirty-four of single

size, and the printseller's address and the date have been defaced. The print of 'The Siddan Carriers' shows the engravers and printsellers moving with the times. When in 1626 the Duke of Buckingham went through the streets of London 'carried on men's shoulders in a Spanish chaire or hand litter' there was much adverse comment, and some protested against men being brought to the servile condition of horses.[11] The word 'sedan' came into the language in the 1630's.

NOTES

1. S. Rowlands, *Greene's Ghost* (1602), Hunterian Club ed. I, 37.

2. *The Pepys Ballads*, ed. H. E. Rollins, I, 47 and his *Pepysian Garland*, p. 30.

3. From a 'Fancy' by Orlando Gibbons, 'The London Cry', British Museum Add. MS. 17792, f. 110.

4. *Deuteromelia*, sig. D4.

5. The three cries cited are from Add. MS. 17795, f. 104; 29376, f. 73; and 29374, f. 86. See on these 'Fancies' Sir Frederick Bridge, *The Old Cryes of London* (1921).

6. In a 'Fancy' in Add. MS. 17794, f. 46 the maiden child is of about the age of six or seven and forty, she was lost between the Standard and the Conduit, and the finder is promised 'four pence for his hier and thats more than shees woorth and gods blessing'. If we go back to 1592, to *Soliman and Perseda*, I, iv, 78, we find: 'Ile haue ten for the crying it.'—'Ten Crownes? And had but sixpence for crying a little wench of thirty years old and vpwards, that had lost her selfe betwixt a tauerne and a bawdie house.'

7. The Museum has a second copy with the words 'And Gods blessinge' removed.

8. It is by no means clear that Wolfe's entry refers to street-cries. The fourpenny fee paid by H. Carr for entering 'The Common Crie of London' on 21 November 1580 suggests that it was a ballad. W. Griffith was certainly entering a ballad 'Buy Bromes buy' in the trade year 1563–4. On the other hand the printseller Francis Leach entered on 12 March 1656 no fewer than forty 'pictures or portraitures' of which no. 29 is 'The common cries of London'. My search in the Registers has been hasty.

9. I am indebted to an excellent article on these counters by L. A. Lawrence in *The British Numismatic Journal* for 1918 (XIV, 49–55). He gave illustrations of both sides of all the extant coins except no. 15 ('Sum broken Breade and Meate') acquired by the Museum in 1929. He also gave reduced facsimiles of the Museum copies of (1), (2), (3), and (5). He did not know of the Pepysian and Bodleian copies, and for his knowledge of the Huntington-Bridgewater copy of (3) he depended on Charles Hindley's *History of the Cries of London* (revised ed. *c.* 1885). For a later examination of (4) and an attempt to date (3) see H. Farquhar in *The Numismatic Chronicle* (1925), 5th ser. v, 78 ff.

10. The printseller's name and address have been altered, and all that can be read of the original imprint is 'Printed and sold by...at the White Horse...by newgat'. This was the address of three successive Overtons, Henry, John and Henry. In the altered imprint John Overton's name can be read. He seems to have moved to the White Horse without Newgate in 1671. *The Weekly Intelligence* may be the London newspaper of that name first published in 1679. For another cry of a bookseller see Pl. IV—'New Bookes newly printed and newly Com forth'. In a draft of a facetious letter of 1579 to Spenser, Gabriel Harvey imagines how a volume of his verses might be cried up at Bartholomew or Stourbridge Fair (*Letter Book*, ed. E. J. L. Scott, p. 59): 'What lack ye Gentlemen? I pray you will you see any freshe newe bookes? Looke, I beseeche you, for your loove and buie for your moonye. Let me yet borrowe on cracked groate of your purse for this same span new pamflett. I wisse he is an University man that made it, and yea highlye commended unto me for a greate scholler.'

11. J. Chamberlain, *Letters*, ed. McLure, II, 630; A. Wilson, *The History of Great Britain* (1653), p. 131.

AN ELIZABETHAN STAGE DRAWING?

BY

R. A. FOAKES AND R. T. RICKERT

When Edward Alleyn was on tour in the provinces acting with Strange's Men in 1593, the year of the great plague, Philip Henslowe wrote some letters to him from London, giving him city and family news. These were preserved, and one of them, now Dulwich College MSS. I. 14,[1] has on it some pen-and-ink sketches. W. W. Greg noted the existence of these drawings in his edition of the *Henslowe Papers*,[2] where he remarked that one was 'apparently for some scenery in perspective'. This sketch, which does not seem to have attracted further attention, is reproduced below slightly reduced from its actual size; it measures about 5 by $3\frac{1}{8}$ in.

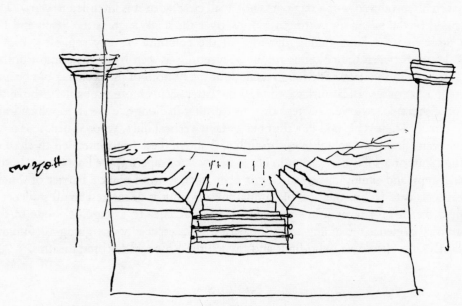

Fig. 1. Henslowe papers, MSS. I. 14: letter from Philip Henslowe to Edward Alleyn, 28 September 1593. Sketch on blank leaf.

The letter was written on a sheet of paper that had been folded once to give four pages; the letter itself occupies two pages. The sketch reproduced above is drawn on the third page in a reddish-brown ink; this page is otherwise blank except for the phrase 'A Imbroydered carpett', written in Henslowe's hand, and in a much darker-coloured ink, to the left of the sketch. The last page, the outer fold of the letter, bears the address, and also, drawn with the paper turned sideways, so that they appear at right angles to the address, sketches of four heads and one full-length figure of an old man leaning on a staff and holding out his hand. Three of the heads are clearly imitated one from the other, and the topmost one, perhaps the one drawn first, has some shading round it which suggests a halo; the others lack this. All the sketches except one of the copies of this head are in a darkish ink, but this one is in a reddish-brown ink similar to, and apparently the same as, that of the drawing overleaf; above it, in the same ink, and apparently in Henslowe's hand, are written 'the things wch I Craves', and, making a separate line, 'ther is'.

It seems likely, then, that the sketch reproduced is by Henslowe, although it is in a different ink from the letter and cannot be dated. Alleyn may have returned Henslowe's letter to him when he came back to London, and the phrase 'A Imbroydered carpett' may be a jotting relating to that part of the letter which deals with a refurbishing of Alleyn s quarters. In any case, he would have brought it back to Henslowe's household, where his wife Joan, Henslowe's step-daughter, was living and anxiously awaiting the return of the 'welbeloued husband' to whom it is addressed.[3] Perhaps the drawings were made soon after their reunion; it seems more probable that Henslowe scrawled on this letter when it was still in his mind than that he returned years later to single it out for such a purpose.[4] But Henslowe lived until 1616.

If the sketch reproduced is of a stage, it is not at all clear what it is intended to show. The two pillars[5] could be the pillars supporting a canopy over the stage, such as the Swan and Fortune theatres possessed; the lines joining the tops of the columns vaguely suggest a roof there. What is drawn between the columns might be a setting as seen from the auditorium, or the theatre as seen from the stage. The long rectangle at the bottom of the sketch could be intended to represent a flat or a vertical surface, though the latter seems more probable. Above this are shown, on either side, two tiers of steps or seats, turning in alongside the steps which lead back from the centre. These stairs end in a number of faint vertical lines, whose purpose is not clear, and some even fainter horizontal lines through and above these seem intended to close off the vista with a hint of a solid background. Three heavy lines superimposed across the bottom of the central steps, and ending in tiny circles or open dots, seem to mark a barrier of some kind.

Whatever its date within the possible limits, this drawing is of interest to all students of the Elizabethan theatre; for if, as seems probable, it has reference to a stage, it is one of the few scraps of visual evidence remaining from the period. It is especially intriguing as coming from the hand of Philip Henslowe, who built and owned the Rose and Fortune theatres.

NOTES

1. See G. F. Warner, *Catalogue of the Manuscripts and Muniments of Alleyn's College of God's Gift at Dulwich* (1881), pp. 10–11.

2. (1907), p. 39.

3. The letters are in the writing of Philip Henslowe, but were sent as joint messages from Joan Alleyn as well. So this letter, dated 28 September 1593, begins 'Righte wealbeloued Sonne...', but is addressed (still in Henslowe's hand), '...vnto my welbeloued husband'.

4. Another letter, from Henslowe to Alleyn, of 26 September 1598 (MSS. I. 24; see Greg, *Henslowe Papers*, p. 47), has on it a sketch of a head and two sentences in Henslowe's writing, 'lamentation is Ever moued to ioy', and 'Hinchlowe is my name & w^t my pen I writt ye same'. He also covered the outer pages of his diary with scrawls and odd phrases, but this diary was in continuous use over many years.

5. The doubling of the line at the right of the left column is due to a fault in the paper.

WAS THERE A MUSIC-ROOM IN SHAKESPEARE'S GLOBE?

BY

RICHARD HOSLEY

The first historian to deal with the problem of a music-room in the Elizabethan theatre appears to have been Edmund Malone. Writing in 1790, Malone said: 'The band...sat (as I have been told by a very ancient stage veteran, who had his information from Bowman, the contemporary of Betterton) in an upper balcony, over what is now called the stage-box' ('An Historical Account of the Rise and Progress of the English Stage', in *The Malone-Boswell Variorum Shakespeare*, 1821, III, 111–12). The words quoted, however, contain an obvious error, as W. J. Lawrence pointed out in 1911:

Unfortunately, Malone did not know, what is well known now, that the Elizabethan theatre, unlike the theatre of his own time, had neither proscenium arch nor front curtain; otherwise he would not have conveyed his information in precisely these terms. The stage boxes in the latter half of the eighteenth century were situated on either side of the 'apron,' or *avant scène*, a little in front of the proscenium arch. It is at least made clear to us, however, by Malone that the ancient 'music-room' was in stage regions and not in the auditorium proper. Most likely, what Bowman's acquaintance meant to convey to him was that the Elizabethan musicians occupied an upper balcony at the back of the stage. Broadly speaking, this tallies with most of the evidence educible on the subject.[1]

I

A music-room over the stage is presumably referred to in Marston's *Sophonisba*, a Blackfriars play of 1606: '*A short song to soft Musique above*' (Q, 1606).[2] A more specific reference by Pepys (cited by Lawrence) to the 'musique-room' at the Red Bull in 1661 is of value because, though of late date, it confirms the implication of a stage-direction in William Rowley's *Shoemaker a Gentleman* that the Red Bull had a music-room over the stage about 1608: '*Musicke heere descends*' (Q, 1638). More important is evidence for a music-room at the Swan in 1611. A stage-direction in Middleton's *Chaste Maid in Cheapside*, printed in 1631 as played at that theatre, requires '*a sad Song in the Musicke-Roome*'. This last reference naturally directs our attention to De Witt's drawing of the Swan (*c.* 1596), the chief of our four pictorial sources for the Elizabethan stage. This shows a row of six windows above and behind the stage, apparently the front openings of boxes (each approximately 6 ft. wide) used generally by spectators but also, upon occasion, by players for the delivery of speeches 'above'—the 'Lords' room' or 'rooms'. Any one of these boxes, if a 'consort' of three or four musicians were placed in it, could have served as the music-room alluded to in our text of the *Chaste Maid*. Similarly either of the somewhat smaller boxes of the Lord's room in the *Roxana* vignette (1632), our second pictorial source for the Elizabethan stage, could have served as a music-room above and behind the stage of the unknown theatre in question.

A music-room is depicted on the frontispiece to the 1711 edition of *Wit at Several Weapons* by Beaumont and Fletcher. (The picture is reproduced by Allardyce Nicoll in *The English Theatre*, 1936, facing p. 38.) The lateness of this evidence makes it of dubious relevance to the Elizabethan stage. Nevertheless it is of value in suggesting survival in the late seventeenth or early eighteenth century of an Elizabethan theatrical custom that we know of from earlier evidence. The picture shows a playing-area, possibly in a hall, on which six dancers are performing, and above and behind this playing-area is a 'room' or box in whose window (approximately 10 ft. wide) four musicians are playing—two violinists, a violist, and a harpist. Thus we have unambiguous pictorial evidence for a music-room directly over a playing-area sometime before 1711.

The Elizabethan music-room was sometimes equipped with curtains. Evidence for these occurs in directions calling for a speech above in Webster and Rowley's *Thracian Wonder*, a play of unknown theatre dated by Chambers about 1600 though not printed till 1661: '*Pythia speaks in the Musick-room behinde the Curtains...Pythia above, behinde the Curtains.*' A curtained music-room above is implied in Brome and Heywood's *Late Lancashire Witches*, a Second Globe play of 1634: '*Arth*[*ur*]. Play fidlers any thing. *Dou*[*ghty*]. I, and lets see your faces, that you play fairely with us. *Musitians shew themselves above*' (Q, 1634). And more general evidence (cited by Adams) for placing musicians behind a curtain occurs in Richard Brathwait's *Whimsies, or A New Cast of Characters* (1631), where the description of a Gamester's behaviour at the theatre contains an allusion to the 'encurtain'd Musique'.

What was the function of the music-room curtains? The answer seems obvious and has been given before: to make the musicians invisible while at the same time permitting their music to be as audible as possible. But why should the musicians have been made invisible? One explanation is that Elizabethans, whether in a theatre or elsewhere, occasionally preferred not to see the source of their music, and here the tradition of a choir-screen in churches may have been influential. Another explanation (which does not necessarily deny the first) is that the attention of a theatrical audience would have tended to be diverted from players to musicians if the latter were visible during the action of a play. If we accept this latter explanation, we may suppose further that a possible secondary function of the music-room curtains was to permit the musicians to be made visible at such times as music would be playing but the action of the play not going forward—that is to say, during act-intervals and before and after the play, when the musicians, instead of accompanying the players as during the acts, would have been performing music for its own sake and thus might have been a legitimate object of the audience's visual as well as auditory attention.

Further evidence for a curtained music-room over the stage is to be found, I believe, in the latter two of our four pictorial sources for the Elizabethan stage, the *Messalina* vignette (1640) and the *Wits* frontispiece (1662). The curtained space over the stage in each of these illustrations is usually interpreted as some kind of an 'upper-stage' (in the former picture perhaps 8 or 10 ft. wide, in the latter about five). Yet neither curtained space resembles the large playing-area (in one modern reconstruction 23 ft. wide) usually connoted by the term *upper-stage*.[3] I would suggest that the curtained space over the stage in each of these pictures is primarily a music-room. This is not to deny that the curtained space over the stage in each picture was sometimes used to discover players 'above'. But the chief function of the curtains over the stage in each picture, I believe, was to conceal musicians, a possible secondary function of the curtains being to reveal the musicians between the acts and before and after the play; whereas discovering players above was only a secondary or tertiary function of those curtains. This proposition follows from the relative infrequency of discoveries above in Elizabethan plays performed at private theatres, most of which (because of the custom of inter-act music) presumably were equipped with a music-room over the stage.

To substantiate this proposition, let us consider the eight extant plays by Massinger that are definitely known, from their title-pages, to have been performed at the Blackfriars. Three of these plays require no action above: *The Fatal Dowry* (1616–19), *The Guardian* (1633), and *A Very Woman* (?—revised 1634). Four plays require each a single action above: *The Duke of Milan*, II, i (1621–2); *The Emperor of the East*, I, ii (1630/1, also performed at the Second Globe); *The City Madam*, V, iii (1632?); and *The Bashful Lover*, V, iii (1636 or 1637). And one play, *The Roman Actor*, requires two actions above, II, i and IV, ii (1626). Thus the eight plays require six actions above, but in only two of these are curtains called for, in I, ii of *The Emperor of the East*, where 'the curtaines' are 'drawne above', discovering Theodosius and his eunuchs who then secretly observe Athenais upon the stage below (Q, 1632); and in V, iii of *The City Madam*, where Lacy and Plenty, having been directed to be 'ready behind' (i.e. behind a curtain, Q, 1659), are discovered above as 'statues'. (The latter action is especially significant and will be referred to again below.) The statues are in view for some two dozen lines, after which Sir John Frugal undertakes to bring them to life by his 'magic' art. He does so and his brother Luke admires the resulting signs of animation. Sir John then orders the statues to descend, whereupon they are directed to enter to the stage: '*Enter Lacie and Plenty. Luke.* Prodigious. *S. John.* Nay they have life, and motion. Descend' (in Q, sig. L4, the direction for re-entrance below is erroneously printed two lines higher than the cue for the descent). Yet each of these eight plays was presumably produced with music during four act-intervals and before and after performance of the play itself. In view, therefore, of the regularly recurring need of these eight plays for a curtained music-room and of their rather infrequent need for a raised playing-area equipped with curtains, it seems probable that, if there was but a single curtained space over the Black-friars stage, that curtained space would have been not an 'upper-stage' but a music-room that might have functioned occasionally as a raised playing-area. Now in both the *Messalina* vignette and the *Wits* frontispiece there is but a single curtained space over the stage. I would suggest that the curtained space over the stage in each of these pictures was primarily a music-room that was used also, upon occasion, for action above requiring curtains.

The identity of a curtained music-room over the stage and a raised playing-area equipped with curtains is clearly implied by the directions earlier quoted from *The Thracian Wonder*. The goddess Pythia speaks '*above, behinde the Curtains*' and then '*Throws down a paper*' of oracular import. Here we have a dramatic action above which does not involve music but which was played, conveniently enough, '*in the Musick-room*'.

That the music-room was occasionally used for an action above requiring curtains is confirmed by Massinger's *City Madam*, mentioned earlier as a Blackfriars play of around 1632. As many writers have observed, a book-keeper's warning note occurs toward the end of Act IV: '*Whil'st the Act Plays, the Footstep, little Table, and Arras hung up for the Musicians*' (Q, 1659). (Presumably the footstep and table are to be 'made ready' for bringing on stage in v, iii; and presumably the arras is hung up in front of a middle doorway in the tiring-house façade.) Then in v, i, the musicians descend, apparently having played 'the Act' (i.e. the act-interval) above in the music-room: '*Musicians come down to make ready for the song at Aras.*' Finally in v, iii we have the music for which the musicians have descended, apparently played behind an arras hung up expressly for the purpose of permitting them to play invisibly yet with maximum audibility. '*Musick. . . Sad music.*' The question immediately arises: Why do the musicians descend to play behind an arras especially fitted up below when they might more conveniently have remained above in the music-room and played, as usually, behind the music-room curtains? The answer, I would suggest, is that the musicians were required to vacate the music-room so that it might be used for the discovery of Plenty and Lacy as 'statues' in a raised playing-area, it still being desirable for the musicians to play, as usually during the acts, out of sight of the audience even though they had descended to stage level.

The problem of an Elizabethan music-room is complicated by the fact that music was not always performed 'above'; in a majority of cases stage-directions call for music to be performed 'within'.[4] W. F. Rothwell, in a study of all Elizabethan plays produced before 1598, finds that off-stage music is invariably noted as 'within', never as 'above' ('Was There a Typical Elizabethan Stage?', *Shakespeare Survey*, 12, 1959). Now I have come across only one example of the term *within* used in the sense of 'out of sight of the audience on the second level of the tiring-house'. This occurs in Beaumont and Fletcher's *The Captain* (1609–12, Blackfriars or First Globe), iv, ii, where a voice 'off' calls a Tavern Boy who is on stage: '*Above within. Why drawer?*' (F, 1647). Presumably other examples exist, but the usage is certainly exceptional. Furthermore I have noticed only three examples of the term *within* used in the sense of 'in sight of the audience on the second level of the tiring-house' (that is to say, in a raised playing-area). The first is in Munday's *Fedele and Fortunio* (c. 1584): '*Fedele and Pedante speake out at a windowe within*' (Q, 1585). The second is in Shakespeare's *1 Henry VI* (1592): '*Enter. . .within, Pucell, Charles, Bastard, and Reigneir on the Walls.*' The third is in Fletcher's *Love's Pilgrimage* (1616?): '*Enter Rodorigo above. . . .Rod. within*' (F, 1647). But these too are isolated instances. In hundreds of cases probably, and in scores demonstrably, the term *within* bears the meaning 'out of sight of the audience on the stage level of the tiring-house'. Evidence for this usage is so abundant that illustration would be superfluous. Clear examples in connection with entrances to the stage may be found in *Julius Caesar*, II, i (1599); *Every Man out of his Humour*, Act v (1599, Q or F); *Measure for Measure*, IV, iii (1604); and *Othello*, v, ii (1604?, Q or F)—all plays designed for the First Globe. Hence we must concede that, although offstage music was sometimes made in a music-room above, it was also sometimes made within the tiring-house on stage level.[5]

What was the rationale behind these variant modes of locating musicians off-stage? The key to the puzzle, I believe, lies in a general distinction between two kinds of music, that which was performed during act-intervals and that which was performed during a play's action. The two kinds may conveniently be called 'inter-act' music and 'dramatic' music. Inter-act music was peculiar to the private theatres, at least down to 1604, the date of Webster's Induction to Marston's *Malcontent* as performed at the Globe, in which 'Burbage' mentions 'the not received custome of musicke in our Theatre' (Q2, 1604)—that is to say, in the men's or 'public' as opposed to the children's or 'private' theatres. For inter-act music the musicians required a permanent station where, even if they played softly, they could be heard reasonably well (and possibly also, upon occasion, seen); and it was desirable also to conceal them within that station. Hence the private theatres developed a music-room over the stage equipped with curtains; and players at private theatres occasionally used the music-room curtains for discoveries above. On the other hand, dramatic music, which of course was common to plays written for both public and private theatres, was the only kind of music 'received' in the public theatres before 1604. Often it was 'military' music, sometimes performed on stage but in any case loud enough to be performed also behind the tiring-house façade ('within'); and often it was an accompaniment for songs or a special effect of some sort, in which case it might be performed on stage, or within the tiring-house behind an 'arras' fitted up in front of an open doorway, or even in particular cases under the stage. But since the special requirement of inter-act music did not exist in the public theatres before 1604, those theatres did not develop music-rooms before that date; and hence also before that date players at public theatres did not, in general, employ the device of discovery above. If the hypotheses here presented are correct, we should expect to find neither music nor discoveries above in public-theatre plays before 1604. In fact we find neither.

A postscript may be added to the foregoing argument. If, in view of evidence for a music-room at the Red Bull around 1608, at the Swan in 1611, and at the Second Globe in 1634, we suppose that inter-act music was introduced to the public theatres sometime after 1604, when approximately may that have been? Evidence of act-division in Elizabethan plays suggests the date 1607 or shortly thereafter, probably 1609 if we are to credit the King's Men with initiating the vogue of act-intervals in the public theatres because of their experience of playing at the Blackfriars. The evidence is conveniently tabulated and sensitively interpreted by Wilfred T. Jewkes in his *Act Division in Elizabethan and Jacobean Plays* (1958). Private-theatre plays are generally divided into acts, whereas public theatre plays printed before 1607 are generally not so divided. 'Somewhere about 1607, however, there must have been a gradual change of practice in the public theatres. After that date, the proportion of divided plays rises sharply, until by about 1616, it appears to be universal' (pp. 100–1). This change of practice Jewkes would attribute in part to the appearance of major dramatists like Middleton and Fletcher who wrote as much for the private theatres as for the public; and in part to the public-theatre players, who began to make use of act-intervals. Presumably they did so in order to interpolate music in the performance of their plays.

II

Although there is no 'external' evidence to determine the question whether there was a music-room in Shakespeare's Globe, a fairly reliable answer is suggested by the 'internal' evidence of a group of plays designed presumably for performance at the First Globe and in no other theatre. These are the thirty extant plays first performed by the Chamberlain-King's Men between the spring of 1599, when the Globe was built, and the autumn of 1608, when the King's Men may have begun using the Blackfriars as well as the Globe. The plays are listed on pp. 36 and 43–4 of *Shakespeare Survey*, 12 (1959).

The 'substantive' texts of twenty-one of these thirty plays make no reference in stage-directions to the location of offstage music (though most of them contain references to music without specifying its location). On the other hand texts of the remaining nine Globe plays make seventeen references in stage-directions to the location of offstage music (in addition to references that fail to specify location):

(1) *Julius Caesar* (1599), IV, ii (F, 1623): '*Low March within.*'

(2) *A Warning for Fair Women* (>1599), sig. D1 (Q, 1599): '*Here some strange solemne musike, like belles is heard within.*'

(3) *Troilus and Cressida* (1602), III, i (F, 1623): '*Musicke sounds within.*'

(4) *All's Well That Ends Well* (1602–3), IV, i (F, 1623): '*Alarum within.*'

(5) *Ibid.* '*A short Alarum within.*'

(6) *Othello* (1604?), II, i (Q, 1622): '*Trumpets within.*'

(7) *King Lear* (1605), I, iv (F, 1623): '*Hornes within.*'

(8) *Ibid.* II, i: '*Tucket within.*'

(9) *Ibid.* II, iv: '*Tucket within.*'

(10) *Ibid.* v, ii: '*Alarum within.*'

(11) *Ibid.* '*Alarum and Retreate within.*'

(12) *Ibid.* v, iii: '*Trumpet answers within.*'

(13) *Macbeth* (1606), I, ii (F, 1623): '*Alarum within.*'

(14) *Ibid.* I, iii: '*Drum within.*'

(15) *Ibid.* III, v: '*Musicke and a Song . . . Sing within. Come away, come away, &c.*'

(16) *Antony and Cleopatra* (1607), IV, iii (F, 1623): '*Musicke of the Hoboyes is under the Stage.*'

(17) *The Devil's Charter* (1607), sig. M2 (Q, 1607): '*Sound a Horne within*'.

With one exception this evidence is unanimous in designating off-stage music at the First Globe as 'within' the tiring-house. The exception, an instance of music under the stage in *Antony and Cleopatra* (item 16), is clearly a special effect imposed by the dialogue of that play, which requires mysterious music when the god Hercules leaves Antony. Now in Elizabethan stage-directions, as noted on p. 116 above, the term *within* usually refers to the stage level of the tiring-house. It is true that this term was used also in reference to the second level of the tiring-house. But verifiable examples of this usage are so few that it may be regarded as a rarely recurring exception. Certainly it would be inadmissible to argue that these sixteen references to music 'within' are *all* exceptions to a usage that is overwhelmingly normal, especially in view of the fact that the thirty plays from which the evidence is drawn (several of them extant in more than one substantive text) contain no evidence whatsoever for the performance of music 'above'.

On the basis of available evidence, then, we may conclude that there was probably not a music-room over the stage at the First Globe before 1609.

But a further question then arises: May the King's Men, under influence of the music-room at the Blackfriars, which they presumably began to use late in 1608 or in 1609, possibly have created a music-room at the First Globe during the period from 1609 to 1613, when the Globe was destroyed by fire? This question is difficult to answer because there is no evidence for the location of off-stage music in the four extant plays known to have been performed at the Globe during this period: *Philaster* (>1610); *A King and No King* (1611), *The Winter's Tale* (1611), and *Henry VIII* (1613). In any case the question depends, I believe, on the corollary question whether the King's Men, perhaps because of prevailing custom at the Blackfriars, introduced inter-act music to their performances at the Globe between 1609 and 1613. Of this in turn we cannot be sure, though it is demonstrable that they did adopt, at the Blackfriars, the private-theatre custom of inter-act music sometime after 1608. Presumably their adoption of inter-act music is reflected in the well-known stage-direction of *A Midsummer Night's Dream*, lacking in the quarto of 1600 but supplied in the folio of 1623, for the four lovers to '*sleepe all the Act*'— that is to say, during an interval for music between Acts III and IV.

Of one thing we may be reasonably confident: If the King's Men wished to create a music-room at the First Globe they could easily have done so by adapting one of the boxes of the Lords' room to that purpose. The capacity of the Globe for such adaptation is suggested by the existence of a music-room at the Swan in 1611, as recorded in our text of *A Chaste Maid in Cheapside*, for the Swan, like the Globe, presumably lacked a music-room in 1604 when Webster, in the Induction to the Globe version of *The Malcontent*, tells us that the custom of inter-act music was not received in the public theatres. Similarly the capacity of the Red Bull for such adaptation is suggested by evidence in *A Shoemaker a Gentleman* that the music-room at that theatre (alluded to by Pepys in 1661) existed as early as around 1608.

What would have been necessary to convert one of the Lords' rooms at the Globe (or at the Swan or Red Bull) into a music-room? The only adaptation necessary would have been to fit up the window of the chosen box with hangings in order to comply with the custom of concealing musicians during the action of a play. So that perhaps the existence of a music-room at the First Globe between 1609 and 1613 is revealed by mention of curtains above in the dialogue of *Henry VIII*, where the King, having entered along with Butts '*at a Windowe above*' in order secretly to observe Cranmer on the stage below, withdraws from the window with the words '*draw the Curtaine close*' (v, ii). We cannot be certain since the text might have been written with the Blackfriars' music-room in mind. But in any case this evidence affords a significant contrast with that of the thirty plays first performed by the Chamberlain-King's Men between 1599 and 1608, for none of these 'Globe' plays requires a curtain above.

III

It remains to consider the theory proposed by Adams, in *The Globe Playhouse* (1942), that the First Globe had a music-room on the third level of the tiring-house. The theory may be rejected on the basis of five considerations.

(1) There is no external evidence for such a third-level music-room. De Witt's drawing of the Swan, our most detailed source of information about the Elizabethan stage and the only one that bears on the question at issue, fails to show such a room and in fact seems to preclude its existence. Adams argues (pp. 299–301) that De Witt intended, but failed, to convey the information that the underside of the stage-cover at the Swan was level with the eaves of the playhouse frame, with the result that the tiring-house façade was three storeys high and thus could have framed a third-level opening beneath the underside of the stage-cover; but the argument is not convincing.

(2) The theory is architecturally and structurally improbable in so far as it requires the under-side of the stage-cover to be level with the eaves of the playhouse frame, a height above ground of over 32 ft. if we accept the specifications of the Fortune contract (1600). C. Walter Hodges, while conjecturing the possibility of a small third-level opening 'tucked up' inside the stage-cover (see his drawing on p. 174 of *The Globe Restored*, 1953), has advanced effective arguments against this proposition.[6]

(3) Adams (pp. 310–23) cites numerous plays alluding in dialogue to music 'hanging in the air' or calling in stage-directions for musicians to '*come down*' or for music to be performed '*above*'—which term he interprets in the undemonstrated sense of 'on the third level of the tiring-house'. However, not a single one of these plays was designed for performance at the First Globe and most of them (on the evidence of date alone) were designed for performance at other theatres: *Four Plays in One* (date and theatre unknown), *The Unfortunate Lovers* (1638), *Love's Changelings Change* (1630), *The Cruel Brother* (1627), *The Sun's Darling* (1624), *The Spanish Gipsy* (1623), *A New Trick to Cheat the Devil* (1639), *1 Henry IV* (1597), *The Faerie Pastoral* (1603, Paul's), *The City Madam* (1632), *The Bondman* (1623), *The Fatal Dowry* (1616), *The Cruelty of the Spaniards in Peru* (1658), *Epicoene* (1609, Whitefriars), *The Roman Actor* (1626), *The Late Lancashire Witches* (1634), and *The Siege of Rhodes* (1656)—the last an error for *The First Day's Entertainment* (see Leslie Hotson, *The Commonwealth and Restoration Stage*, 1928, p. 150). Clearly Adams' evidence for music 'above' has no bearing on the question whether there was a music-room in Shakespeare's Globe.

(4) As has been pointed out in an earlier section of this article, the thirty extant plays designed for performance at the First Globe between 1599 and 1608 contain no evidence whatever for music 'above', although they do contain considerable evidence for music 'within'. Four additional plays presumably designed for performance at the Globe between 1609 and 1613 also contain no evidence for music above although one of them, *Henry VIII*, contains an allusion in dialogue to curtains above which may indicate a music-room at the Globe in 1613. If so, however, the Globe music-room must be postulated as on the second level of the tiring-house, in view alike of the standard meaning of the term 'above' in Elizabethan stage-directions and of evidence for a music-room directly over the stage in such pictorial sources as the *Messalina* vignette, the *Wits* frontispiece, and the frontispiece to *Wit at Several Weapons*.

(5) Finally, Adams argues (pp. 302–7) that Elizabethan plays occasionally require a playing-area above the second level of the tiring-house and that such a playing-area must have been a third-level music-room. This argument supports his interpretation of the term 'above' in the sense of 'on the third level of the tiring house'. However, none of the five plays named in evidence was designed for performance at the First Globe or is even likely to have been performed in that theatre; and the actions in those plays cited by Adams as requiring a third-level playing-area may equally well have employed the second level of the tiring-house or some other station higher than the second level but not within the tiring-house.

The first of these actions is in *1 Henry VI* (1592, Rose): '*Enter Pucell on the top, thrusting out a Torch burning...Enter...within, Pucell, Charles, Bastard, and Reignier on the Walls.*' Adams suggests that the earlier entrance by Joan '*on the top*' is at a higher level than the later entrance by Joan and others '*within...on the walls*'—this entrance evidently being in a regular playing-area on the second level of the tiring-house. This may be. On the other hand, Joan's first entrance may have been in the same second-level playing-area as the later entrance (that is to say, in one of the Lords' rooms), or in another such second-level playing-area (in another of the Lords' rooms), the term 'top' referring to the gallery over the stage as 'the top' of the tiring-house proper; or her first entrance (if indeed at a level higher than the Lords' rooms) may have been at a window in the 'hut' over the stage-cover or in the 'top' gallery for audience on either side of the stage.

The second action occurs in *Claudius Tiberius Nero* (1607, theatre unknown): '*Enter Germanicus and Piso* [as below the walls]...*Enter Vonones as upon the walles*....*Germanicus and Piso scale the walles*,...*Vonones and his sonne flie* [i.e. exit from the raised playing-area, in which Germanicus remains]...*Vonones on the Keepe* [i.e. he enters at a different raised playing-area from the original one, in which Germanicus is still located; from a distance Vonones then challenges Germanicus to single combat]....*Germanicus comes down to the Stage*...*Vonones commeth down, they fight*' (Q, 1607). Adams suggests that the entrance of Vonones *on the Keepe* is at a higher level than the station of Germanicus *upon the walles*. This may be, but it seems just as likely that 'keep' and 'walls' were represented by two different playing-areas on the second level of the tiring-house (that is to say, by two separate Lords' rooms), especially since earlier in this play two different playing-areas are called for on the same upper level: '*Enter Caligula at one end of the stage, and Sejanus at the other end below. Julia at one end aloft, and Tiberius Nero at the other.*'

The third action occurs in *The Double Marriage* by Fletcher and Massinger (c. 1621, Blackfriars or Second Globe): '*Enter Boteswain and Gunner*...*Bots*....Ho, in the hold. *Enter a Boy*.... *Botes*. To th' main top boy...Here's Gold...*Exit Boy*. *Bots*. Come sirs, a queint Levet. *Trump. a levet*. To waken our brave Generall...*Enter Duke of Sesse above and his daughter Martia like an Amazon*. *Sess*. I thank you loving mates; I thank you all. There's to prolong your mirth,... *Daugh*. Take this from me, you'r honest valiant friends,...*Bots*. Call up the Master, and all the Mates. *Enter below the Master and Saylers*...*Boy a top*...*Boy above*. A Sayle, a Sayle... *Mast*. Up, up another,...*Exit Sayler*...*Sayl. above*. Ho...*Sess*. [To the Boy and Sailor] Down,...*Mart*. I swear Ile be above sir, in the thickest, And where most danger is, Ile seek for honor' (F, 1647).

This is obviously a complex sequence of action. Adams interprets the entrance of the Duke and Martia *above* as in a second-level playing-area, that of the Master and Sailors *below* as on the stage. This interpretation, seemingly satisfactory at first glance, neglects two or three minor requirements of the dialogue. First, the Duke and Martia distribute largess immediately upon entrance, and this action, since there is no hint of throwing down money from a raised playing-area to the stage, suggests that they are on the same level as the Boatswain and Gunner. (In contrast to the stage-direction *above*, the dialogue nowhere implies that the Duke and Martia are on a higher level than players on the stage.) Then the Duke and Martia have a long conversation (nearly a hundred lines) in which he narrates several events of his past life to her, and to this conversation the Master easily listens, as though in close attendance and hence on the same level. Finally, toward the end of the action Martia swears that in the anticipated engagement she will be 'above' in the thick of things.

These considerations raise the question whether a different interpretation of the evidence is possible. I believe that one is. When the Boy first enters he comes from 'the hold', and thus we may suppose that he enters by a trap-door in the stage. Later the Master and Sailors are called 'up', and again we may suppose that their entrance is by trap, the direction *below* meaning 'from beneath the stage'. (A near analogue occurs in a Second Globe play by the same authors, *The Prophetess*, 1622, where the term *below* is used in the sense of 'beneath the stage' immediately before an entrance by trap: '*Musick belowe…Enter a Spirit from the Well*', F, 1647.) And correspondingly we may suppose that the Duke and Martia enter to the stage by one of its doors, the direction *above* in this instance meaning 'on the stage, as opposed to "from beneath the stage" as in the direction next following'. Thus the Duke and Martia are on stage along with the Boatswain, the Gunner, and the Master, with the result that they can hand money directly to the Boatswain and Gunner (as the Boatswain earlier gives gold to the Boy), the Master can listen easily to the conversation between the Duke and Martia, and Martia's vow to be 'above' in the thick of the fight becomes more readily intelligible. (The absence of any indication in dialogue that the Duke and Martia are at an elevated station is also accounted for.) According to this interpretation, only the Boy and Sailor appear above the stage, in a regular playing-area on the second level of the tiring-house.

We may now return to Adams' interpretation, according to which the Duke and Martia appear in a second-level playing-area. Adams suggests that the Boy and Sailor appear at a higher station. This is possible, but another station on the second level would serve the purposes of the action equally well (though perhaps not quite so 'realistically'), it being remembered that the term *top* is here relevant to the fiction and thus may have no special theatrical significance. (Louis B. Wright, in 'Elizabethan Sea Drama and its Staging', *Anglia*, LI, 1927, accepts the location *above* for the Duke and Martia but is not certain of the precise location of 'a-top'; he suggests that the Boy might have climbed above the level of the Duke by means of a rope-ladder or simple rigging in the upper balcony, or that at the Globe he might simply have used an adjacent balcony.) Or, if we insist upon a higher station for the Boy and Sailor, the hut at the Second Globe or the trap in the underside of the 'heavens' (referred to as '*the top of the Stage*' in Greene's *Alphonsus King of Aragon*, *c.* 1587, Q, 1599) at Globe or Blackfriars might here have been used as the 'main-top' from which they call down their information; or they might have reappeared in the 'top' spectators' gallery at the Globe.

The fourth action occurs in Heywood and Rowley's *Fortune by Land and Sea* (c. 1607?, Red Bull): '*Enter young Mr. Forrest, like a Captain of a ship, with Sailors and Mariners, entering with a flourish…young For.…*Climb to the main-top, boy, see what you kenne there. *Boy.* I shall, I shall Sir…*Above, Boy.* Ho there…A sayl…*young For.…*Boatswain with your whistle command the Saylors to the upper deck to know their quarters, and to hear their charge… [To the Boy] Come descend' (Q, 1655). Because the preceding action takes place on the deck of another ship and because the dialogue of this action refers to 'the upper deck', Adams suggests that Forrest and his Sailors enter in a second-level playing-area and that the Boy, having gone 'off', re-enters in a third-level playing-area as though on the 'main-top'. This interpretation seems unlikely in view of the absence of an 'above' from the direction for Forrest's initial entrance, as well as in view of the ambiguity of his reference to the 'upper deck': it may be that the Boatswain is expected to command the Sailors to a deck higher than the one he is standing on, or, if he is to command them to the same deck he is standing on, that may be simply the main deck of the ship, which of course would be higher than several other decks. A more likely interpretation (proposed by Wright in 'Elizabethan Sea Drama' and by George F. Reynolds in *The Staging of Elizabethan Plays at the Red Bull Theater*, 1940) is that Forrest and the Sailors enter on the stage as though on deck, and that the Boy re-enters in a regular second-level playing-area as though on the main-top.

The fifth action is in the anonymous *Lady Alimony* (*c.* 1640?, theatre unknown but evidently designed for a public theatre). The performance begins with an induction in which Presenters discuss the ensuing play. One of them, Trillo, decides to watch the play and later interrupts the third and fourth acts to applaud the 'author' Timon's genius (Q, 1659): '*Tril.* May the Poets day prove fair and fortunate: full Audience and honest Door-keepers. I shall perchance rank my self amongst your Gallery-men... *Trillo from the high Gallery....He takes his Seat again ...Trillo from the Gallery.*' Since the play proper requires a second-level playing-area, Adams suggests that Trillo's two later appearances are in a third-level playing-area of the tiring-house, but his alternative suggestion that Trillo appears in the top spectators' gallery is surely more likely in view of Trillo's evident intention to station himself among the audience.[7]

NOTES

1. Lawrence, 'Music and Song in the Elizabethan Theatre', in *The Elizabethan Playhouse* (1912), p. 91.

2. Dates of plays are generally, as appropriate, from E. K. Chambers, *The Elizabethan Stage* (1923), W. W. Greg, *The Shakespeare First Folio* (1955), and G. E. Bentley, *The Jacobean and Caroline Stage* (1956).

3. The paucity of evidence for an Elizabethan 'upper-stage' is pointed out in my 'Gallery over the Stage in the Public Playhouse of Shakespeare's Time', *Shakespeare Quarterly*, VIII (1957).

4. Music was also, of course, occasionally performed on stage. I assume that music for the Elizabethan jig was generally so performed. (This particular problem is not dealt with by Lawrence in his essay on the jig in *Pre-Restoration Stage Studies*, 1927, or by C. R. Baskervill in *The Elizabethan Jig*, 1929.) The custom of locating musicians on stage is recorded in the Van der Venne print, reproduced by Richard Southern in 'A 17th-century Indoor Stage', *Theatre Notebook*, 9 (1954).

5. The performance of music within the tiring-house is alluded to by Jonson in the Induction to *Cynthia's Revels* (1600, Blackfriars). The Third Boy asks the whereabouts of the Author, and the Second Boy replies: 'Not this way, I assure you Sir, we are not so officiously befriended by him, as to have his Presence in the Tiring-house, to prompt us aloud, stampe at the Booke-holder, sweare for our Properties, cursse the poore Tire-man, rayle the Musique out of tune, and sweat for every veniall trespasse we commit, as some Author would, if he had such fine Ingles as we' (Q, 1601).

6. Hodges writes: '...if the "shadow" were to be raised high up to the eaves-line, it would necessitate elongating, in what I think is a most improbable way, the two pillars supporting it in front. Clearly the two pillars in the Swan sketch are intended to be in the classical style and proportion. But to raise them in anything like classical proportion to the height of approximately thirty feet (which is what would be required) would be to make them unwieldily massive for their job. On the other hand, to make them of that height but slender, would be to add structural difficulties to architectural improbabilities; for two such tall, slender single-piece shafts of timber would not only be unsuitable for carrying a permanent weight but, moreover, would not be easy to get. And even if, as Adams suggests, ships' masts could be satisfactorily used for the job, the result would still have been so out of character with the Elizabethan style and method of building that I, for one, think it more likely the pillars were kept pretty well within the classical proportion, that they therefore did not rise to the eaves-line, and that people in the top galleries whose view was consequently impaired by the "shadow", were obliged to make the best of it, as we have to do today in some of the upper galleries of our own theatres' (*The Globe Restored*, pp. 31–2).

7. This article was written during tenure of a Research Fellowship of the University of Missouri.

INTERNATIONAL NOTES

A selection has been made from the reports received from our correspondents, those which present material of a particularly interesting kind being printed in their entirety, or largely so. It should be emphasized that the choice of countries to be thus represented has depended on the nature of the information presented in the reports, not upon the importance of the countries concerned or upon the character of the reports themselves.

Australia

In 1958 in Australia there was no production such as the 1957 Elizabethan Theatre Trust *Hamlet* which was seen in each of the States; but each capital city, and some others, saw one or more performances by local companies, amateur or professional. In Sydney, for example, both the Independent Theatre and the Sydney University Players performed *Titus Andronicus* (the former in a production by John Alden), while the Poetry Society of Australia sponsored several performances of *Hamlet* (produced by Norma Polonsky, with Keith Buckley as the Prince). In Adelaide, *As You Like It* was produced by the Teachers' College; in Hobart, *The Merchant of Venice* by the Repertory Theatre Society (producer, Barbara Manning); in Melbourne, *Henry IV Part I* by the combined Church of England Grammar Schools; and in Brisbane, *King Lear* (on an Elizabethan-type stage) by the Twelfth Night Theatre, and *Richard II* by the Arts Theatre.

To mark Shakespeare's birthday, the Australian Broadcasting Commission presented a radio performance of *Hamlet*, with an Elizabethan Theatre Trust cast headed by Paul Rogers as Hamlet and Zoe Caldwell as Ophelia, the producer being Neil Hutchison.

Perhaps the most interesting experiment was a tour of N.S.W. in a station waggon and caravan, made by a party of five actors under the sponsorship of the Elizabethan Theatre Trust and the N.S.W. Division of the Arts Council of Australia, with the support of the Department of Education. The five actors presented to school audiences *Henry V* and *Hamlet*, in performances of about one and a half hours, the chosen scenes being linked by narration. The basic costumes were jeans, white shirts and gymnasium shoes, supplemented if necessary. The idea, as explained by the Execu-

tive Director of the Trust, Hugh Hunt, was to emphasize the importance of the spoken word, and not the spectacle, in the plays the audience were studying. The touring company was led by Clement McCallin, the other members being Eleanor Elliot, Bruce Barry, Guy LeClaire and Roger McDougall.   H. J. OLIVER

Austria

After an interval of twenty-three years, *King Lear* was produced at the Burgtheater, Vienna; it was the fifth production in the 178-years tradition of the house. Although there are a number of *Lear*-translations of much better quality (such as the recent German rendering by Richard Flatter), the early nineteenth-century translation of Wolf Graf Baudissin was used. The producer, Adolf Rott, conceived the play as a tragedy of character, and presented the story of a superman, who was the absolute centre of attention. Owing to the over-emphasis placed upon the Lear scenes and the outstanding performance and dominating personality of Werner Krauss as Lear, the other figures appeared as weak shadows moving either on the periphery or in the background, a fact that was forcefully brought home also by the optical grouping of the persons around Lear. As scenes, only projections (big walls, towers, stormy skies, etc.) were used and all of them tended to convey not only relentless power but also a mood of forceful gloom. Many critics, however, felt that the production was in the tradition of the nineteenth century, that it emphasized the external and did not try to grasp the spiritual significance of the tragedy.

If *King Lear* was the most ambitious production of the year at the Burgtheater, the performances of *Measure for Measure* were the most memorable. The play was repeated in the 1956 production by Leopold Lindtberg with only a few changes in arrangement and cast. The most interesting feature of the production was perhaps the highly successful attempt to give local colour to the story: the characters spoke the type of modified standard German that had been adapted for the stage by Ferdinand Raimund and Johann Nestroy, and even St Stephen's Cathedral was there in a prospect. While the play thus attained immediacy and intensity, it reached depth and scope by the masterful blending of tragic and comic moods.

The most unusual production of the year was that of *The Taming of the Shrew* by the Washington Players Incorporated (producer Leo Brady) at the Landestheater in Salzburg. It was felt that this American interpretation of Shakespeare was determined by a high degree of disrespect for the dramatist. In this production *The Taming of the Shrew* became a turbulent farce rather than a comedy, with a good deal of extemporizing, without a definite style, and in the manner of an American musical. As a critic put it, the Washington Players did not play Shakespeare, but played with Shakespeare.

The great popularity in Austria of *A Midsummer Night's Dream* was again demonstrated this year by two productions of the play. While the performance of the comedy at the Renaissancetheater in Vienna (arranged for the Theater der Jugend) failed to find the appreciation of a teenager audience accustomed to the naturalism and scenic effects of the cinema, the production of the play by Ludwig Andersen in the garden of the Castle at Graz, Styria, a regular feature of the Graz Summer Festival, found unanimous approval. A performance of Acts II and III of the play by the Bühnenstudio of the Zurich Schauspielschule (producer Leopold Lindtberg) reached only a small audience and showed one unusual feature, namely the rendering of Oberon by an actress.

Twelfth Night was performed by a company of lay-actors at Friesach, Carynthia, during the Friesach Festival; *Romeo and Juliet* was produced at the Stadttheater in Klagenfurt, and the Berliner Theatergastspiele visited Lindau, Vorarlberg, with *The Merchant of Venice* in July 1958.　　　　SIEGFRIED KORNINGER

Belgium

Shakespearian productions in Belgium throughout 1957–8 were limited to the Flemish and French National Theatre and to the Flemish Theatre in Brussels. Of particular interest is the fact that both the Flemish and French sections of the National Theatre brought out productions of *The Merchant of Venice*—the Théâtre National anticipating the National Toneel by a few months. Of the two, the former proved to be artistically

the better. Guest producer Denis Carey deserves credit for his faithful treatment of the text, for his characterization and for his rhythm and movement. The only criticism which might be made is that there was too much allowance of physical brutality by the Venetians in dealing with Shylock, even in the presence of the Doge and the city elders. The settings served to permit the play to move swiftly; the costumes were colourful and functional. Herman Closson's translation aspired to be a reconstructional essay in poetic prose.

The production of the National Toneel unfortunately lacked style and above all unity of form. Over-elaborate and insignificant pieces of business were substituted for the simplicity and effectiveness of the original Shakespearian lines, and one felt that all the accent was on cleverness. Noise, low comedy and shouting affected even Shylock, the Prince of Morocco and Portia, while there was utter failure in the Jessica and Lorenzo parts. The 'groundlings', however, seemed to like this version of the play. The translation by Bert Voeten was excellent.

The touring company of the National Toneel, Het Reizend Volkstheater, presented in a series of open-air performances Rik Jacobs' well-balanced production of *Othello* in a translation by L. J. Burgersdyk, while the Royal Flemish Theatre in Brussels brought out an interesting *Taming of the Shrew*.　　DOM. DE GRUYTER

Bulgaria

In Bulgaria interest this year has centred in *Lear*. The appearance of Ognyanov's translation was followed by a production of the tragedy at the National Theatre in yet another version by the poet N. Liliev, in which two of the best known actors of the old guard played the title part alternately.　　M. MINCOFF

Canada

The Stratford Ontario Festival still continues to dominate the Shakespearian scene in Canada.

In the 1958 season it produced a group of three plays—*1 Henry IV*, *Much Ado About Nothing* and *The Winter's Tale*. Michael Langham, now the resident manager, was the director of the first two of these and Douglas Campbell, another Old Vic immigrant, directed the third.

1 Henry IV was a somewhat dull production, not helped by the director's juggling with the text nor by an imported American actor, Jason Robards Jr., whose speaking of verse reminded one more of the Bowery than of the Boar's Head. The second of Langham's productions was, however, brilliant, with Christopher Plummer as Benedict and Eileen Herlie as Beatrice.

Both speak verse well and both have a natural gift for comedy—a gift which did not preclude them later from both exploiting the tragic overtones of their parts in *The Winter's Tale*, in which they played Leontes and Paulina respectively.

So established now is the Stratford Festival that its first five years have been recorded in a book written by Herbert Whittaker, the drama critic for the Toronto *Globe and Mail*. Entitled *Stratford, the First Five Years*, the book gives a generous selection of pictures of the various productions, with Whittaker providing a running commentary at once witty and informative.

Another book dealing with the Festival, but in quite a different way, was by Diana Valk, the widow of Frederick Valk who made such a success in Canada as Othello (at the Crest Theatre of Toronto, 1956) and as Shylock at Stratford in that same season. In *Shylock for a Summer* Mrs Valk prints some of her late husband's letters to his family showing how he approached the character of Shylock and how he grew into it as the hot summer advanced.

Apart from these manifestations from Stratford, there have been other Shakespearian activities, including the tenth Shakespearian season by the Earle Grey Players in the quadrangle of Trinity College, Toronto.

The Canadian Players, a touring group formed out of the Stratford (Ontario) company, have also been travelling with a production of *As You Like It* directed by Dennis Carey, and one of *Romeo and Juliet* directed by Tony Van Bridge. The standard of the Canadian Players has deteriorated, however, in the past two or three years from the taut and spare productions which they did when they began.

Canadian Shakespearian productions reflect, as Canada itself reflects, the strong influence of England and English manners. But as the immigrant actors and directors settle down and become Canadians, a Canadian form of Shakespearian production seems to be evolving.

ARNOLD EDINBOROUGH

Czechoslovakia

There were three major events in the Shakespearian life of Czechoslovakia this year. The National Theatre in Prague produced *King Lear* in a new translation by E. A. Saudek which was warmly welcomed by the press. Unfortunately, both actors who play the title part, Zdeněk Štěpánek and Jaroslav Průcha, were taken ill and so the play has now disappeared from the repertory. This is the greater pity as *King Lear* had not been staged here for a considerable time and the interest in it was widespread: Saudek's new translation published as a

paper-back in the 'World Literature' series went immediately out of print—as did both the first and second printings of Jan Vladislav's translation of the *Sonnets* some time ago. Another important publishing venture will bring to the reader for the first time in the history of Czech literature Shakespeare's complete works: the State Publishing House is dedicating several volumes of its series 'Masterpieces of Czech Translation' to Josef Václav Sládek's translations of Shakespeare (see *Survey*, 9, pp. 103–5). Notes and introductions are provided by Otakar Vočadlo. Jiří Trnka has finished his puppet-film version of *A Midsummer Night's Dream*—a poetic transcription into music, ballet and colour, which gives Bottom and his colleagues full scope and, incidentally, reward. Bratislava's National Theatre staged *Macbeth* and Prague saw the first night of Jan Hanuš's ballet *Othello* (National Theatre) and a very good chamber-music-like production of *A Midsummer Night's Dream* in the Realistic Theatre with an excellent Puck in Emil Kadeřávek.

BŘETISLAV HODEK

Finland

The two significant Shakespeare productions of the 1958–9 season were *Julius Caesar* at the National Theatre and *King Lear* at the Turku Municipal Theatre.

Julius Caesar had been previously played at the Finnish National Theatre in 1880 and 1904. The 1959 production, by Edvin Laine, aimed at a well-balanced synthesis of the many constituent elements: political pageantry, mob and battle scenes, intrigues between the conspirators and the supporters of Caesar, and individual character studies. The play was performed on the large new revolving stage. The setting, by Leo Lehto, aimed at massiveness. In the Roman scenes the dominant features were two heavy marble pillars in the centre, with stairs descending forwards. In the battle scenes the stage was surrounded by black drapery. Carefully planned elevated planes and the deep valley in the background produced an illusion of mountainous country. In the mob scenes some 150 persons were brought on. Careful attention was paid to the rhythmic movement and composition of the groups. The part of Brutus was played by Leo Riuttu; Cassius was Matti Ranin, Antony Jussi Jurkka, and Casca Ekke Hämäläinen. This production was certainly one of the most remarkable stage achievements of recent years.

The *King Lear* of the Turku Municipal Theatre was the fourteenth Shakespeare production of Jouko Paavola during his eighteen-years-long career. This time the production presented unusual technical difficulties because the theatre is temporarily housed in the Turku

Concert House while its own new building is under construction. The play opened with a prologue, which is really a monologue by the Fool transferred from within the play. By cutting the text and combining scenes the total number of the scenes was reduced to eleven. The remarkably simple stage-design consisted of several planes, the one on the right, with Lear's throne, being the highest. The heath scenes were played in the middle. The stage effects were achieved by using black drapery in addition to the lights. The central idea of the production was to underline the contrast between good and bad. Lear's part as played by Hemmo Airamo stressed the symbolic significance of Lear's tragedy, showing his way through anguish, suffering, and sorrow towards the final catastrophe and the concluding peace and serenity.   RAFAEL KOSKIMIES

France

René Planchon's two parts of *Henry IV*, originally presented at the Théâtre de la Cité of Villeurbanne, a suburb of Lyons, were played in succession during May and June 1959, at the Théâtre Montparnasse: this was the major event of the Shakespeare season in Paris, and it is undoubtedly the most imaginative production since Jean Vilar's *Richard II* and *Macbeth*. It is influenced by Brecht's theory and practice, but in no servile way. The choice of the drama itself is deliberate: not a tragedy, but an epic showing the interplay of social forces, and history in the making. Planchon's technique aims at reconciling realism with the conventions involved in rapid changes of time and place. He was helped in achieving this by René Allio who suggested, with an unerring artistic sense, the three dimensions of reality by setting upon an abstract structure a few natural or man-made objects which seemed roughened by wind and weather or polished by use. He also made characters more solid and convincing by using the costumes to reveal condition and temperament, and choosing their material, colour, degree of wear and tear, with the same loving care. Similar praise should go to Planchon's sense of rhythm and tempo, of group and movement, to the company's high level of acting and the quality of the team-work.

At the same time Planchon deliberately gave his production a polemic and didactic twist by introducing silent episodes suggesting the sufferings of the common man or the harshness of the ruling classes. Whether this is necessary or not can be discussed, but it does not affect the text. In last year's report I quoted his statement that the poetic quality of the speeches had to be toned down. This was done by cuts, or by making the charac-

ters' behaviour contradict the nobility of their language, more often than not by making them eat gluttonously while they spoke. Since so much of the essential truth of Shakespeare's picture of the relationship, and struggles, of king, barons and prelates came to life in this production, and Planchon believes that nothing is too good for a popular theatre, it is to be hoped that he will do away with such unworthy tricks, let the poet speak for himself, and the audience be its own judge.

While Shakespeare is boldly handled by gifted young men like Planchon, Guy Rétoré and his company, La Guilde, confessed that while preparing *Macbeth* for the Théâtre de Ménilmontant they trembled with the fear of betraying the play's meaning and beauty. I have already praised here the courage of the Guilde, and told of the merits of their *King John*. The costumes in *Macbeth* were in bad taste, and the sound and lighting effects in the witch scenes did not quite come off, but while there was a good deal of amateurish acting, Raymond Garrivier as Macbeth was far more convincing than Vilar or Alain Cuny in the T.N.P. performances, and the production showed real insight into the tragedy of the guilty couple.

The Tempest was played for a few nights only by an amateur company, l'Equipe, at the Salle Valhubert, before a public composed for the most part of railwaymen with their wives, children and friends. Henry Demay, who played Prospero and is the company's Prospero, also believes that Shakespeare must be given a chance to deliver his own message. With modest means, and actors of no exceptional talents, Demay achieved a performance which was more moving and more true to Shakespeare's spirit than anything I have seen upon a French stage. Of course the actors and the thoroughly unsophisticated audience were in tune, which was a marvellous help, but the secret of success was humility, and a true insight into the poetry and symbolism of the play.

John Blatchley's production of *A Midsummer Night's Dream* was presented by the Comédie de Saint-Etienne, in a translation by Jules and Jean-Louis Supervielle, at the Foyer de la Culture of Sassenage, near Grenoble, and then under a circus tent in nineteen neighbouring small towns (20 May–10 June 1958). The Comédiens de Provence also toured their province with *King Lear* (28 June–14 August) after playing it in Toulon. I saw it in the public square of the beautiful village of Tourrettes. R. Lafforgue was responsible for the production and took the leading part: he meant well, but I am sorry to say it was the most ludicrous piece of ham-acting I ever watched.

Jean Deschamps's *Tempest* was given the same summer in the vast open-air Théâtre de la Cité at Carcassonne. A background of towers and battlements was rather a hindrance, ambitious lighting and stereophonic effects were used, with large-size puppets for the masque. Georges Wilson also gave *All's Well that Ends Well* at the 'petit théâtre', during the same festival.

Mlle Rose-Marie Moudouès must be thanked for her usual kindness in placing the resources of the Centre de Documentation Théâtrale at my disposal for the preparation of these notes.   JEAN JACQUOT

Germany

With altogether 2674 performances of his plays during the year 1958 Shakespeare is still by far the most popular of all dramatists on the German stage. Not even the 200th anniversary of Schiller's birthday in 1958 could reverse this order of succession, for in spite of many Schiller-festivals, Schiller reached only a total of 2076 performances. If, moreover, Shakespeare operas like Verdi's *Otello* and Shakespeare ballets are included, no fewer than 3021 Shakespeare performances can be recorded in 1958.

During the past few years, however, a certain decline of new productions of Shakespeare's tragedies and histories may be noted: the comedies have been more frequently produced, probably because they offer fewer difficulties for performance in small or medium-sized theatres. Thus in 1958, there were twenty-eight new productions of tragedies, compared with seventy-three of the comedies. Of these *The Taming of the Shrew* was produced by fourteen theatres, *Much Ado About Nothing* by twelve, *Twelfth Night* and *As You Like It* each by ten. Of this last play the Schauspielhaus at Düsseldorf presented a particularly impressive production by Karl Heinz Stroux with Joana Maria Gorvin in the part of Rosalind. The same play received an interesting though perhaps not wholly convincing interpretation at Gelsenkirchen, where a stage version by Otto Falckenberg was presented. According to Falckenberg's conception, Orlando very soon recognizes the disguised Rosalind and she, too, becomes aware that she has been discovered, but both conceal their knowledge. That *Hamlet*, in earlier years Shakespeare's most often played tragedy, appeared only in two new productions on the German stage was by some critics attributed to the influence and success of Sir Laurence Olivier's film, which may have made it difficult to stage the play in the same season. But this may also be due to other reasons, particularly to the often deplored fact that it is becoming increasingly difficult to find a whole *ensemble* of qualified actors for producing one of Shakespeare's great tragedies.

Experiments designed to offer Shakespeare's plays on the television screen have not yet proved quite successful, as in the television series of six Shakespearian comedies, arranged by Ludwig Berger, which was concluded by *A Midsummer Night's Dream*. Although the fairies here, by some technical device, were presented in miniature size, the impression remained faint, and only the clowns' scenes produced a lively and convincing effect. On the other hand, some endeavours to arrange Shakespeare's plays as radio dramas have been quite successful. A notable performance was *King Lear* arranged by Wilhelm Semmelroth for the 'Westdeutsche Rundfunk'. Here Fritz Kortner, in the title-role, together with such excellent actors as Bernhard Minetti, Claus Clausen, Maria Becker gave force to the play on the auditory level and strongly appealed to the imagination of the listeners.

As a symptom of Shakespeare's growing popularity the wide circulation of cheap editions of Shakespeare's plays in large numbers in the S. Fischer, Rowohlt and Goldmann series may also be recorded. The cheap bi-lingual editions of single plays recently published by Rowohlt contain introductions by Walter F. Schirmer, Ernst Theodor Sehrt and Wolfgang Clemen. At the ceremonial annual meeting of the Bavarian Academy of Sciences in the winter of 1957–8 Shakespeare formed the main theme, since the public address, given by Wolfgang Clemen, was on the subject of 'Appearance and Reality in Shakespeare'.

There was no general meeting of the German Shakespeare Society in 1958, but the meeting of 1959 at Bochum, the 95th anniversary of the Society's foundation, was celebrated through a public lecture by Allardyce Nicoll on 'What do we do with Shakespeare?' and a lecture by Ernst Theodor Sehrt on Shakespearian comedy. The warning pronounced in Nicoll's lecture against the danger of distorting Shakespeare's meaning through an exaggerated craving for novelty in some modern productions coincided in substance with some of the points raised in a strong public protest which was launched by the editors of the *Shakespeare Jahrbuch* and other Shakespeare scholars against Hans Rothe's German versions of Shakespeare's plays. In the opinion of these scholars Rothe takes far too many liberties with the original texts, inserting many passages of his own, altering and rearranging whole scenes and acts, omitting or adding characters, and rendering many crucial phrases in a way which obviously misrepresents Shakespeare's own intention. The Shakespeare scholars therefore raised the question whether versions of Shakespeare's plays which contain so many serious alterations, unnecessary additions and deviations from the original text should be allowed to go under Shakespeare's name.

WOLFGANG CLEMEN
KARL BRINKMANN

Hungary

Othello kept the stage during the theatrical season of the National Theatre in Budapest. In the year 1959 *The Merry Wives of Windsor* was revived there and was a great success. Ferenc Bessenyei, the well-known tragic actor, added to his distinction by proving a convincing and highly amusing Falstaff. T. Major's colourful direction emphasized the burlesque and grotesque elements of the play.

The new theatrical season of Békéscsaba was opened in 1958 with a rather good production of *Romeo and Juliet*, while in the nearby town of Szeged the opening play was *King Lear*, which had a fairly long run. The powerful rendering of Lear by Ferenc Kiss, the great tragic actor, was one of the memorable events of the year.

Marcell Benedek, the senior critic and literary historian of Hungary, published a 400-page volume on Shakespeare in 1958. This was the first over-all book to appear on the subject in Hungary since the end of the last war. It gives a very readable, careful and reliable interpretative analysis of every play of the author and sketches in the history of pre- and post-Shakespearian drama as well.

LADISLAS ORSZÁGH

Israel

The Habima Theatre, under the guidance of its guest-director, Tyrone Guthrie, has given the Israeli theatre-goer a novel and interesting production of *The Merchant of Venice*. Unlike the performance of some twenty years ago, this was given in modern dress. The tragic, comic, and romantic elements were interwoven and very well presented by the whole cast, which was headed by Aaron Meskin and Simon Finkel, both interchanging in the role of Shylock and each, naturally, giving his own interpretation of the role; Raphael Klatzkin played Antonio and Shoshanna Ravid was Portia. The actors not only spoke the lines of Simon Halkin's well-polished Hebrew version very fluently and eloquently, but every movement was well planned to fit in with Tanya Moiseiwitsch's set; the occasional music of Gari Bartini helped to create the atmosphere desired.

This year another play was added to our shelf of Shakespearian plays in Hebrew translation. Nathan Alterman has given us his version of *Julius Caesar*, which was published by the Hakibbutz Hameuchad Publishing House.

REUBEN AVINOAM

Italy

The Merchant of Venice has always been a favourite with the Italian public, and it is no wonder that the well-known composer Mario Castelnuovo-Tedesco has chosen this play for a musical opera which won the Campari Prize in April 1958. On the other hand two Shakespearian plays little known to the theatre-going Italian have been adequately appreciated for the first time thanks to two memorable performances, *La commedia degli equivoci* at the Teatro Antico of Ostia, and *Molto rumore per nulla* in the park of Villa Castelnuovo at Palermo. Both performances took place in the summer of 1958, in mid-July at Ostia, in mid-August at Palermo, in the enchanted setting of a summer night of the South. No doubt this circumstance has contributed to the success, particularly at Ostia, where a light scenic set in the shape of a prospect of open loggias had been fitted to the ancient theatre. At one moment the orchestra was transformed into a market-place with a crowd of vendors and picturesque heaps of wares such as one sees in a Neapolitan *presepio*: the liveliness of the setting, the adequacy of the translation (by Gerardo Guerrieri)—an adequacy easy to obtain since the text of this play does not rise above the common run of sixteenth-century Italian drama—the excellent acting (particularly by Franco Parenti as Dromio of Ephesus and Arnoldo Foà as Dromio of Syracuse), all contributed to make of this performance one of the best Shakespearian revivals on the Italian stage. Tonino Pierfederici gave an original interpretation of Antipholus of Syracuse, with a touch of the dream-like quality of the Prince in Calderón's *La vida es sueño*—one who had nothing on earth and suddenly is stunned by a succession of windfalls—although unfortunately the conventional *dénouement* robs the character of this fairy-like halo. Mario Ferrero has certainly scored here one of his best successes as producer. Alessandro Brissoni, the producer of *Molto rumore per nulla*, had already become interested in the play fifteen years ago when he was only a beginner: this is his fourth attempt at producing it, and the magic of the summer night and the park have combined to invest this performance with a magic of its own. The translation was by Cesare Vico Lodovici, the cast, of the Compagnia dei Giovani, included Rossella Falk as a stimulating, tomboyish Beatrice, Giorgio De Lullo as a slightly self-confident Benedick, Romolo Valli as a Don John with a touch of irony under his impassive mask of a villain, Glauco Mauri as an exuberant, blatant Dogberry.

Two more translations of *Hamlet* have been added to a long list of such painstaking and on the whole impossible undertakings. This time it is the turn of Gabriele Baldini (*Amleto*, Rome, Angelo Signorelli, 1958: 'Le Opere di Shakespeare in versione italiana con testo a fronte') and Alfredo Obertello (Biblioteca Moderna Mondadori). Baldini's version is clear and fluent, but even a close rendering of the original fails to convey the quality of its language, as for instance when Baldini translates lines 79–80 of Act II, scene i: 'le calze sudice e senza giarrettiere, che gli pendevano alle caviglie come fossero ceppi', which, to say the least, is lengthy and prosy. Obertello, years ago, gave a sample of his uncommon verbal skill in his rendering of *The Alchemist*; but his prose version of the famous passages in *Hamlet* falls short of expectation. This *Tragedia di Amleto* was published in June 1958; in October the same translator gave a version of *Measure for Measure*, thus adding to his previous achievements, which include versions of *Richard II, Julius Caesar, Antony and Cleopatra, Coriolanus, Romeo and Juliet*, and the *Sonnets*.　　MARIO PRAZ

Japan

A particularly important production in 1958 was that of *Macbeth* by the Bungakuza company. In a translation by the director, Tsuneari Fukada, this was presented in Tokyo Hall, with the well-known Hamlet, Hiroshi Akutagawa, in the title-role.　　JIRO OZU

The Netherlands

Apart from a not inconsiderable number of sometimes most commendable amateur performances—among which the traditional summer repertory at the village of Diever must not be overlooked—the Dutch theatregoer could view five major professional productions in the course of the 1958–9 season. Two of these consisted of variations on the theme of *The Merchant of Venice*, and thereby gave rise to extensive discussions on the possibility or impossibility for a mid-twentieth-century European audience of seeing the comedy dispassionately. The 'Haagse Comedie', in Laseur's gallant effort at suggesting the essential lightness of the play as a whole, showed a Shylock whose hall-mark was a deeply-felt conviction of the fatality of his condition coupled with a consistent understatement of all outward effects inherent in the part. The 'Youth Theatre Company', 'Arena', on the other hand—contracted to perform for secondary schools throughout the country—concentrated under Erik Vos on letting both the poetry of

the text and the dramatic qualities of the plot speak for themselves. The Arnhem company 'Theater' produced *The Tempest*, directed by Cruys Voorbergh according to the well-known translation by the late Martinus Nijhoff, in the open-air theatre at Velp. And the new company 'Ensemble' delighted Eindhoven with a sparkling performance of *The Taming of the Shrew* in the combined Quarto and Folio version, as produced by guest-director Michael Warre, whose success with Dutch actors seems to have become well established.

In 1958 the *Hamlet* translation by Bert Voeten, used by the 'Haagse Comedie' in the previous season, appeared in pocket-book form and in 1959 the translation of the *Sonnets* by Gerard Messelaar. The present writer is engaged in preparing an acting-version of *Hamlet*, with running commentary. In 1959 also, Voeten, who since the end of the war has produced popular translations of several other Shakespearian plays, was awarded the Nijhoff prize for translation into Dutch of literary masterpieces in a foreign tongue. This official recognition—perhaps testifying as much to the eagerness with which 'modern' translations of Shakespeare are being bought in the Netherlands as to the skill of the translator—thereby offers a significant contribution to the great debate on the translatability of classic poetry now raging in Dutch academic circles.

An important event was the great Elizabethan Exhibition at The Hague, which was inspected by Queen Elizabeth and Prince Philip on the occasion of their State Visit in April 1958. Here an entire hall was devoted to music and drama.　　A. G. H. BACHRACH

Norway

A Midsummer Night's Dream was performed at two theatres in 1958: at the 'Nationaltheatret', Oslo, on 27 March, and at 'Den Nationale Scene', Bergen, on 9 June. Both theatres used a new translation by the poet André Bjerke—a translation of such a superior quality that it seemed no translation at all but a new play written in the most genuine, natural and original Norwegian. This brilliant text must have been an inspiration to the actors, carrying them irresistibly away into the world of imagination and giving to the whole performance an exuberant air of gaiety and merriment.

Another feature to be noted in the Oslo performance was the very brilliant Puck created by Toralv Maurstad —a young faun in cunning opposition, ironically submissive, witty, swift, a demon performing incredible feats of athletics, leaping suddenly from a treetop, bounding down a flight of stairs like a tiger. In short an article fit for exportation.　　LORENTZ ECKHOFF

South Africa

There was a notable open-air production by Leslie French at Maynardville, Wynberg, Cape, of *The Winter's Tale*. Leontes was played by Philip Birkinshaw, Hermione by Cecilia Sonnenberg and Paulina by Rene Ahrenson. The play ran for a month and attracted audiences of over 10,000.　　　A. C. PARTRIDGE

Sweden

Two plays, almost new to the present generation of Swedish theatregoers, were staged last season.

Richard II, acted at Norrköping, has not been given since 1902. Olof Widgren both produced the play and performed the title-role. *Measure for Measure* at the 'Little' Dramaten was the event of the year. Except for a production of the play at Hälsingborg's stadsteater in 1946 it had not been on the stage since the first performance 1884. Karl Ragnar Gierow, the manager, had adroitly revised Hagberg's classical translation: never have I heard the Swedish blank verse run smoother. The production, by Alf Sjöberg, was excellent, and the scenery, by Lennart Mörk, greatly added to the success of the drama. This ran for eighty-two performances.

In the spring season Alf Sjöberg also produced *Twelfth Night* at Göteborg's stadsteater. This displayed a fine balance between the lyric and comical elements in the play.

An interesting version of *The Taming of the Shrew* was produced at Hälsingborg's stadsteater, where the induction and the epilogue—the Sly episode—were arranged as a musical pantomime.　　　NILS MOLIN

Switzerland

Six of Shakespeare's plays were performed in the course of 1958 in various parts of the country and in different circumstances. *Richard III* was acted in February at Zurich, *Much Ado* at Bern in March, *Julius Caesar* at Zurich in September and at Bern in December, *As You Like It* at St Gall in October when it ran for twenty nights, all at the respective municipal playhouses. The Sion (Valais) High School or Lycée, which has a long tradition of play-acting, and gives every year in the early summer one or two plays in the public gardens, chose *A Midsummer Night's Dream* for their representations on 6 and 7 June. Every Tuesday night in July and August *Twelfth Night* was performed with unabated success in the main courtyard of Cillon Castle by a youthful company of professionals—Le Théâtre du Pays Romand—under the skilful direction of J. P. Stemmer: exquisite costumes designed by an artist of original

talent, tuneful music specially composed for the occasion, with the ancient walls encompassing actors and spectators, combined to create an atmosphere in which the absence of scenery appeared to be the right thing.

The production of *Julius Caesar* at Bern gave Rudolf Stamm, who had just been appointed to the chair of English at Bern University, the opportunity of launching a powerful attack against Hans Rothe's versions of Shakespeare. He had opposed the choice of this translation in preference to Schlegel and Tieck's. Not only was his advice disregarded, but the Director of the Theatre, feeling that his decision was being resented by many, invited Rothe to come to Bern and give a public lecture in defence of his work on the eve of the first performance of the tragedy. When this was announced, Stamm felt it as a personal challenge. On the day of the lecture, 1 December, he justified his opposition by brief but scathing criticisms published in *Der Bund*, the chief local paper and one of the most widely read papers in the country. He followed it up by a public lecture at the University and an elaborate article in the 8 February Sunday issue of the *Neue Zürcher Zeitung*, Switzerland's leading newspaper, which is also widely read in Germany. Though Rothe's so-called translations had already met with a good deal of adverse criticism on the part of Shakespearian scholars and critics, no detailed study of any of them had yet been published. Stamm's examination of his *Julius Caesar*, conducted with severity but scrupulous fairness, shows conclusively that by calling it a translation the author deceives his public. Rothe has altered Shakespeare's general conception of his tragedy, freely cut his text, suppressed secondary characters, turned Brutus into a different character, dropped the poetry in favour of increased spectacular effects, and generally used a language which, in its poverty and frequent vulgarity, is poles apart from Shakespeare. The popularity of his adaptations Stamm explains as being due to their doing away with anything that might be thought beyond the powers of understanding of the lower classes of spectators, and to the freedom they give both stage-managers and actors to do what they like with them.

For their inaugural lectures, both Rudolf Stamm and Adrien Bonjour, who now holds the chair of English at the University of Neuchâtel, chose Shakespearian subjects. The former spoke of the theatrical aspect of the plays (Die theatralische Physiognomie), the latter of the art with which the poet uses apparently simple lines to convey his basic themes. Stamm's lecture was summarized in *Der Bund*, Bonjour's published by his University under the title of *Résonances shakespeariennes*.

With this lecture and his book on *The Structure of Julius Caesar* (published by the Liverpool University Press, with a preface by Kenneth Muir) Bonjour proves himself one of our best Shakespearian scholars.

GEORGES BONNARD

Turkey

During the last twelve months Shakespearian activities in this country were noteworthy in quality if not in quantity.

In May Miss Yildiz Kenter's production of *The Taming of the Shrew* was carried to the festivals of Hierapolis and Pergamum and gathered an enthusiastic public from the Ægean district after it closed at the National Conservatoire of Ankara. The antique theatre of Asclepion was booked mostly by the people from Izmir.

The most interesting offering of the season was the production of *King Lear* at the larger playhouse of the National Theatre of Ankara, staged by Cüneyt Gökcer who is the new Director General of the same theatre and who assumed the title-role. His Lear was exquisite. The public and the critics were unanimous in his praise. It must, however, be admitted that the production suffered from the fact that the director was also the principal actor. As a result some parts were not so effectively interpreted—and in Shakespeare no part is a minor part.

Irfan Sahinbas' new version of *King Lear*, which has just been published in a series of 'British Classics' by the Ministry of Education, is in excellent Turkish prose. The third impression of the present writer's *Merchant of Venice* and the second of *Julius Caesar* have also been issued in this series during this year. NUREDDIN SEVIN

U.S.A.

The regular U.S.A. festivals continue to serve still greater audiences and break their past attendance records. The most important, The American Shakespeare Festival Theatre and Academy, offered *Hamlet*, *A Midsummer Night's Dream*, and *The Winter's Tale* for a fourteen-week season ending on 14 September 1958, and attracted 170,000 theatregoers—20,000 more than in the previous season. The New York City Shakespeare Festival entertained about 75,000 in a free, open-air amphitheatre in Central Park. Hundreds were turned away nightly. By dinners, donations, benefits, and requests for donations from the stage, enough money was obtained to present *Othello* and *Twelfth Night* from 2 July to 30 August. The Shakespeare-wrights who offered *Julius Caesar* during the regular season presented *King Lear* as the year ended.

The Oregon Shakespeare Festival is building a new theatre for what is the oldest regular festival in the U.S. In its eighteenth season *Much Ado About Nothing*, *The Merchant of Venice* and *Troilus and Cressida* were seen by more than 29,000 in thirty-nine days—an increase of 5000 over the previous season. With *Troilus and Cressida* the Festival joined the ranks of the half dozen companies which have completed the plays of the First Folio.

The San Diego Festival in the Globe 'replica' also broke a record in its 400-seat theatre and entertained 16,000 in six weeks. *Macbeth*, *Much Ado*, and *Antony and Cleopatra* were the plays in this ninth season. Another Globe 'replica' stage, designed by Adams nine years ago, was in 1958 set up for the first time in the new theatre constructed on the Hofstra College campus. *Hamlet* was the featured play. A brief but equally successful festival was the second annual of the Phoenix Little Theatre in Arizona. There, as in Oregon and San Diego, the plays are surrounded by Elizabethan fanfare on the adjacent grounds. *Othello*, *The Taming of the Shrew* and *Twelfth Night* were shown in April for three performances each. The last of the widely known annual festivals is the newly established Colorado Shakespeare Festival. In thirteen days *Hamlet* and *The Taming of the Shrew* attracted well over 7000 spectators. The latter production was distinctive in that the play was staged before Christopher Sly as a play-within-a-play in *commedia dell'arte* style with the actors wearing masks.

LOUIS MARDER

U.S.S.R.

During the past year more than twenty new Shakespeare productions were presented in the U.S.S.R. Of particular note were those of the various 'national' theatres. In Kaunas (Lithuanian S.S.R.) N. Bukhman directed an interesting *Merry Wives of Windsor*; the Tarta (Estonian S.S.R.) public warmly applauded a new effort of the 'Vainemuine' theatre, *The Merchant of Venice*; in Erevan (Armenian S.S.R.) O. Karapetian directed a vigorous and temperamental *Taming of the Shrew*.

The oldest theatre of Uzbekistan—the Taskkent Khamz Theatre—chose for its fifth Shakespearian production *Julius Caesar* and succeeded in developing an original and appealing approach to the play—a testimony to the continuing growth of this theatre's creative power; two actors of long experience, Sh. Burchanov as Brutus and K. Khodshaev as Caesar, shared honours with a young actor, N. Kasimov as Antony.

Among the productions in central Russia that of *King Lear* in the Kuibshevsk 'Gorki Theatre' (director

V. Galitskii) deserves first mention; in this V. Kuznetsov took the part of Lear. In the Orlovsk dramatic theatre a young actress, I. Rostova, won particular success in the role of Perdita.

Of the Moscow Shakespeare productions *King Lear* at the Mossovet Theatre attracted most attention, as presented by a woman director, I. Aksimova-Vulf; the title-role was interpreted by the well-known Shakespearian actor N. Mordvinov, *Hamlet* at the Maiakovski Theatre and the same play at the Vakhtangov Theatre were given on the same evenings and vied in popularity with *The Merry Wives of Windsor* in the Mossovet Theatre.

The chief item of interest in the field of scholarly studies is the appearance of the *Shekspirovskii Sbornik*

(*The Shakespearian Miscellany*), published by the All-Russian Theatre Society. Here are twenty-four articles, including essays by A. Smirnov on 'Shakespeare's Mastery', G. Meri on *Antony and Cleopatra*, A. Anikst on 'Shakespeare as a popular writer', a series of articles by men active in the Soviet theatre (K. Zubov, S. Mikhoels, Iu. Zaradski and others) concerning experiments in the production of Shakespeare's plays, and impressions by M. Tsarev, F. Bondarenko and the present writer of Shakespeare productions in England and Canada.

In addition to this work the third volume of a general commentary on Shakespeare's work has recently been published.
IU. SHVEDOV

SHAKESPEARE PRODUCTIONS IN THE UNITED KINGDOM: 1958

A LIST COMPILED FROM ITS RECORDS BY THE SHAKESPEARE MEMORIAL LIBRARY, BIRMINGHAM

JANUARY

27   *As You Like It:* Intimate Theatre, High Wycombe. *Producer:* DAVID RUSH.

28   *Henry V:* The Play House, Nottingham. *Producer:* VAL MAY.

FEBRUARY

3   *Much Ado About Nothing:* The Playhouse, Sheffield. *Producer:* GEOFFREY OST.

11   *Macbeth:* Birmingham Repertory Theatre. *Producer:* BERNARD HEPTON.

11   *Macbeth:* The Library Theatre, Manchester. *Producer:* DAVID SCASE.

19   *King Lear:* The Old Vic Company, at The Old Vic Theatre, London. *Producer:* DOUGLAS SEALE.

24   *King Lear:* The Oxford University Dramatic Society, at the Oxford Playhouse. *Producer:* STEPHEN AARON.

MARCH

1   *As You Like It:* The Eton Players, at Eton College. *Producers:* B. REES and R. PAYNE.

7   *Love's Labour's Lost:* The Norwich Players, The Maddermarket Theatre, Norwich. *Producer:* IAN EMMERSON.

10   *King John:* The Marlowe Society, at The Arts Theatre, Cambridge. Producer and actors are anonymous.

11   *Hamlet:* Northampton Repertory Theatre. *Director:* LIONEL HAMILTON.

17   *Hamlet:* Wimbledon Repertory Theatre. *Producer:* JOHN McKELVEY.

17   *Macbeth:* The Civic Theatre, Chesterfield. *Producer:* RICHARD SCOTT.

APRIL

1   *Twelfth Night:* The Old Vic Company at the Old Vic Theatre, London. Later at the Edinburgh Festival. *Producer:* MICHAEL BENTHALL.

8   *Romeo and Juliet:* Shakespeare Memorial Theatre at Stratford-upon-Avon. Later in Moscow and Leningrad. *Producer:* GLEN BYAM SHAW.

14   *Much Ado About Nothing:* The Bankside Players at the Chiswick Empire, London, and on tour in England. Afterwards as the Ariel Theatre Company, at the Open-Air Theatre, Regent's Park, London. *Producer:* ROBERT ATKINS.

15   *The Merchant of Venice:* Liverpool Repertory Company at the Playhouse, Liverpool. *Producer:* WILLARD STOKER.

16   *Henry IV, Part I:* The Bankside Players at the Chiswick Empire, London, and on tour in England. *Producer:* ROBERT ATKINS.

19   *Henry IV, Part II:* The Bankside Players at the Chiswick Empire, London, and on tour in England. *Producer:* ROBERT ATKINS.

22   *Hamlet:* Bristol Old Vic Company, at the Theatre Royal, Bristol. *Producer:* JOHN MOODY.

APRIL

22   *Twelfth Night:* Shakespeare Memorial Theatre at Stratford-upon-Avon. Later in Moscow and Leningrad. *Producer:* PETER HALL.

MAY

3   *Henry VIII:* The Old Vic Company, at the Old Vic Theatre, London. Afterwards on tour in France, Belgium and Holland. *Producer:* MICHAEL BENTHALL.

19   *Macbeth:* Oldham Repertory Theatre Club at the Coliseum, Oldham. *Producer:* HARRY LOMAX.

JUNE

3   *Hamlet:* Shakespeare Memorial Theatre at Stratford-upon-Avon. Later in Moscow and Leningrad. *Producer:* GLEN BYAM SHAW.

5   *A Midsummer Night's Dream:* The Amateur Dramatic Company, at the A.D.C. Theatre, Cambridge. *Producer:* CHRISTOPHER RENARD.

6   *The Merchant of Venice:* Harrow School. *Producer:* RONALD WATKINS.

16   *A Midsummer Night's Dream:* The Oxford Play House Company at the Arts Theatre, Cambridge. Afterwards on tour in Europe. *Producer:* FRANK HAUSER.

23   *The Taming of the Shrew:* The Ariel Theatre Company at the Open Air Theatre, Regent's Park, London. *Producer:* LESLIE FRENCH.

JULY

4   *Twelfth Night:* Maddermarket Theatre, Norwich. *Producer:* FRANK HARWOOD.

8   *A Midsummer Night's Dream:* Bristol University Dramatic Society Players, at Milverton, Somerset, and on tour. *Producer:* JOHN HYDE.

    Pericles, Prince of Tyre: Shakespeare Memorial Theatre at Stratford-upon-Avon. *Producer:* TONY RICHARDSON.

12   *Othello:* Festival Phoenix Company in The Century Theatre at Shrewsbury Summer Festival. *Producer:* ADAM O'RIORDAN.

14   *As You Like It:* Ariel Theatre Company at the Open-Air Theatre, Regent's Park, London. *Producer:* LESLIE FRENCH.

AUGUST

26   *Much Ado About Nothing:* Shakespeare Memorial Theatre at Stratford-upon-Avon. *Producer:* DOUGLAS SEALE.

27   *Troilus and Cressida:* Youth Theatre, London, at the Moray House Theatre, Edinburgh. for the Edinburgh Festival. *Producer:* MICHAEL CROFT.

SEPTEMBER

22   *Romeo and Juliet:* Little Theatre, Middlesbrough. Arts Council Company on tour. *Producer:* JORDAN LAWRENCE.

29   *Much Ado About Nothing:* Wolverhampton Repertory Company, at the Grand Theatre, Wolverhampton. *Producer:* JAMES GILLHOULEY.

30   *As You Like It:* Bristol Old Vic Company, at the Theatre Royal, Bristol. *Producer:* JOHN MOODY.

OCTOBER

7   *Julius Caesar:* The Old Vic Company, at the Old Vic Theatre, London. *Producer:* DOUGLAS SEALE.

NOVEMBER

3   *Hamlet:* Ipswich Theatre. *Director:* JOHN HALE.

4   *A Midsummer Night's Dream:* Library Theatre, Manchester. *Producer:* DAVID SCASE.

7   *The Tempest:* Norwich Players, at the Maddermarket Theatre, Norwich. *Producer:* IAN EMMERSON.

10   *Romeo and Juliet:* Guildford Repertory Theatre. Producer not known.

15   *A Midsummer Night's Dream:* The People's Theatre, Newcastle-upon-Tyne. *Producer:* WILLIAM SCOTT.

17   *Antony and Cleopatra:* Theatre Royal, Lincoln. Producer not known.

DECEMBER

17   *Macbeth:* The Old Vic Company, at The Old Vic Theatre, London. *Producer:* DOUGLAS SEALE.

THREE ADAPTATIONS

BY

JOHN RUSSELL BROWN

The Old Vic's production of *The Tempest: or the Enchanted Island* in June 1959 was intended to honour the tercentenary of the birth of Henry Purcell who, in 1695, composed music for this adaptation of Shakespeare's *Tempest*. But the revival was also timely in that, during the same month, two variously accomplished and modern adaptations of Shakespeare's plays were being presented at the Memorial Theatre, Stratford-upon-Avon. So an act of reverence towards one artist, involving careful research and editing, has been the occasion for comparing the ways in which different ages have amplified, altered, and curtailed the work of another.

The text of *The Enchanted Island* was a collaborative effort. A theatre-manager was the first to see that Miranda's meeting with Ferdinand gave an opportunity for presenting a novel kind of sexual encounter which Shakespeare had not exploited. He enlisted the help of a poet, John Dryden, and their version was performed in November 1667. In a preface to its first edition of 1670, Dryden explained how

Sir *William Davenant*, as he was a man of a quick and piercing imagination, soon found that somewhat might be added to the Design of *Shakespear*, ... and therefore to put the last hand to it, he design'd the Counterpart to Shakespear's Plot, namely that of a Man who had never seen a Woman; that by this means those two Characters of Innocence and Love might the more illustrate and commend each other. This excellent contrivance he was pleas'd to communicate to me, and to desire my assistance in it. I confess that from the very first moment it so pleas'd me, that I never writ any thing with more delight. I must likewise do him that justice to acknowledge, that my writing received daily his amendments. ... The Comical parts of the Saylors were also his invention, and for the most part his writing.

The new scenes, so busily written, give Miranda a younger sister, Dorinda, who has likewise grown up in island seclusion, and give Prospero an infant ward, Hippolito, who is the rightful Duke of Mantua. The two girls are sprightly and inventive, and their reactions are frank, selfish and deceitful, often prudent and always rapid. Hippolito first appears on release from solitary confinement and tutored to believe that women are beautiful and mortally dangerous; when he meets Prospero's daughters he is, in quick succession, awed, incredulous, devoted, ambitious, insatiable, simple and brave. Shakespeare's comedies often invite their audiences to laugh at the fine and precarious idealism of men and women who are in love, but here the laughter is provoked by the appetites and selfish cunning of beings who are ideally 'innocent' in the affairs of love. Today most critics and theatre-directors see little that is amusing in Miranda and are content, with Ferdinand, to admire and wonder at her; but the theatre-manager and the poet of the Restoration had noticed that Shakespeare directs her to 'prattle something too wildly' and to insinuate, needlessly, 'Sweet lord, you play me false'; and it is this vein that they have developed.

The Old Vic followed the original production and an almost unbroken eighteenth-century tradition in casting a young actress for Hippolito. As played by Christine Finn, he was pert and wide-eyed in curiosity and warm in sentiment, and yet, in assurance, he was insecure and unprotected; the ambiguities of a travesty performance well presented the adult in the child, insistence in innocence. Miranda and Dorinda were played by Natasha Parry and Juliet Cooke: the elder was rightly more deliberate—'I had rather be in pain nine Months, as my father threaten'd, than lose my longing'—and the younger more gauche—'O Sister, there it is, it walks about like one of us'. These performances suggested that the three parts are nicely differentiated within a consistent idiom. Ferdinand, who woos Miranda with some of Shakespeare's words, is obviously intended as a more temperate and stable element, and possibly it was only Gordon Gardner's constrained movement and unmusical speaking which occasionally made him too graceless for such company.

Among the characters of the subplot, Caliban has a number of Shakespeare's lines, but he does not instigate an attack on Prospero as in the original. Instead he is involved in a struggle for supremacy in the island between Trincalo, the bosun, and Stephano and his new followers, Ventoso and Mustacho. This development introduces some slight political satire of elections and deputed power, and a marriage of convenience between Trincalo and Sycorax, Caliban's sister, whom the fools believe to be 'inheritrix' of the island. Of Shakespeare's other characters, Sebastian has been omitted and Antonio does not plot anew against Alonzo; Gonzalo is reduced to a few, scarcely individualized, lines. In the Prologue, Dryden protested that

> Shakespear's Magick could not copy'd be,
> Within that Circle none durst walk but he,

and, in keeping with this judgement, the revisers have not embellished Prospero's magical powers nor modified the role of Ariel, his spirit: almost always they have been content to cut and rearrange, so that Prospero as a magician makes a briefer and simpler appearance, and the masque of Ceres and Juno has disappeared. But Davenant had written and directed court masques, and Dryden was ambitious to succeed in the newly-opened theatres, and so they converted the spirits who appear to Alonzo and his companions into a few singing devils and apparitions, and gave to Ariel a new echo-song and a fellow spirit, Milcha, with whom to dance a saraband at the close of the play.

Once Davenant and Dryden had treated Shakespeare's *Tempest* so boldly, many other adapters were ready to follow them, and by the end of the eighteenth century eight different versions had been performed.[1] Several of these indulged the taste for operatic embellishments still further: the one published in 1674 (and from which John Rylands prepared the text for the present Old Vic production) was basically the first adaptation with added directions for a spectacular storm and aerial flights by Ariel and Milcha, and with new dances and songs for the spirits and a concluding masque of Neptune and Amphitrite. All this was very much in the contemporary fashion: in 1701, when Granville adapted *The Merchant of Venice* and added an elaborate masque, the Epilogue recollected:

> How was the Scene forlorn, and how despis'd,
> When *Tymon*, without Musick, moraliz'd?
> *Shakespears* sublime in vain entic'd the *Throng*,
> Without the Charm of *Purcel*'s Syren Song.

The Enchanted Island, as performed at the Old Vic in the sophisticated colours and ornate lines of Finlay James' set, demonstrated almost the full range of these new attractions.

But this lively play-with-music-and-dance is scarcely a satisfactory whole. The concluding masque gratifies a taste but does nothing to sum up, reflect or comment upon the preceding action; possibly, as a final splendid irrelevance it is useful in ensuring a thoroughly inconsequential reception for the whole entertainment. Prospero is a divided character—partly a tactlessly repressive nursemaid and tutor, partly a powerless father and guardian, partly a potent enchanter, seer and duke. The broad comedy of the subplot—despite the expressive and practised agitation of Miles Malleson as Trincalo at the Old Vic—has only the slightest connection with the main plot in the 'monstrous', yet innocent, love-making of Sycorax. And there is little motive for the characters from the two plots to assemble together at the close of the play. The Old Vic's producer, Douglas Seale, seemed to be attempting a fuller, deeper close, for his text restored Prospero's 'Our revels now are ended...' immediately after the final masque; but this Prospero could speak the words as a showman only, not as Shakespeare's Prospero.

A reminder of the original text brings an immediate recognition of the subtle complexity and unity of Shakespeare's plot, and of the peculiarity of the dramatic experience which his play provides. Its development does not encourage a full meeting between the audience and all the dramatis personae: the picture is continually changing, situations are not consistently built up, reactions are not fully expressed or exploited; the audience's attention is steady only upon Prospero, and much of his struggle takes place in silence while he walks 'a turn or two' to 'still' his beating mind. Introducing J. P. Kemble's version of the play (which retains Hippolito and Dorinda, but not Trincalo and Sycorax), Mrs Inchbald commented that 'it would never have become a favourite on the stage without the aid of Dryden's alteration. The human beings in the original drama had not business enough on the scene to make human beings anxious about them; and the preternatural characters were more wonderful than pleasing.' If Shakespeare's play is judged by normal eighteenth-century standards, this may be fair comment upon its individual characterizations; but, as a criticism of the play as a whole, it fails to recognize that there are some modes of dramatic experience in which human interest is not intended to be indiscriminate, and in which wonder is no less relevant than pleasure. The authors of *The Enchanted Island*, and those of later adaptations of *The Tempest*, have all tried to make their own terms with the material of Shakespeare's comedy; they have not had the patience and humility to accept and study the original text, and to allow it to reveal the appropriate modes of presentation and reception.

One peculiarity in the records of performances of *The Enchanted Island* suggests that Shakespeare's achievements are not easily displaced. Most of the critics of the recent revival expatiated about the quartet of frank and innocent lovers, but, in conclusion, reverted to the maimed portrayal of Prospero. And it would seem that earlier audiences, for whom the new characters may well have lost their gloss with repeated performances, found their attention reverting to the same centre. Three illustrations appear in early editions of these adaptations and each of them depicts Prospero as the dominant figure—presenting Ferdinand to Miranda, or disclosing Ferdinand and Miranda to Alonzo and his followers, or calling for Ariel.[2] He always has a staff and is dressed in a long gown; and in one picture a magic circle is traced around him.

*   *   *

Three productions were in the repertory at Stratford-upon-Avon while *The Enchanted Island* was being revived in London. That of *Othello* was tame and, possibly, under-produced in the central and final scenes, and its director, Tony Richardson, seemed interested only in catching the eye by elaborate crowd-scenes (busy with lights, massive dogs, men-at-arms and prostitutes), and by a deformed and apoplectic Duke of Venice. The other two productions were more determined and thorough adaptations.

Since Dryden's day, Shakespeare's plays have been much studied in schools and elsewhere, so that public opinion has turned against large-scale rewriting. (Translators, however, still cut, alter and add to please themselves, as Hans Rothe in Germany and Matej Bor in Yugoslavia.) This means that in England, at any rate, poets are no longer employed to alter Shakespeare and the responsibility has devolved entirely upon theatre-managers and directors. Of course, their scope is still considerable. Tyrone Guthrie, directing *All's Well that Ends Well* at Stratford in 1959, made some additions to the dialogue to fill out those scenes which had particularly attracted him: so a major-domo instructs lesser servants about 'hastening the musicians' and moving a platform 'more to the left', a courtier inquires about the 'good old king' and there are many 'Quite so's', 'Hear, hear's', petty oaths, orders and exclamations; more ambitiously, the Duke of Florence enquires 'Is this the machine?' But Guthrie's invention—in keeping with the present reluctance to accept rewriting—was more plainly shown in numerous dumb-shows, excisions, actions in contradiction to what is said, and deliberate and effective mis-speaking of Shakespeare's lines.

Yet after he had taken all this trouble, it was hard to see his leading purpose in adapting the play. During the first half, the scenes in which the Countess appears were set in and around an elegant Chekhovian mansion: in a tender, brownish light, a grove of bare and slender trees bend gracefully, from both sides of the stage, towards a summer-house, and, while its inhabitants are voguish and precise in dress, from classical urns dead leaves and tendrils hang untended. At the end of the play the same house becomes, surprisingly, a vast hall, sketchily furnished in trivial blue, white and gilt. The King's Court at Paris is a dark ballroom, glittering occasionally with lights and dancing figures but, more often, empty and comfortless, so that its inhabitants protect themselves with tall leather screens. All these scenes were presented as if the action took place just before the First World War, but in later scenes among the soldiers in Florence the stage was set as for the Second World War: there is a microphone and a megaphone of the latest design, and the men are dressed in khaki shorts, the officers in tunics, black ties and berets. The widow's household was presented in a mixture of the two periods: for, gaping and giggling at the soldiers, the girls are dressed in housecoats and headscarves, and one sucks a fruit lolly; but for travelling, Diana appears in an Edwardian coat and hat, to match Helena's, who has come, unchanged in her style of dress, from the other part of the play.

The treatment of the text was as various as that of the setting. At one extreme, Lavache, the old clown, is cut completely, and at the other, the Countess is played by Edith Evans with assured dignity, feeling and intelligence, in keeping with the sense and music of Shakespeare's lines. The King, both when dying and when restored to health, is a tetchy princeling: in Robert Hardy's performance, he has nothing of the Countess' assurance, but strives continually to exert himself; he toys with Helena and pats his courtiers; his lines are ingeniously spoken so that 'I fill a place, I know't' is a petulant rebuke, 'My son's no dearer' an affected self-advertisement, and 'the inaudible and noiseless foot of Time' a jest that amuses its speaker. Diana, who is called a 'young gentlewoman...of most chaste renown' and claims to be descended from 'the ancient Capilet', is played by Priscilla Morgan for restless comedy: on her first entrance she looks as if she passed her days reading cheap magazines and staring at men, and this appearance is half-reconciled with her lines about virginity, virtue and pity in that she speaks them with a pert and knowing avidity. Angela Baddeley, as her widowed mother, keeps the audience laughing by little tricks which emphasize her decrepit old-age and prudence to the exclusion of everything else. The bizarre effect of mingling these interpretations may be exemplified from the final scenes: here Parolles takes his proper place as Lafeu's fool without the encounter with Lavache to establish his new status; the king does not sit in judgement, but moves continually among his courtiers, so that he often steps up to a character before addressing him; only the Countess is unmoving and dignified and so, in the continual bustle, draws all eyes to herself— but there seems to be little purpose in this, for Shakespeare has written few words for her in this scene. In this disorder, some expectancy is awakened for Helena's final entry by sweet and soothing music played off-stage.

Guthrie's liveliest invention was reserved for an interpolated dumb-show in Act III, sc. iii. In Shakespeare's play this is a brief moment when the audience is shown the Duke of Florence welcoming the boy Bertram as a man and soldier of worth, and without any of the references to his father's virtues which he has always heard before. As such it is a step forward in the presentation of Bertram, but Guthrie has used it for introducing an entertaining episode in which a comic duke (a grotesque caricature of General Smuts, short-sighted and falsetto) inspects a comic army (a pair of trousers threaten to fall down, someone catches a sword between his legs, a flag slips from its staff as the general salutes, and most of the words are inaudible); this farce lasts six or seven minutes, in which time less than a dozen of Shakespeare's lines are heard, or partly heard. Similar comic invention was utilized every time the soldiers appeared after this, so that the braggart Parolles is shown up as a coward and liar among soldiers that could never fight a battle, and the audience has to suppose that Bertram achieves 'the good livery of honour' in a crazy-gang army. Of course the whole economy of Shakespeare's play has been altered, its proportions, tempo, tensions, emphases, and its comic spirit.

Shakespeare's progressive presentation of the relationship between Helena and Bertram is particularly subtle, yet Guthrie has freely changed this in accordance with his own conception. In the original, Helena hesitantly approaches each of the King's other wards before she confronts Bertram, and then, realizing the presumption of demanding him as husband, she only gives herself to him:

> I dare not say I take you; but I give
> Me and my service, ever whilst I live,
> Into your guiding power.

In Guthrie's version, Helena's choice is made while she engages in a series of lively and senti-mental dances: Bertram offers himself, unprompted, as her partner for the last dance and Helena of course is delighted, and, when the dance concludes, addresses him in modest joy, not in fearful resolution; Bertram relinquishes her hand later, only when the King insists that he must call her wife. Here Guthrie has lessened the nervous embarrassment of Helena, and directed the audience's attention away from her and her feelings; he has also introduced some entertaining *divertissements* and heightened the sense of surprise. When the King demands their marriage, overriding everyone's wishes, Guthrie has directed Bertram to walk right across the stage in a general silence and, after a pause, to say the line Shakespeare has given him, very deliberately: 'I cannot love her, nor will strive to do't.' Again this heightens the dramatic excitement through suspense, but it alters Shakespeare's portrayal of Bertram, making him appear so deliberate that it is no longer credible that, in his inexperience, his action is 'but the boldness of his hand...which his heart was not consenting to'. Next, Guthrie played confidently for pathos: numerous courtiers take silent leave of Bertram, as if sympathizing with him, and then Bertram and Helena walk together across the empty hall towards the marriage ceremony, and are followed by the far brisker steps of Longaville who has been ordered to conduct them. Shortly afterwards an entirely new scene has been added, the re-entry of Helena and Bertram as from their marriage, holding ceremonial candles and attended by a priest. In all these mute actions, Bertram treats Helena with a quiet, dazed tenderness which is in direct contrast with the brusque, reiterative words Shakespeare has given to him: 'I take her hand.... Although before the solemn priest I have sworn, I will not bed her....O my Parolles, they have married me! I'll to the Tuscan wars, and never bed her.' For immediate dramatic gains of suspense or pathos, or in order to introduce dance and movement, the director has altered the presentation of Helena and Bertram.

Whether he was following Shakespeare's text, or deliberately misconstruing it, or introducing some new incident, Guthrie was continually in command of the whole stage; and if his adaptation fails (like Davenant and Dryden's *Enchanted Island*) to sustain any comprehensive dramatic interest, it is always (again like the earlier adaptation) diverting, varied and spirited. If this was the full scope of Guthrie's intentions, he has been brilliantly successful—with the proviso that his version is seen once only. The third or fourth time it is seen, the additions and alterations cease to hold the playgoer's attention, and those parts where he has followed Shakespeare most closely tend to dominate everything else: Zoe Caldwell's tense and emotional Helena in the earliest scenes and Anthony Nicholls's unvariedly elegant Lafeu both gain in stature and interest when they are seen without the new distractions, and Edith Evans's Countess still more realizes the human understanding and poetic utterance which have always been the hall-marks of Shakespeare's original plays.

*   *   *

The other memorable adaptation performed at Stratford in the same month was Peter Hall's production of *A Midsummer Night's Dream*. Like *The Tempest*, this comedy has always been a favourite with adapters. In the summer of 1933, for instance, Max Reinhardt produced it in the open-air at South Park, Headington, cutting the text severely, adding lines for the comics, introducing several ballets and so altering the emphasis that it was 'no longer...a story of mortals in this world behind whom an enchantment has arisen...[but] a tale of sprites and goblins pursuing the natural life of their own dwelling-place, into which men and women have blindly wandered'.[3] Six and a half years later, an adaptation[4] was produced in New York for which the scene was changed to New Orleans in the 1880's; the cast of two hundred included Louis Armstrong as Bottom, Maxine Sullivan as Titania and the Dandridge Sisters as three fairies; the scenery was inspired by Walt Disney and there were three bands, including the Benny Goodman Sextet.

At first sight, Peter Hall's Stratford adaptation seemed modest in comparison. His setting, by Lila de Nobili, looked very much like an illustration of 'the Elizabethan Theatre' from one of the older text-books. It was constructed of unpainted wood, and, between two inward-turning stairways, it had an 'inner' and an 'upper' stage. For the woodland scenes, the painted backcloth depicting an Elizabethan interior was lit from behind so that it became transparent, and a grove of saplings was visible above the steps. The costumes were conservatively Eliza-bethan, some of them being copied from Hilliard miniatures. Moreover, Hall made no additions to Shakespeare's text and introduced no extensive dumb-shows.

His work as an adapter centred in his treatment of the quartet of young lovers. Shakespeare has given them dramatic poetry which is verbally conceited and decorated, with occasional colloquialisms, yet musically pure and clear. All four lovers are presented as ardent and inexperi-enced: they have 'most rare visions' of love and, in consequence, are successively (though in varying order and to varying degrees) courteous, rude, awed, foolish, presumptuous, devoted, incredulous. To the normal hazards of very young love are added those of fairy influence, but before the close of the play their amazement and struggles begin to grow towards 'something of great constancy':

> *Demetrius.* These things seem small and undistinguishable,
>   Like far-off mountains turned into clouds.
> *Hermia.* Methinks I see these things with parted eye,
>   When every thing seems double.
> *Helena.*   So methinks;
>   And I have found Demetrius like a jewel,
>   Mine own, and not mine own.
> *Demetrius.*   Are you sure
>   That we are awake? It seems to me
>   That yet we sleep, we dream. Do you not think
>   The duke was here, and bid us follow him?
> *Hermia.* Yea, and my father.
> *Helena.*   And Hippolyta.
> *Lysander.* And he did bid us follow to the temple.
> *Demetrius.* Why, then, we are awake: let's follow him;
>   And by the way let us recount our dreams.

Bottom, the weaver of Athens, also has strange dreams in the wood, yet he will not 'discourse wonders'; he has not a lover's imagination and faith, and so dares not risk ridicule.

This presentation of young love held little interest for Peter Hall: he was content to direct the quartet to be young, foolish and clumsy. In his adaptation their verse is absurdly guyed, with exaggerated, unmusical stresses and with coarse tone and high pitch. Their actions are consistently clownish: for instance, as soon as Helena enters to Demetrius in the first woodland scene, she reaches towards him, misses, and collapses on the floor; before long, she is screaming and both are sitting on the floor, legs straight before them, on the other side of the stage. All four chase up and down the stairs, lunge at each other, trip up, and spend much of the time on their backsides. When Lysander is charmed to love Helena and exclaims, with a show of reason, 'who will not change a raven for a dove?', he lays hold of Helena and pulls her round to face him, and soon Helena is lying on the stage with Lysander crouching close over her; his desire to read 'love's stories' in her eyes (which are for him 'love's richest book') and his attempts to 'honour Helen and to be her knight' lead only to horse-play, repetitive and crude. Presenting the lovers in this manner, it is no wonder that Hall cut entirely their quartet of amazement and determination as they are about to return from the wood; the strange thing is that he presumably thought the audience would prefer the continual, unrelieved and not very resourceful burlesque to a fuller rendering of the play Shakespeare wrote.

But clearly he had great faith in this kind of fooling. Anthony Nicholls, as Theseus, was encouraged to speak most of his lines musically and without intrusive comic action, yet he was given an Hippolyta who leers knowingly as she speaks to her intended husband of 'the night of our solemnities'. Theseus himself was occasionally given odd, schoolmasterly mannerisms; so, having said that love and 'tongue-tied simplicity in least speak most', he points to himself and then adds 'in *my* capacity', with a sage nod of the head. Possibly a Theseus who has to countenance such young rowdies must be more than a little unsubtle in feeling.

Certainly Peter Hall did not pursue contrasts rigorously. Among the fairies, Titania was the only one to give a counterbalance to the rough and tumble. As played by Mary Ure, she is a frail, vain, thin-faced creature, speaking carefully (almost as if she were trying to be understood in some foreign language), and striving to keep her dignity and show off her glittering costume. Here, of course, the director neglected much of Shakespeare's Titania and he seemed to acknowledge this by cutting her long speech about the 'progeny of evils' which come from her 'dissensions' with Oberon:

> The ox hath therefore stretch'd his yoke in vain,...
> The seasons alter: hoary-headed frosts
> Fall in the fresh lap of the crimson rose,...

The other fairies, in this adaptation, are like a pack of squabbling children. Oberon, the 'King of Shadows', is scarcely distinguishable in character and manner from Puck: so, when he demands 'Why should Titania cross her Oberon?', he speaks in a mocking, wheedling voice, like one naughty child to another. The lesser fairies are, like the young lovers, played consistently for a burlesque humour: the 'First Fairy' announces that she has to 'hang a pearl in *every* cowslip's ear' as if she were some slut about to continue an endless and boring chore; and even when the fairies intend to dance 'solemnly' at Theseus' wedding, they arrive somersaulting and falling on the floor. Ian Holm's Puck, looking and behaving curiously like a 'dirt-imp' in a detergent advertisement, hardly seems to deserve the epithets 'knavish' or 'mischievous', for the whole fairy world runs that same way.

Hall's invention did not, however, reach to the mechanicals: these amateur actors of Athens are played, as they usually are, slow in wit and clumsy in action, and straightforward in 'simpleness and duty'. Bottom, played by Charles Laughton, is a little unusual: he is a soft-hearted old codger, self-satisfied rather than ambitious or awed at his adventures in the wood; his meeting with Titania is punctuated by what is presumably meant to be the mating-call of an ass. Nevertheless, the encounter between the weaver and the Queen of Fairies did provide one of the rare moments of dramatic contrast in this adaptation, and its humour therefore had a wider range than that of the rest of the play. But Bottom, like every other character, suffers from

PLATE V

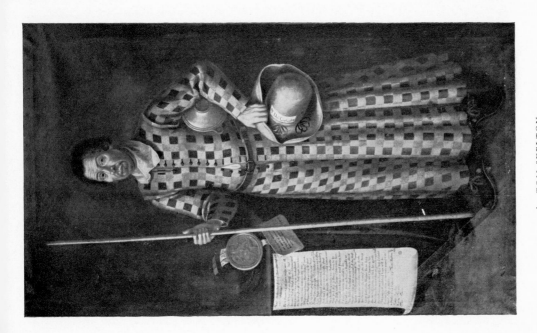

A. TOM SKELTON
Muncaster Collection

B. TOM SKELTON
The Shakespeare Institute

PLATE VI

A. The Widow, Diana and Helena   B. The Countess and Rinaldo

C. Parolles unmasked

'ALL'S WELL THAT ENDS WELL', SHAKESPEARE MEMORIAL THEATRE, 1959

Directed by Tyrone Guthrie, designed by Tanya Moiseiwitsch

PLATE VII

A. The King and Helena   B. Bertram and Helena

'ALL'S WELL THAT ENDS WELL'

C. Titania and her attendants   D. Oberon and Puck

'A MIDSUMMER NIGHT'S DREAM', SHAKESPEARE MEMORIAL THEATRE, 1959

Directed by Peter Hall, designed by Lila de Nobili

PLATE VIII

A. FRONTISPIECE FROM 'THE TEMPEST, BY MR DRYDEN' (1735)

B. MASQUE OF NEPTUNE AND AMPHITRITE

The Tempest: or The Enchanted Island, The Old Vic, 1959. Directed by Douglas Seale, costumes and scenery by Finlay James, choreography by Peter Wright

Hall's treatment of the text; his singing to show the others that he is 'not afraid' loses its point because the wood is never mysterious enough to exact a 'distracted fear'; and the clumsy acting of Bottom and his fellows in the 'tedious, brief scene' of *Pyramus and Thisbe* is so like the burlesque 'performances' of the young lovers that its type of humour has already been devalued by constant and needless repetition.

Unlike Guthrie's and Davenant and Dryden's adaptations, *A Midsummer Night's Dream* at Stratford did not provide varied entertainment. As well as ignoring the humanity and poetry of Shakespeare's comedy, Peter Hall also missed its width of appeal (it is a play in which these three qualities are more than usually interdependent); it would seem that he pursued liveliness—or perhaps he would call it 'raciness' or 'burlesque'—too thoroughly; probably he was so bored with routine productions of this popular work that, in devising his adaptation, he became too narrowly concerned with being brightly amusing.

This adaptation, like Guthrie's, had all the attention to detail and all the expense which are customarily bestowed on productions at the Memorial Theatre, Stratford-upon-Avon. Both gave the impression that everything had been effected as their creators had wished, so that both directors have every reason to be pleased with the results, and their public will have been able to judge the value of such adaptations in the most favourable circumstances. As this article goes to press, two more plays are yet to enter the 1959 repertory at Stratford, *Coriolanus* and *King Lear*, and it is to be hoped that they will show that the choice is not merely between new adaptations and routine, dull, 'straight' productions—deeply considered, imaginative, inventive and freshly observed productions of Shakespeare's plays are still a possibility.

NOTES

1. Cf. C. B. Hogan, *Shakespeare in the Theatre*, II (1957), 636–8.
2. Cf. *The Tempest, by Mr Dryden* (1735), *The Tempest...As it is Acted at...the Duke of York's Theatre* (1733), and *The Tempest:...adapted ...By J. P. Kemble* [?1811]; the illustration from the 1735 edition is reproduced on Pl. VIII A.
3. *The Times*, 16 June 1933; for a fuller description, see *The Birmingham Mail* of the same date. Reinhardt also produced the play in Germany, Italy and the United States.
4. *Swingin' the Dream* was adapted by Gilbert Seldes and Erik Charell, and produced at the Center Theatre on 29 November 1939.

THE YEAR'S CONTRIBUTIONS TO
SHAKESPEARIAN STUDY

1. CRITICAL STUDIES

reviewed by BERNARD HARRIS

Twelve years ago, in the first review of this series, Una Ellis-Fermor noted 'certain tendencies which may prove characteristic of the post-war revaluation'. These included the revival of allegedly 'old-fashioned' modes of interpretation, and the reappraisal of modern approaches. Her remarks hold good, for a common feature of recent work is the continual revision of methods of inquiry, bringing both fresh rewards and relapses.

The persistence of the latter has sent John Crow[1] on a rare rantipole against the vulgar errors of excess humility, of arrogance, pedantry, over-simplification, puritanism, optimism and creative subjectivity. Dryden was charged 'that I make debauch'd Persons...my protagonists', and Crow admits a reader's difficulty in distinguishing between 'what I say as my *credo* and what I invent as the ludicrous statements of honest men who hold views which differ from mine'. He believes that Shakespearian critics must be proven theatregoers, and their published work supervised by robustly humorous censorship, finding that 'The criticism of Shakespeare was formerly an attempt to give assistance to the young. Now we are forced to use it to impress our elders. What started out in life as a crutch has come to maturity as a banner with a strange device.' The metaphor finally takes to its bed with 'what seems to me a disease. I can suggest no cure.'

We are recalled to our business by Miss Helen Gardner,[2] in six lectures primarily concerned with the historical approach to literature. 'How to make a proper use of historical and biographical information and of the facts of literary history', she observes, 'is a fundamental problem for the critic', whose ultimate task is elucidation. Typical of her accomplishment is the discussion of Cleanth Brooks' essay on the 'naked babe' in *Macbeth*. Using Shakespeare to commentate on Shakespeare 'rather than personal associations aroused by the image, she refutes Brooks' desired paradox of pity as both humanly helpless and angelically avenging. The conclusion here, as in the longer commentary on *Hamlet*, is reached through questions which arise out of the work itself, whose final test is of context. As a result her criticism penetrates equally the world which art makes and the world in which it is made. 'In trying to set *Hamlet* back into its own age,' she remarks, 'I seem to have found in it an image of my own time', and it is the strength of her approach that the historical view includes the contemporary. Elsewhere she makes clear that her quarrel with the 'new critics' is over method, not intention, since 'The discovery of a work's centre, the source of its life in all its parts, and response to its total movement—a word I prefer to "structure", for time is inseparable from our apprehension of works of literature—is...the purpose of critical activity'.

G. Wilson Knight has always found the distinction between time and space 'insubstantial',

---

[1] 'Deadly Sins of Criticism', *Shakespeare Quarterly*, IX (summer 1958), 301–6.
[2] *The Business of Criticism* (Oxford at the Clarendon Press, 1959).

and time inseparable from structure. The last chapter in his final collection[1] of Shakespearian criticism examines 'Some Notable Fallacies', and restates critical principles which have preoccupied him for thirty years. The consistency with which Knight has developed his opinion, stated in his first 'manifesto' of 1928 and reprinted here, that Shakespeare's plays 'demand and provide the now necessary synthesis of religious and aesthetic experience' may be seen in the most important chapter of the book, a study of *All's Well that Ends Well*. The climate of thought which Knight finds prevailing is that of the evaluation of honour, in terms of its complex and different connotations for man and woman: we are 'faced by a peculiar antagonism and interweaving of male and female values'. The central action is seen in the miracle of the King's cure, and its correspondence in the preservation of Bertram's honour. We are required to accept Helena as 'almost beyond the human, with the kind of idealization accorded Thaisa, Marina and Hermione', but it is the merit of Knight's analysis that he does not allow his recognition of Helena's symbolical function, or his esoteric view of her as a medium, wholly to replace attention to her as a person. In performing the cure 'Helena claims no power of her own. Even on the plane of nature, it is clear that no health is given; it is there already; only the obstruction is removed, so that nature, the full cosmic powers, may function unimpeded.' If we do not respond to Helena's achievement we shall 'merely rank ourselves beside Bertram as one who fails to recognize the transcendant when he meets it', but as Knight adds, 'True, we need not wish to be married to it, and a difficulty remains'.

Other chapters in the book, such as those on the names of Shakespeare's characters and the theme of royalism, are more interpretative than critical, if one may apply Knight's distinctions within his own work. But critical objections to the interpretative method may be momentarily answered by the unexpected witticism of his retort that 'The only perfect way of keeping everything in its context is to remain silent'.

Another way, no doubt imperfect, is the limitation of critical discussion to the context afforded by an individual play, and this is adopted by Adrien Bonjour,[2] Salvatore Rosati[3] and G. R. Elliott.[4]

Bonjour is concerned with *Julius Caesar* as a 'drama with opposing elements so mixed in it that its antithetical theme and its antithetical motives form its very texture', and specifically with the role of motives and imagery within that structure. Nothing usually so unbalances a critic as the weighing of thesis and antithesis, but Bonjour's modestly argued case for the ambivalence of *Julius Caesar* is given particular support by a number of original points he makes about the role of superstition, suicide and sleep in the tragedy.

Rosati's act by act, scene by scene, analysis of *Lear* gives preliminary attention to such matters as the doctrine of nature, the folk-play, and the special sources, and there is both apt citation of literary references from Shakespeare's time and also recourse to modern research. The reading of the play is seldom far from the circumscribed implication of the book's title, with its general movement towards the inevitable conclusion upon the final scene that 'In tale atmosfera spirituale, i protagonisti muiono felici, e il mondo di questa tragedia, così buio e tormentoso, riesce anche, alla fine, così consolante'.

[1] *The Sovereign Flower* (Methuen, 1958).   [2] *The Structure of 'Julius Caesar'* (Liverpool University Press, 1958).
[3] *Il Giro della Ruota* (F. Le Monnier, Firenze, 1958).
[4] *Dramatic Providence in 'Macbeth'* (Princeton University Press, 1958).

The reading of *Macbeth* undertaken by G. R. Elliott deduces from particular and related images a total pattern of meaning. Elliott believes that 'The doctrine of Grace had a very special fascination for Shakespeare', though less as 'a Christian dogma than a human experience': it is not clear why it could not be both. Elliott studies the operation of grace, concentrating not upon religious disputation but upon 'the *dramatic* phenomenon neglected by criticism: the constant striving of heaven, in various ways, to induce Macbeth to repent'. Wilson Knight has noted that those who 'insist on treating every minute particular contextually and as part of a sequence, trying to show how everything in turn points on or back to this or that, end by composing unreadable essays'. It is a danger Elliott runs, for instance, when he quotes

> I am in blood
> Stept in so farre, that should I wade no more,
> Returning were as tedious as go o'er—

and cannot resist the footnoted comment that 'returning' is 'a well known Christian synonym for repentance, derived from Isaiah xxx. 15, "In returning and rest shall ye be saved".'

It is the kind of extra-dramatic reflection from which Paul N. Siegel[1] derives his assumption that Shakespeare wrote 'for an audience accustomed to think analogically and to regard the history of humanity as a repeated illustration of the truths of the Gospel story'. He finds the basis of Shakespearian tragedy 'explicitly Christian', where divine providence operates, biblical events have dramatic analogies, heaven and hell are implicit, and the guilty are punished with propriety. Edward Hubler[2] takes exception to this reasoning in the work of Bethell and Siegel, and particularly to their verdict on *Othello*. Siegel's reply[3] is to change weapons and fight over the same ground.

One cannot, unfortunately, see an end to dogmatic schematization. Miss Rebecca West[4] claims that 'Shakespeare's work gives impressive testimony against a heresy which had been revived by the Renaissance...Pelagianism'; thus, the pessimism of *Hamlet* is 'extreme', and shows us how 'To our species all gates to innocence are barred'. For historical and moral reasons the play has been consistently misread for centuries. 'Goethe was able to fly in the face of the text because he was the child of his time': Miss West, Salvador de Madariaga, and perhaps T. S. Eliot, are not. We learn that Calvin's voice echoes all through *Hamlet* ('never more strongly than in the "What a piece of work is man" speech'), but at least 'Calvin promised that some of this clay would be translated to predestined glory, while Shakespeare is silent and leaves his damned world damned for ever on his page'.

The Christian critic, disquieted by the spectacle of his fellows acting as God's spies without any apprehension of the mystery of things, will remember the late Charles Williams,[5] who saw that 'The trouble about Shakespeare is that he is both Christian and non-Christian', and urged 'Let us—O let us leave that great ambiguous figure his own ambiguity!' Williams counsels us to remain content with 'half-knowledge', the 'irritable reaching' after identity of doctrine is as dangerous on one side as the other. The plays are the cloudy frontier where much meets, and their definitions are always and only in themselves.'

[1] *Shakespearean Tragedy and the Elizabethan Compromise* (New York University Press, 1957).
[2] 'The Damnation of Othello', *Shakespeare Quarterly*, IX (summer 1958), 295–300.
[3] *Ibid.* Correspondence, pp. 433–5.   [4] *The Court and the Castle* (Macmillan, 1958).
[5] *The Image of the City and Other Essays*, Selected by Anne Ridler (Oxford University Press, 1958).

There is similar wisdom in Philip Edwards's[1] judicious observations upon the criticism of the last plays, whose cloudy frontiers have long been disputed and defined by critics 'accustomed to think analogically' and anagogically. There will be general concurrence with Edwards's opinion that 'It is a disservice to Shakespeare to pretend that one is adding to his profundity by discovering that his plots are symbolic vehicles for ideas and perceptions which are, for the most part, banal, trite and colourless'. Edwards asks that criticism of the last plays should pay attention to 'the formal requirements of romance and the emotional response of the audience' as the best safeguard against 'falsifying those moments in these fantastic plays when Shakespeare's verse rarefies the air and we know perfectly well that something important is being said'. Thus, 'from modest beginnings, and taking each of the plays on its own, we might learn a critical language capable of interpreting the Romances'.

Two essays in the same volume, in their different ways, contribute to this desired end. J. P. Brockbank,[2] reading *Cymbeline* by the light of its source material, provides many illuminations: of how, in the use made of disguise and garments 'Shakespeare could keep one eye here on the chronicle and the other on the fashionable theatre', of how the themes of the chronicle 'are portentous and had Shakespeare engaged with them too profoundly he would have tested the resources of the language and the responsiveness of the audience too severely': and of how, haunted as we are by 'intimations of profound significance' in *Cymbeline*, the 'apocalyptic destiny of Britain cannot be reconciled with the form of pastoral-romance on any but the terms which Shakespeare offers'. Clifford Leech[3] has made an original approach to the structural problems of the last plays, finding in *Pericles* and *Henry VIII* 'an approximation to the purely cyclic representation of time, and in the others an attempt to reconcile the notions of cycle and crisis'. While taking each play on its own, the discussion affords a new basis for all of them, concluding that 'Only *The Winter's Tale*—his major achievement, surely, at this time of his life—successfully combines the sense of flux, of cycle, in its presentation of Florizel and Perdita, with the sense that some actions are uniquely determining, are matters of crisis, as was Leontes' rejection of the oracular word'.

These problems are raised again in an erratic, but frequently profound, study by John Vyvyan,[4] which traces the pattern of tragedy in *Hamlet* and *Othello* and of regeneration in *Measure for Measure* and *The Winter's Tale*. Vyvyan believes that Shakespeare was consistent in his ethical ideas and increasingly fascinated by them, so that in the later plays he sacrificed stage effects to pursue ethical rather than dramatic problems. The principles of construction which Vyvyan finds followed in the tragedies are those of a noble, fatally-flawed soul, its characteristic temptation and yielding to it despite conflict, a second temptation which results in the tragic act, the realization of horror, and death. Such a generalized scheme has the virtue of accommodating the special structures of individual plays. The resolution of tragedy is more complex, and Vyvyan observes that 'remarkable as the achieved resolutions are, the ascending souls have still not the tremendous power and conviction of those that fell'.

Among many discussions one might particularize that of *The Winter's Tale*, and the relations

---

[1] 'Shakespeare's Romances: 1900–1957', *Shakespeare Survey*, 11 (1958), 1–18.

[2] 'History and Histrionics in *Cymbeline*', *ibid*. pp. 42–9.

[3] 'The Structure of the Last Plays', *Shakespeare Survey*, 11 (1958), 19–30.

[4] *The Shakespearean Ethic* (Chatto and Windus, 1959).

ship of Act IV to the whole. Leech notes how the 'new departure characteristic of fourth Acts' is 'here much more firmly underlined', but finds the chorus-speech of Time a 'casual presentation of time-healing': and though the ultimate denouement is prepared, Hermione's survival is kept secret from Leontes and from the audience, a situation 'unique in Shakespeare's works'. Vyvyan finds the chorus-speech indicative of more than a time-lapse, and the 'self-born hour', he thinks, 'could well be a period of inward or imaginative creation', which is 'an allegory of the healing of the tragic wound' and a reconstruction of Leontes' inner world. In this manner, Hermione, though unmentioned, is not forgotten.

As Leontes is kneeling, day after day in the chapel, in contrition and tears, a new birth is taking place within him which is shown to us as an allegory in an idyllic world. In the guise of Florizel, he woos his lost wife again, in the person of Perdita, who is Hermione's second self. Again he, that is Florizel, is tempted to break faith; and again the agent of his temptation is Polixenes. But he has learnt by his experience of remorse and anguish; and this time he makes the perfect answer: 'I am nothing altered; what I was, I am.'

Vyvyan emphasizes that when Leontes' 're-creation—a word he uses of himself—is inwardly perfected, it may be outwardly expressed. The statue comes to life. And Florizel and Perdita slip back into their parents, like fresh perfections of their former selves, fated to excel them.' Psychoanalysis is not new in Shakespearian study, but the allegory which Vyvyan constructs is that of the self and the soul, and as such it is based in human character and personality.

Since the most important criticism of the year has been concerned with the tragedies and the late plays, and with critical principles, we may note here some conclusions of D. J. Enright[1] that future studies 'will be characterised by the effort to remove the barriers which imagery-hunting, excessively ingenious "ambiguity" studies and the taste for abstract "symbolism" have in their turn set up between the author and his audience. Perhaps a more overt concern with character and realistic motivation—but chastened by the work of the great critics of the past forty years—will be part of the means to this.'

It is a prophecy already fulfilled in an absorbing book by Bernard Spivack;[2] described by its author as 'unabashedly archaeological', its findings occupy the mind rather than the museum. Spivack explores the prehistory of Iago, not in the Bradleian sense of his human life, but in terms of 'a partially concealed order of motivation we no longer recognise', deriving from the history of his predecessors in earlier drama. Iago is both villain and Vice. It is only the literal Iago

circumstantially related to the other characters of the play, individualized as a person in time and space, and impelled by the conventional motives of human nature—that the Elizabethan playgoers of 1604 were prepared to accept in tragedy. That is why he was draped on top of a primordial figure of the stage who still titillated them powerfully.

Spivack traces this primordial figure through the formidable territory of medieval drama, providing a most substantial study of precise ways in which the generalizations of such concepts

[1] 'The Next Step in Shakespeare Interpretation', *Hiroshima Studies in English Language and Literature*, vol. 5, no. 1 (1958), 1–7.

[2] *Shakespeare and the Allegory of Evil* (New York: Columbia University Press; London: Oxford University Press, 1958).

as Honour, Lust, Covetousness or Conscience evolve towards the concreteness of character achieved in the secular theatre. In this history of the emergence of the individual conscience, of metaphors becoming men, Spivack never loses sight of his ultimate aim, the delineation in depth of Iago. The question of why he hates the Moor is answered 'where the whole Eliza-bethan drama of evil found its first principle: in the moral dualism of the Psychomachia'. Where the generalized figure of mankind had been a moral vacuum, the object of struggle between vices and virtues, men and women 'carry their moral qualities inside them', and to the extent that they are good they 'attract the enmity as well as the aggression of the allegorical foe'. Shakespeare found in his source a story of villainy highly susceptible to such a dramatiza-tion and 'deliberately undertook to give new brilliance to the old stage image'. Spivack succeeds in doing a critical task of the same nature.

Othello, once a neglected tragedy, continues to be the one most discussed at present. John Arthos[1] corrects some over-simplifications in our view of the hero, whose 'knowledge of the self is also a growing thing, not at all an abstraction'.

Objections to *Macbeth* have been brought by T. B. Tomlinson,[2] who finds confirmation within uncertainties of the verse for his impression that 'Shakespeare's attempt to raise subtle intro-spection to the status of tragedy must fail'. By neglecting Aristotle's precepts, and necessarily in ignorance of Racine's example, Shakespeare produced 'a tragedy manqué and a clear example of the danger of an introspective approach to play writing'. C. W. Davies[3] retorts that if a certain conception of tragedy 'is not wide enough to include [*Macbeth* and *Hamlet*] it is the conception that is at fault'. Sailendra Kumar Sen[4] objects that Shakespeare does not quite make Coriolanus 'a Shakespearian tragic hero; he has in some measure remained Plutarch's Roman patrician', and he believes Coriolanus to be 'Shakespeare's experiment in the broad and simple style of characterization' resembling more the heroes of Greek tragedy. Several impressive records of the production of *Coriolanus* by the Piccolo Teatro della Città di Milano have been issued in the 'Collana Letteraria Documento', together with a stimulating essay by the producer, Giorgio Strehler.

B. T. Spencer[5] believes that at the end of *Antony and Cleopatra* Shakespeare 'held to the paradoxical and ironic as a tonic chord' and hence we have the paradox 'of nobility in failure and pettiness in success, of magnanimity in passion and calculation in reason'. What may with justice be claimed here becomes an over-ingenious paradox discerned by T. A. Stroud[6] in the 'curiously ironic way' that Chekhov may have intended *The Seagull*, so that 'a play which inverts a tragedy, stands it neatly on its head, must be a comedy. And not just any tragedy, but *Hamlet*!' Barbara Hardy[7] uses Coleridge's critical insights in a convincing manner to suggest that his brevity and 'fragmentariness often obscure a sensibility and an analytical method which would not have much to learn from later criticism'. Coleridge availed himself of 'linguistic

[1] 'The Fall of Othello', *Shakespeare Quarterly*, IX (spring 1958) 93–104.
[2] 'Action and Soliloquy in *Macbeth*', *Essays in Criticism* (April 1958), pp. 147–55.
[3] *Essays in Criticism*, Correspondence (October 1958), pp. 451–3.
[4] 'What Happens in *Coriolanus*', *Shakespeare Quarterly*, IX (summer 1958), 331–45.
[5] '*Antony* and the Paradoxical Metaphor', *Shakespeare Quarterly* IX, (summer 1958), 373–8.
[6] '*Hamlet* and *The Seagull*', ibid. pp. 367–72.
[7] '"I have a smack of Hamlet": Coleridge and Shakespeare's Characters', *Essays in Criticism* (July 1958), pp. 238–55.

evidence in his psychological analysis', and saw that 'language is the medium which presents character and not merely an appropriate donation to each dramatic figure'.

A perceptive attention to linguistic evidence is provided in Francis Berry's[1] approach to the problems of person, time and mood in poetry. Only part of his book concerns Shakespeare, and only parts of Shakespeare, but it is a highly original and fruitful study. It is demonstrated that the 'verbal dynamics' of Sonnet 129 ('Th'expence of Spirit') 'articulate a recurrent experience', that the form of the verb which controls the whole plot of *Macbeth* is the Future Indicative, but that the dominant verb form is Subjunctive; that in no work more than *Henry IV* 'save perhaps in *Hamlet*—is Shakespeare so aware of process, or so aware of a corrupt present being—beyond choice—the issue of a corrupt, and still corrupting, past'. Comments such as that 'The axis of Play-Tenses, on which *Henry IV* revolves, is Past-Present-Past. Gone now is the Romance innocence of the Continuous Present; gone too is Chronicle Time conceived of in terms of merely outward change' are typical of the new kinds of judgements to be found in this examination of the poetic meaning of grammar.

Among studies of style must be mentioned J. H. P. Pafford's[2] account of 'Words used only once in Shakespeare', with its useful table of incidences, and the analysis by Clifford Leech[3] of the occurrence of Shakespeare's prologues and epilogues, and the implications of their absence from his major tragedies.

Very little attention has been paid to the histories recently, though it is interesting to see the results of thinking about them applied to the further understanding of the tragedies in particular. J. A. Barish and Marshall Waingrow[4] provide a useful comment on the concept of 'Service' in *King Lear*, where Lear 'proves himself a bad king even before he proves himself a bad father and master. And this first failure may be regarded as the failure of a servant—the chief servant of the state.' A general study of Shakespeare's history plays has been made by Zdeněk Stříbrný,[5] who does not find too neat a pattern in the history plays, and is responsive to their conflicting tendencies, even though he finds them eventually 'transcended in a great synthesis of national unity'. But it is the struggle which forms the material of the plays, and Stříbrný places proper emphasis upon Shakespeare's achievement as a 'victory of poetical truth and of historical truth as well'.

The nature of Shakespeare's development as an artist in these early plays is rarely analysed in detail, though it is fashionable to refer to their 'rhetorical' mode without precisely defining it. R. F. Hill[6] notes our assumptions that 'Elaboration of utterance seems alien to the profound emotions of tragic experience' but holds that a proper relationship of verbal artistry and human passion is possible 'on the level above life of rhetorical tragedy at which self-conscious word artistry becomes a means of tragic expression'. Hill has some important points to make about the 'natural psychology' which underlies the relationship between intense feelings and artificial language, finding that

Deep emotion, particularly grief, gives rise to a desire to ease the troubled mind, but at the same time inhibits the faculty of speech. At a naturalistic level the dramatist may solve the problem by counter-

[1] *Poets' Grammar* (Routledge and Kegan Paul, 1958).   [2] *Notes and Queries* (June 1958), pp. 237–8.

[3] *Studies in Honor of T. W. Baldwin*, edited by D. C. Allen (University of Illinois Press, Urbana, 1958).

[4] '"Service" in *King Lear*', *Shakespeare Quarterly*, IX (summer 1958), 347–55.

[5] *Shakespeare's History Plays* (Czechoslovak Academy of Sciences, Prague, 1959).

[6] 'Shakespeare's Early Tragic Mode', *Shakespeare Quarterly*, IX (autumn 1958), 455–69.

feiting simple, broken speech; or he may, as Shakespeare sometimes did, extend the emotion to insanity, thus making possible a different kind of articulation. At a rhetorical level, the tortured mind could be imaged in tortured word-play, the stunned mind in hypnotic iteration.

This study takes account of naturalistic as well as rhetorical modes in Shakespeare's early style, finding *Richard II* 'the only near-perfect essay in rhetorical tragedy in the whole canon' and *Romeo and Juliet* 'pivotal in the development of Shakespeare's tragic style'.

Further studies in Shakespeare's language have come from Charlotte Ehrl,[1] who transforms and enlarges the usual discussion of character-delineation by speech to include the creation of atmosphere and the formulation of a dramatic theme, and from Kurt Schluter[2] who provides a detailed account of Shakespeare's narrative art in all its manifestations. Clifford P. Lyons,[3] in a brief study of related material to Schluter's, draws attention to the ways in which the 'controlling narrative structure' ought to provide a ruling emphasis in the interpretation of a play's theme.

Some of this concern informs L. G. Salingar's[4] essay on *Twelfth Night*. This is a full analysis, using source materials as the basis for a well-organized clarification of the play's complications, arguing that 'the first half of Shakespeare's comedy dwells on self-deception in love, the second half stresses the benevolent irony of fate'. A fresh study of the role of the Shrew is most entertainingly written by Miss M. C. Bradbrook,[5] who looks back to *Johan Johan* and forward to *The Silent Woman* to find perspective for her views. She observes that Katherine, unlike older shrews, has never been in league with society, but at odds with it and 'Henceforth her relations to others, as she shows in Act v, are to be through Petruchio': Katherine is not transformed into the image of Bianca, rather the younger sister 'clearly assumes the scold'. The logic of it pleases. Terry Hawkes[6] briefly considers that the Hero–Claudio and Benedick–Beatrice wooings show conventional and informal distinctions, which are part of a greater division between their worlds in the play as a whole. W. W. Lawrence[7] finds Lucio sacrificed in *Measure for Measure*, as Falstaff had been, with only 'the saving grace of a ready wit at the moment of disaster'. Lawrence believes that the Jacobean audience 'did not care a straw whether the bed-trick was morally justifiable', but assumes that it is 'of course highly unpleasant to modern feelings'. On such matters, particularly Falstaff, E. M. W. Tillyard[8] has a just comment: 'The way you feel on this old controversy depends on how far you allow your head to intervene in the promptings of the heart, and perhaps too on how far you can put yourself in the place of Shakespeare's contemporaries'. In his summary of the diversity of Shakespearian comedy Tillyard puts in a much needed word for *The Merry Wives*.

Among translations attention must first be given to the French edition being edited by Pierre Leyris and Henry Evans,[9] which has reached volume 5. This prints the text of the Cambridge

[1] *Sprachstil und Charakter bei Shakespeare* (Quelle and Meyer, Heidelberg, 1957).
[2] *Shakespeares Dramatische Erzählkunst* (Quelle and Meyer, Heidelberg, 1958).
[3] 'It Appears so by the Story'', *Shakespeare Quarterly*, IX (summer 1958), 287–94.
[4] 'The Design of *Twelfth Night*', *Shakespeare Quarterly*, IX (spring 1958), 117–39.
[5] 'Dramatic Role as Social Image: A Study of *The Taming of the Shrew*', *Shakespeare-Jahrbuch* (1958).
[6] 'The Old and the New in *Much Ado About Nothing*', *Notes and Queries* (December 1958).
[7] 'Measure for Measure and Lucio', *Shakespeare Quarterly*, IX (autumn 1958), 443–53.
[8] *The Nature of Comedy and Shakespeare* (Presidential Address, The English Association, 1958).
[9] *Œuvres Complètes de Shakespeare*, vol. 5 (Formes et Reflets, Paris, 1959).

New Shakespeare on the facing page, and accompanies each play with critical prefaces, textual commentaries and glossaries and translators' notes. Despite the numerous translators a very real consistency has been achieved in this most important part of a formidable undertaking. The clarity and dramatic strength of Armand Robin's *Othello* and Pierre Jean Jouve's *Macbeth* deserve particular mention.

Turkish editions of *The Merchant of Venice* and *Julius Caesar* have come from Nureddin Sevin,[1] and a Polish reprint of Tarnawski's *Tempest* has an introduction by Stanisław Helsztyński,[2] well based on recent discussion of the play. From Poland too has come what is in many ways the most impressive foreign contribution of the year, Wiktor Hahn's[3] Bibliography of Shakespeare in Poland, whose 2500 entries range from the first productions in Warsaw, by John Green's company in the mid-seventeenth century, down to the year 1955. It is a remarkable book, covering such related aspects of the criticism of Shakespeare, productions and translations of the plays, and the translations of works of criticism in foreign languages: notable sections, which other bibliographies might well include, list music and illustrative material and film versions. The non-Polish reader is assisted by the courtesy of translating the system of abbreviations and by excellent indexes. Hahn's work confirms the extent to which Shakespearian interest and knowledge have become part of Poland's cultural independence.

Finally, a process similar to that begun in Poland centuries ago may be seen in the establishment at Munich of a Ukrainian Shakespeare Society. Ukrainian translations of *Romeo and Juliet* and of the *Sonnets* have been made by E. G. Kostetzky,[4] and despite difficulties in book production the volume of the *Sonnets* reproduces some interesting portraiture in its commentary, and that of *Romeo and Juliet* accompanies its text with theatrical records illustrative of its stage history.

2. SHAKESPEARE'S LIFE, TIMES AND STAGE

reviewed by R. A. FOAKES

In her genial history of Charlecote,[5] Alice Fairfax-Lucy makes the most of the supposed connection between Shakespeare and Sir Thomas Lucy, but with proper brevity. The family and the house, which remained relatively unaffected by, and isolated from, major wars and political changes until modern times, are the theme of a book which celebrates the attachment of the country gentleman to his land. The author has a good deal of quiet fun with the mediocrity or downright silliness of many of the Lucys, but writes charitably, and out of a deep affection for a way of life that has all but passed. Shakespeare removed himself from their influence by going to London, but he no doubt took some Stratford mannerisms with him, and Hilda Hulme[6] provides some further examples of local usages and dialectal forms which may help to explain obscurities in the poet's language. The sonnets seem to reflect something of Shakespeare's early

[1] *Venedik Taciri*, and *Julius Caezar* (Maarif Basimevi, Ankara, 1958).
[2] Władysław Tarnawski, *Burza* (Wrocław, 1958).
[3] *Shakespeare w Polsce* (Wrocław, 1958).
[4] *Romeo and Juliet* (Munich, 1957) and *The Sonnets* (Munich, 1958).
[5] *Charlecote and the Lucys. The Chronicle of a Family* (Oxford University Press, 1958).
[6] 'Shakespeare of Stratford', *Review of English Studies*, n.s. x (February 1959), 20-5.

life in London, but the identity of the youth addressed remains a mystery; Dick Taylor Junior,[1] illustrating the ambition and forcefulness of the Earl of Pembroke from the age of 15 when he came to court, seeks to show that he 'in no way resembled any of the several youths who might be extracted from the Sonnets as they were printed in 1609'.

If nothing new has turned up about Shakespeare's life this year,[2] our knowledge of him is steadily increased by the continuing exploration of his reading and knowledge. The fullest study is R. R. Simpson's *Shakespeare and Medicine*,[3] which provides a guide to all medical references in the plays and poems. This is a serious book by a doctor who knows a lot about the history of medicine, and who concludes that 'Shakespeare was well-acquainted with the medical knowledge of the day—and probably also with the literature'. It is difficult to assess the validity of this statement, since an acquaintance with medical knowledge may have been common among literate people, but the evidence gathered in the book will be useful. The learned amassing of evidence by Rolf Soellner,[4] who thinks Shakespeare consciously employed an ancient way of regarding the passions, and by Warren D. Smith,[5] who shows that the Elizabethan authorities were on the whole sceptical about astrology, seems to lead nowhere. The pairing of the passions in opposed sets, joy and grief, hope and despair, is common, and seems an obvious device for any poet, while Warren Smith's attack on 'the usual generalization that Shakespeare's practice reflects personal belief in astrology' is justified only if people really are as silly as he supposes, and usually make such rash generalizations.

On the other hand, J. Leeds Barroll[6] does throw light on Shakespeare's treatment of Roman history by drawing attention to a traditional view of Augustus as an ideal emperor; this leads him to argue that 'it is difficult to believe that even Shakespeare would have glorified Antony and Cleopatra at the expense of Augustus'. C. J. Sisson[7] helps us to understand the function of Prospero, whom he sees as 'a visible Providence' rather than a magician, by showing that there is no parallel for his activities in the feats of contemporary magicians. The interesting background to Caliban is filled in by R. H. Goldsmith's study[8] of the 'wild man' in literary history. In his attractive account of a portrait (apparently of the Moorish ambassador who visited Queen Elizabeth in 1600) now in the Shakespeare Institute, Bernard Harris[9] suggests that it may have some bearing on *Othello*, on the presentation of a Moor on the Elizabethan stage.

Other studies in the background to Shakespeare include Gisela Dahinten's book[10] on ghost-

---

[1] 'The Earl of Pembroke and the Youth of Shakespeare's Sonnets: An Essay in Rehabilitation', *Studies in Philology*, LVI (January 1959), 26–54.

[2] H. A. Shield pursues further tenuous 'Links with Shakespeare' in *Notes and Queries* (December 1958), pp. 526–7.

[3] Edinburgh and London: E. and S. Livingstone, 1959.

[4] 'The Four Primary Passions: A Renaissance Theory Reflected in the Works of Shakespeare', *Studies in Philology*, LV (October 1958), 549–67.

[5] 'The Elizabethan Rejection of Judicial Astrology and Shakespeare's Practice', *Shakespeare Quarterly*, IX (spring 1958), 159–76.

[6] 'Shakespeare and Roman History', *Modern Language Review*, LIII (July 1958), 327–43.

[7] 'The Magic of Prospero', *Shakespeare Survey*, 11 (1958), 70–7.

[8] 'The Wild Man on the English Stage', *Modern Language Review*, LIII (October 1958), 481–91.

[9] 'A Portrait of a Moor', *Shakespeare Survey*, 11 (1958), 89–97.

[10] *Die Geisterszene in der Tragödie vor Shakespeare* (Palaestra, Band 225: Göttingen: Vandenhoeck and Ruprecht, 1958).

scenes in pre-Shakespearian tragedy, which seeks to show how he used existing conventions stemming from Seneca, and endowed them with new life. It is a pity that what seems a fairly well-documented work relies on Fleay for its dating of plays, and accepts, for instance, his not very probable 1586 for *Locrine* (Chambers dates it *c.* 1591), a play given much prominence as marking a new departure in the integral use of ghost-scenes, and as pointing towards Shakespeare's development of them. This hardly inspires confidence in the general argument of the book. Friedrich Hoffmann[1] argues that recurring scene-patterns were expected by the Elizabethan theatre audiences, but many of his examples seem to be basic situations of drama at all times. More convincing is Clifford Leech's theory[2] that *Tamburlaine* established a vogue for two-part plays describing the rise and fall of a hero, a pattern Shakespeare replaced in *2* and *3 Henry VI* by a continuous action. He believes that Shakespeare did not conceive a trilogy, which would have been altogether a new departure, but revised an old play to make *1 Henry VI*, so that the first three-part play was made up from 'a particularly adventurous two-part play together with a fore-piece written later by another dramatist'.

A number of notes bear further on Shakespeare's background. Lawrence J. Ross[3] observes precedents for references in the plays to Lucifer as a name for the devil, which Noble thought were lapses in Shakespeare's knowledge of the Bible. Peter G. Phialas[4] claims that there is a quibble on 'de(v)il' in 'Colevile of the dale' (*2 Henry IV*, IV, iii), and J. G. McManaway[5] interestingly cites evidence that sand was employed to teach handwriting, so that Lavinia's writing in the sand in *Titus Andronicus* may have seemed familiar and pathetic, as equivalent to writing on a slate now. The evidence is very circumstantial that 'Robin' had a bawdy or phallic meaning traditionally, and Harry Morris,[6] who finds in the name 'bonny sweet Robin' a clue to Ophelia's sexual frustration, is seeing what no audience would notice. B. R. Morris[7] has observed an allusion to Troilus as the central figure in the story as early as 1590, which is interesting since the emphasis in pre-Shakespearian versions is usually on the faithlessness and miserable end of Cressida.

A few notes concern dating and authorship. I. A. Shapiro[8] argues well that Sir Edward Hoby's letter of December 1595 referring to 'K. Richard' cannot be used to date *Richard II*, but may refer to *Richard III*, or possibly not to a play at all. The argument put forward by three scholars[9] for dating *Hamlet* in late 1600 or 1601 rests shakily on the assumptions that the comments on a picture in v, i of *Antonio and Mellida* give Marston's age in 1599 as 24; that Marston could not have written three plays in one winter; and that *Antonio's Revenge* and *Hamlet* draw indepen-

---

[1] 'Die typischen Situationen im Elizabethanischen Drama und ihr Pattern', *Shakespeare-Jahrbuch*, XCIV (1958), 107–20.

[2] 'The Two-Part Play. Marlowe and the Early Shakespeare', *Shakespeare-Jahrbuch*, XCIV (1958), 90–106.

[3] 'Two Supposed "Defects in Shakespeare's Biblical Knowledge"', *Notes and Queries* (November 1958), pp. 462–3.

[4] 'Coleville of the Dale', *Shakespeare Quarterly*, IX (winter 1958), 86–8.

[5] 'Writing in Sand in *Titus Andronicus*, IV, i', *Review of English Studies*, n.s. IX (May 1958), 172–3.

[6] 'Ophelia's "Bonny Sweet Robin"', *P.M.L.A.*, LXXIII (December 1958), 601–3.

[7] 'Thomas Watson and "Troilus and Cressida"', *Notes and Queries* (May 1958), pp. 198–9.

[8] '*Richard II* or *Richard III* or . . .', *Shakespeare Quarterly*, IX (spring 1958), 204–6.

[9] John Harrington Smith, Lois D. Pizer and Edward K. Kaufman, '*Hamlet*, *Antonio's Revenge* and the *Ur-Hamlet*', *Shakespeare Quarterly*, IX (autumn 1958), 493–8.

dently on the *Ur-Hamlet*. Kenneth Muir[1] strongly asserts Shakespeare's part-authorship of *The Two Noble Kinsmen*, adducing as new and interesting evidence the appearance in the play of some characteristic Shakespearian image-clusters. He also reconsiders the evidence concerning the lost *Cardenio* and Theobald's *Double Falsehood*,[2] but finds it inconclusive. Finally, John P. Cutts[3] forcibly attacks Richard Flatter's view that the Hecate scene in *Macbeth* is entirely by Shakespeare, and lays emphasis on the evidence that the songs are an interpolation borrowed from Middleton's *The Witch*.

As far as sources are concerned, the most important new work is undoubtedly volume II of Geoffrey Bullough's projected five-volume collection of the major sources and analogues of Shakespeare's plays.[4] This volume deals with the mature comedies, excluding *Troilus and Cressida*, and follows the pattern of the first, except that the editor has been more generous, if anything, in printing source-material, and has amplified his own introductions to individual plays. Excerpts from seven different analogues and possible sources are given for *The Merry Wives of Windsor*, a play for which Kenneth Muir, in his *Shakespeare's Sources*, found no certain source, and to which he devoted only brief comment. It is excellent to have these items, some of them relatively inaccessible, gathered together, so that the reader can use his own judgement. Bullough and his publishers deserve praise for including more than most users will expect to find, for instance, summaries of Cinthio's *Epitia*, Secchi's *L'Interesse*, and excerpts from *Sir Clyomon and Clamydes* (this last in relation to *As You Like It*). The first two volumes have appeared in successive years, and this speed of production excuses a few minor lapses and errors, and makes remarkable the general quality of the editor's own contribution, in which he comments judiciously on the relevance of the sources to each play, and, particularly for *Much Ado* and the later plays, provides a good deal of reference to recent critical estimates. Altogether, this is an admirable collection, and will clearly be a standard work of reference.

Except in relation to *Much Ado*, where a borrowing from *The Faerie Queene*, Book II, has long been suspected, Bullough makes little reference to Spenser. Abbie Findlay Potts,[5] however, believes that after 1600, Shakespeare used Spenser's themes and ideas to give 'ethical meaning' to his plays, and she pursues all the analogies she can find in seeking to show what few are likely to accept. Paridell is linked with Parolles, Archimago gives birth to Iago and Iachimo, and Hamlet, who is all things to all men, carries a smack of Marinell, Scudamour, Guyon and Prince Arthur. What is significant tends to be lost in the spate of guesses, and the book's force diminished by the curious critical attitude which divides Shakespeare's work into two, regards *As You Like It* as lacking an 'ethical dimension', and this and all plays written before it as dealing with 'pawns', not 'persons'. The author is also concerned to make a comparative study of the ethical basis of *The Faerie Queene* and Shakespeare's later plays, and this was well worth doing, even though it is not likely to persuade anyone that Shakespeare needed to know Spenser's long poem in order to develop a concern with 'weightier purposes'; if anything, it does more

---

[1] 'Shakespeare's Hand in *The Two Noble Kinsmen*', *Shakespeare Survey*, 11 (1958), 50–9.

[2] 'Cardenio', *Études Anglaises*, XI (July-September 1958), 202–9.

[3] 'Who Wrote the Hecate-Scene?', *Shakespeare-Jahrbuch*, XCIV (1958), 200–2.

[4] *Narrative and Dramatic Sources of Shakespeare*, volume II, The Comedies, 1597–1603 (Routledge and Kegan Paul, 1958). Volume I was reviewed in *Shakespeare Survey*, 12 (1959), 141–2.

[5] *Shakespeare and The Faerie Queene* (Ithaca, New York: Cornell University Press, 1958).

for Spenser, in reminding us of the truly dramatic nature of the spiritual ordeal his heroes undergo.

In her essay on *Troilus and Cressida*, M. C. Bradbrook[1] sees Shakespeare 'correcting' Chaucer in order to dwell on the 'pettiness of evil: the squalor and meanness and triviality of betrayal'. Arthur M. Z. Norman[2] cites one or two interesting parallels in seeking to prove the influence of Daniel on *Antony and Cleopatra*, but Thomas H. McNeal[3] relies too much on similarities of phrasing that are quite commonplace in suggesting that Shakespeare adapted a scene from the old play *Leir* to establish the relationship of Suffolk and Margaret in *1 Henry VI*. There may nevertheless be something in his general argument. Kenneth Muir[4] presents a reasoned case that Shakespeare conflated three passages from Holland's Pliny for a speech in *Othello*, and elsewhere[5] throws doubt on the view sometimes held that the poet made use of Anthony Copley's jest-book, *Witts Fittes* (1595). One further note, by Terry Hawkes,[6] shows that extracts of Ficino's writings were available in translation to Shakespeare in a popular manual of letter-writing published in 1568.

In his sumptuously produced *Shakespeare and the Artist*,[7] W. Moelwyn Merchant interprets the work of illustrators of editions, painters inspired by Shakespeare's text, and scene designers, to build up a visual history of the production of the plays. This is fascinating material, and though the author deviates rather a lot in pursuit of minor discoveries of his own, the detail accumulates to fortify and make convincing the general story. It is his purpose to establish that a unity of style prevailed in theatre *décor* in all periods from 1660 to the end of the last century, a unity connected with an accepted interrelationship of art and the theatre; he then goes on to lament the divorce in this century of artists from the stage, and the lack of critical attention paid to *décor*. He wishes we could regain 'the vitality of the visual tradition which lies behind the contemporary theatre'. He realizes, of course, that the artist needs to subdue his vision to 'interpreting or reinforcing the power of a Shakespearian theme', and admits that no single production can 'hope to stress visually more than one major aspect' of a play; but clearly it is better that they should do these things than be merely decorative or gimmicky. Part II of the book consists of a group of essays on individual plays which illustrate the interaction of visual and literary elements; the most interesting are on *Timon*, *Coriolanus* (the staging of which was traditionally much influenced by a painting of Poussin) and *Henry VIII*, where the dramatic significance of a traditional grouping in the trial of Katherine is well brought out.

In his sympathy for the visual aspects of theatre art, Merchant wants us to reject the notion of a neutral background at the Globe, and emphasizes the richness and varied significance of the stage façade there. His claims for it seem exaggerated, especially when he later argues, for instance, that Romantic sets showing, for a history play, representations of old English streets, were analogous in effect to the background at the Globe. There seems an important distinction to be made here; the Globe façade was a contemporary one, and absolutely constant for any

[1] 'What Shakespeare did to Chaucer's *Troilus and Criseyde*', *Shakespeare Quarterly*, IX (summer 1958), 311–19.
[2] 'Daniel's *The Tragedie of Cleopatra* and *Antony and Cleopatra*', *Shakespeare Quarterly*, IX (winter 1958), 11–18.
[3] 'Margaret of Anjou: Romantic Princess and Troubled Queen', *ibid.* pp. 1–10.
[4] 'Shakespeare's Use of Pliny Reconsidered', *Modern Language Review*, LIV (April 1959), 224–5.
[5] '"Witts Fittes" and Shakespeare', *Notes and Queries* (May 1958), pp. 186–7.
[6] 'Ficino and Shakespeare', *ibid.* pp. 185–6.   [7] Oxford University Press, 1959.

play (in this sense it was more neutral than Merchant allows), whereas an historical set for a history play is at once limiting and prescribing. Perhaps the danger is just this, that by rendering *one* aspect of a play an artist is bound to annoy many persons because he limits it; but if it be granted that we must have *décor* in the modern theatre, then Merchant urgently and well makes his case.

Two articles have a bearing on Merchant's book; one,[1] by him, describes an original set of Hayman's drawings for Hanmer's edition of Shakespeare, now in the Folger Library; the other, by Kalman A. Burnim,[2] shows how some letters of Hayman's reveal details of Garrick's staging of *Lear* and *Othello*. Studies relating to the stage in Shakespeare's own time include Allardyce Nicoll's well-presented argument[3] that the last plays were not influenced by the court masque except in 'imaginative vistas inspired by its soul'; he notes that there is no evidence that any of them were presented at the Blackfriars theatre. G. P. V. Akrigg[4] thinks the clown's remarks to Malvolio in *Twelfth Night*, IV, ii, describe an actual hall, which was the scene of performance, and which can be identified with one of the Inns of Court, but not with Whitehall. Richard Bernheimer[5] has found an interesting illustration of a theatre, which he identifies as a converted tennis-court, in a book by Robert Fludd published on the continent in 1619. This has some analogies with features of London stages, but the author presses these too far in treating what may be a fanciful drawing as a representation of a real 'structure of a generally Elizabethan type'. In an important note, S. P. Zitner[6] shows that most of Gosson's celebrated account of the behaviour of the audience in an Elizabethan theatre was drawn from Ovid's *Art of Love*.

Glynne Wickham's *Early English Stages*,[7] volume 1, has no direct reference to Shakespeare, but in its implications for the study of the plays and the Elizabethan theatre, it is the most ambitious and important book since Chambers's *Elizabethan Stage*. Its full significance will only emerge in the second volume, which will deal with the period after 1576, but already the drift of Wickham's general argument is clear. It traces the development of Elizabethan drama from 'two basic and distinctly independent sources of dramatic entertainment in medieval England: worship and recreation', as represented by, on one hand, the miracle play, on the other, the tournament and civic pageant; the greatness of the drama of Shakespeare's time is seen as arising out of the fusion of these two traditions for a few years when 'the professional actors obtained their long-sought-after popular audience...and began to lose the intelligentsia almost simultaneously'. The lines of development are perhaps distinguished too clearly, but the perspective in which the Elizabethan drama is here placed, as an end, not a beginning, as the culmination of a long and elaborate process, not a sudden flowering out of nothing, is most valuable. For this is to see the drama in its full historical setting, and thence to recognize that the 'appearance of the first proscenium-arch stage at Court in 1605' was a crucial event, beginning the transformation of a theatre of poetry and suggestion, which had reached its perfection and widest appeal only a short time previously, into the modern theatre of 'pictorial realism and prose'. In

---

[1] 'Francis Hayman's Illustrations of Shakespeare', *Shakespeare Quarterly*, IX (spring 1958), 141–7.

[2] 'The Significance of Garrick's Letters to Hayman', *ibid.* pp. 149–52.

[3] 'Shakespeare and the Court Masque', *Shakespeare-Jahrbuch*, XCIV (1958), 51–62.

[4] '*Twelfth Night* at the Middle Temple', *Shakespeare Quarterly*, IX (summer 1958), 422–4.

[5] 'Another Globe Theatre', *Shakespeare Quarterly*, IX (winter 1958), 19–29.

[6] 'Gosson, Ovid and the Elizabethan Audience', *Shakespeare Quarterly*, IX (spring 1958), 206–8.

[7] *Early English Stages 1300–1660*, volume 1, 1300–1576 (Routledge and Kegan Paul, 1959).

presenting this argument with much detailed evidence correcting and amplifying the work of Chambers, Wickham has made out a most convincing case; and if the boldness of his style and sharp oppositions of his picture make the reader cautious in accepting some of his particular conclusions, this is all to the good. From a literary point of view the most interesting section is that which develops a new and very attractive interpretation of some of Lydgate's text for 'mummings'.

A most useful little book has been written by A. M. Nagler on *Shakespeare's Stage*;[1] this excellent introductory account is sceptical where it should be, and firm in its handling of available evidence. It aims to establish an 'ideal type' of Shakespearian stage, and its most original feature is a wide range of reference to continental practice, which enables the author to make a good case for a curtained alcove, tent or pavilion as the central feature at the rear of the stage, something movable rather than a fixed recess. He draws attention to the evidence in Henslowe's lists and in court records for a considerable use of scenery, and though the main emphasis is on the Globe and Blackfriars, there are sections on masques, costume, acting, and on the audience. This is a first-rate handbook for students. Richard Hosley[2] describes the 'Elizabethan' façade designed by Richard Southern for the Bankside Players to act against; their concern for reproducing original conditions of production is not shared by Jean Jacquot, who, with André Veinstein, presents another collection of essays on the theatre,[3] this time on the staging of old plays. He accepts as inevitable that many in a modern audience seeing *Macbeth* will not have any acquaintance with the historical or critical background to the play, and that their concern will be 'le drame moral du protagoniste'. In addition to essays on problems of interpretation, and on documents of the theatre, there are some descriptions of actual productions, including one by Gabriel Monnet[4] on a production of *Hamlet* before the castle of Annécy.

Reports on current productions of Shakespeare's plays grow more numerous every year.[5] Roy Walker's account[6] of *Timon* at the Old Vic and *Julius Caesar* at Stratford should please W. M. Merchant, for he is particularly good in his critical remarks on the settings of these plays. The fullest and most valuable review is undoubtedly that by Muriel St Clare Byrne[7] of recent productions at the Old Vic and Stratford; she is especially interesting on the Old Vic's *Henry VIII*, which prompts her to note that 'the charge of degeneration' brought against much of the

---

[1] New Haven, Connecticut: Yale University Press, 1958.

[2] 'An Elizabethan Tiring-House Façade', *Shakespeare Quarterly*, IX (autumn 1958), 588.

[3] *La Mise en Scène des Œuvres du Passé* (Paris: Centre National de la Recherche Scientifique, 1957); Jacquot's essay, 'Les Études Shakespeariennes, Problèmes et Méthodes: l'exemple de "Macbeth"', occupies pp. 176–209.

[4] 'Sur une Mise en Scène de "Hamlet"', *ibid.* pp. 233–9.

[5] Among these are accounts of the New York season, by Alice Griffin, *Shakespeare Quarterly*, IX (autumn 1958), 531–4; of the festivals at Stratford, Connecticut, and Phoenix, Arizona, by Claire McGlinchee and Anson B. Cutts respectively, *ibid.* pp. 539–42, 549–53; of a new festival at Boulder, Colorado, by Robert L. Perkin, *ibid.* pp. 555–9; and of productions in Germany and Switzerland, by Karl Brinkmann and Lydia Benz-Burger respectively, *Shakespeare-Jahrbuch*, XCIV (1958), 233–52. Karl Brinkmann also reviews the Russian film on *Othello*, *ibid.* pp. 252–5; S. Prema has a note on what may be the first Indian performance of scenes from *Julius Caesar*, *Shakespeare Quarterly*, IX (summer 1958), 395–6; and Alice Griffin provides a check-list of productions from October 1956 to October 1957, *Shakespeare Quarterly*, IX (winter 1958), 39–58.

[6] 'Unto Caesar: A Review of Recent Productions', *Shakespeare Survey*, 11 (1958), 128–35.

[7] 'The Shakespeare Season at the Old Vic, 1957–8, and Stratford-upon-Avon, 1958', *Shakespeare Quarterly*, IX (autumn 1958), 507–30.

verse of early seventeenth-century playwrights is 'meaningless in the dramatic context, if what the play substance requires is closer approximation to the conversational note, where so-called "poetic" weakness can in fact mean idiomatic strength'. Other valuable reviews are contributed by Arnold Edinborough[1] on the season at Stratford, Ontario, and Gloria E. Johnson[2] on the Ashland, Oregon, festival, where all Shakespeare's plays have now been produced.

A feature of recent work on Shakespeare has been the discovery and study of early music associated with the plays. John P. Cutts[3] has found two seventeenth-century settings of sonnets from *The Passionate Pilgrim*, and Peter J. Seng[4] has turned up in a copy of a book of 1609 what may be music for the Fool's song in *Lear*. The same author has discovered an early version in lute tablature of Desdemona's willow song, dating from about 1572.[5] In a very interesting article, Frederick W. Sternfeld[6] identifies the allusion in Silence's 'Do me right, And dub me knight, Samingo' (*2 Henry IV*, v, iii, 79) to a popular song, 'Mounsier Mingo', which appeared in a collection by Lasso, published in 1570. He notes four other references to this final phrase of the song in Elizabethan plays. The use of music in Shakespeare's last plays is discussed by J. M. Nosworthy,[7] who believes that it reflects a 'concept of divine order which informs the dramatic pattern at all points'. Andrew J. Sabol's edition of sixty-three items of music from court masques[8] does not directly concern Shakespeare, but will be of interest to Shakespearians. It is prefaced by a substantial introduction on the masque and the use of music in it, which valuably stresses the variety and range of the masque, and its character as an independent art form.

Two further articles deserve attention. In one, Norman N. Holland[9] argues that the recurrence of references to ears in *Hamlet* is significant for the interpretation of the dumbshow in the play within the play; Claudius, he thinks, 'must see and understand, but not be overcome', for Hamlet is here making the punishment fit the crime by pouring poison into his ears. The other, by Margaret Farrand Thorp,[10] comments on a problem which does not seem to have drawn as much study as it deserves, namely, how to transfer Shakespeare's plays adequately to the screen. She notes that, in the United States at any rate, the only opportunity many people have to see the plays is in the cinema; and she goes on to consider some difficulties of filming Shakespeare, and the solutions adopted by outstanding directors like Laurence Olivier. Now that the plays are being seen also on television screens, it is to be hoped that the questions she raises will receive more consideration.

[1] 'A Lively Season at Canada's Stratford', *ibid.* pp. 535–8.
[2] 'Shakespeare at Ashland, Oregon—1958', *ibid.* pp. 543–7.
[3] 'Two Hitherto Unpublished Settings of Sonnets from *The Passionate Pilgrim*', *Shakespeare Quarterly*, IX (autumn 1958), 588–94.
[4] 'An Early Tune for the Fool's Song in *King Lear*', *ibid.* pp. 583–4.
[5] 'The Earliest Known Music for Desdemona's "Willow Song"', *Shakespeare Quarterly*, IX (summer 1958), 419–20.
[6] 'Lasso's Music for Shakespeare's "Samingo"', *Shakespeare Quarterly*, IX (spring 1958), 105–16.
[7] 'Music and its Function in the Romances of Shakespeare', *Shakespeare Survey*, 11 (1958), 60–9.
[8] *Songs and Dances for the Stuart Masque* (Providence, Rhode Island: Brown University Press, 1959).
[9] 'The Dumb-show Revisited', *Notes and Queries* (May 1958), 191.
[10] 'Shakespeare and the Movies', *Shakespeare Quarterly*, IX (summer 1958), 358–66.

3. TEXTUAL STUDIES

reviewed by JAMES G. McMANAWAY

For the third time in a decade, a British scholar has produced an independent text of Shakespeare, truly a notable record. The latest, *The London Shakespeare*,[1] an annotated and critical edition of the complete works, with glossary, in six well-printed volumes, is the work of J. J. Munro, who unfortunately did not live to see it through the press. The General Introduction, by G. W. G. Wickham, is warmly recommended for its account of Shakespeare's life (I, xi–xvii). That Munro was able in less than ten years to pick up the threads of Shakespeare scholarship laid down thirty years before at his entry into service in the First World War and make a critical text of the Works is extraordinary. He read most of the right authorities and familiarized himself with the new critical approaches. It would be interesting to know whether he edited the individual titles in the order in which they appear in print, for in the later volumes he appears to take more serious account of certain kinds of evidence than in the earlier, when it was perhaps not properly evaluated. He never seems at home, for example, in matters bibliographical, though there are occasional references to such studies. C. K. Hinman is not included among the authorities consulted, and though W. W. Greg's *The Shakespeare First Folio* is listed, citations are to the earlier *Editorial Problem in Shakespeare*.

What is puzzling is the kind of reader for whom the edition was intended. Format and typography suggest the general reader, as does the inclusion of the Glossary. Such a reader needs prefaces to date each work, necessary details about sources and genre, a brief statement of the textual position and identification of copy text, guidance in interpretation of incident, fable and characters, and perhaps a little stage history. He has no use for, or comprehension of, textual variants—here given in profusion—and no competence to choose among them, much less to infer the unstated reasons for editorial preference. To what good purpose, then, has Munro recorded variants and other textual minutiae? Would not a general statement of textual practice have sufficed?

Some of the Introductions are admirable, and there are occasional observations of importance. Such a one is the description (IV, 1146–7) of a hitherto unnoted metrical characteristic that bears on the authorship of *Henry VIII*. In Shakespeare, Munro writes, but rarely in Fletcher, the verse

is interlaced frequently by orthodox 5-foot lines made up of the latter end of a run-on or lightly-pointed line which follows a pause, and the beginning of the next line preceding a pause, at which point an extra syllable often occurs. Speeches which begin or end in a half-line have often, for this reason, the effect of opening or closing on a full line [compare I, i, 13–38 or I, ii, 68–88 with II, i, 100–36 or Katharine's speeches in III, i]. Both the normal line and the straddling line carry the fundamental measure, which is reinforced by this repetition and overlapping; but in places, as in V, i, 163–9, the straddling line may be the dominant.

There are, however, notable omissions or oversights. In the discussion of *Pericles*, for example, there is no reference to Philip Edwards's important essay in *Shakespeare Survey*, 5 (1952) or to Kenneth Muir's Introduction (1953) to the reprint of *The Painfull Adventures of Pericles Prince*

[1] John J. Munro, ed., *The London Shakespeare* (London: Eyre and Spottiswoode; New York: Simon and Schuster, 1957), 6 vols.

of Tyre. The Introduction to *Macbeth* makes no use of J. Q. Adams' edition or of H. N. Paul's *Royal Play of Macbeth*. There is no reference to Harry Hoppe's account of the change of printers of the first quarto of *Romeo* or to McKerrow's evidence that variations in the speech headings in Q2 are proof that Shakespeare's foul sheets served as printer's copy. Neglect of the bibliographical description of the Folger fragment of *Passionate Pilgrim* in J. Q. Adams' facsimile edition leads to the acceptance of the second edition as the first. There is no reference to my study of the scene omitted from the first issue of *2 Henry IV* or to arguments by M. A. Shaaber and others about whether Part II is a pre-conceived continuation of Part I or a sequel called into existence by the theatrical success of Falstaff. Of *1 Henry IV* Munro gives a transcript of the title of Q1 (i.e. Greg 145 (*b*)) and adds that 'Four leaves of sheet C found in a binding and containing one original reading are now found in the Folger Library'. In a footnote he mentions Halliwell-Phillipps' opinion that the fragment represents a lost edition, earlier than Q1, but he dismisses the suggestion with the words: 'it may be a cancelled proof.' Now in his Variorum edition (1936) S. B. Hemingway (pp. 344–5) adduces bibliographical evidence of the primacy of the Fragment that Greg (*Bibliography*, I, 238) accepts and amplifies. Whether Munro's failure to take account of these two discussions was caused by sheer inability to digest the great mass of textual detail in the time at his disposal or to his inability to recognize the validity of certain kinds of evidence, it is clear that the text of the London Shakespeare has not the authority that was hoped for.

The Heritage Shakespeare[1] presents the plays in three beautifully printed and attractively bound, yet inexpensive, volumes. It has the revised text of Peter Alexander and also his special Introduction to each play. The prefatory essay to *The Comedies* is by Tyrone Guthrie; that to *The Histories* by James G. McManaway; and that to *The Tragedies* by George Rylands.

Two volumes have been added to the New Arden Shakespeare. In editing *All's Well*,[2] which appears to have been printed from the author's foul papers (or a transcript of them), G. K. Hunter has been generally conservative, rejecting many of the emendations that have accumulated in favour of the Folio readings. In many places he restores what may be presumed to be Shakespeare's lineation that Jaggard's compositors altered because of miscalculations in the counting of difficult copy. It is disturbing, therefore, to see signs of bibliographical indecision about the pattern of composition of the text. Hunter believes that composition proceeded in abnormal fashion, from the outside towards the middle (p. xi, note 2). No supporting evidence is given, and it may be doubted whether it exists. There is doubt, too, about the identification of the compositors who set quires V and X and the proposed distribution of work between them. Hunter is correct in attributing the concluding pages of the play, $Y1^{r \text{ and } v}$, to B. These pages were printed at a considerable time later than quires V and X,[3] and, Hunter observes, there is a remarkable change in speech-tags in them. The Countess and her son, who on $X6^{v}$ had been labelled *Old La.* and *Ber.* become, in the middle of a scene, *Coun.* and *Ros.* consistently. The explanation of the change may be, as Hunter suggests, that after a long interval B forgot the identity of the dramatis personae and simply followed copy, whereas in earlier pages he had attempted to regularize the functional speech-tags of Shakespeare's foul sheets (elsewhere,

[1] Peter Alexander, ed., *The Heritage Shakespeare* (New York: The Heritage Club, 1958, 1959), 3 vols.
[2] *All's Well That Ends Well*, New Arden (Methuen, 1959).
[3] See J. W. Shroeder, *The Great Folio of 1623*, pp. 70, 73.

for example, the Countess appears as *Mo.*, *Cou.*, *Coun.*, *Old Cou.*, *La.*, depending partly on her relations to the others present at the time). If *B* made such an attempt at normalizing speech-tags in *All's Well*, the effort was unique, for there are no signs of such activity elsewhere. And if the doubt that *B* set any pages of the play before Y I should be sustained, Hunter's explanation falls to the ground. In any case, it fails to account for the sudden appearance of *Coun.* and *Ros.* on Y I. Is it possible that this change is connected in some way with the failure to complete work on *All's Well* and that when Jaggard's shop returned to the play *B* was given different kind of copy from that used in quires V and X?

Timon of Athens,[1] edited by H. J. Oliver, is another play set from manuscript and first printed in the Folio. Like *All's Well*, the text has the irregularities characteristic of a state anterior to the preparation of the fair copy or the prompt-book. The Folio compositor is identified as *B*. From a careful analysis of spelling variants, Oliver believes that portions of the text (I, i, 176–end; I, ii; III, ii, iii, iv, v; IV, iii parts, including 461–end, v, i–end—see p. xix) were in a transcript of Ralph Crane, possibly because the author's papers were at these points too difficult for use in the printing house. If so, he argues, the difficulties disappear that editors have had in explaining the variant forms of such names as Apemantus and Ventidius. The Shakespearian foul sheets, he thinks, had the spellings, *Ventid(d)ius* and *Apemantus*, while Crane's transcript used the forms *Venti(d)gius* and *Apermantus*. Oliver doubts, incidentally, that compositor *B* made any attempt to normalize these spellings (as Hunter thinks he did with certain names in *All's Well*), and, correctly in my opinion, he takes no account of the supposed interruptions in the printing of *Timon* that Shroeder describes in *The Great Folio of 1623* (p. 91). Shroeder's schedule of printing, based as it is on the study of rules and headlines, that is, the elements of the skeleton forme applied during imposition, can give no information about the order of composition. This doubtless proceeded, column by column, in the normal fashion, as described by Hinman.[2] Shakespeare had no collaborator or reviser, according to Oliver. The extraordinary mixture of verse and prose and of good and bad verse represents an imperfectly completed play. As such, it throws light on Shakespeare's method of composition. '*Timon* would suggest that thoughts often came to him in a kind of incomplete verse form, sometimes in prose and sometimes (interestingly) in rhyme, and that only on revision did the text evolve into predominantly blank verse. It might also suggest, I think, that he wrote scenes as he felt in the mood for them, not bothering to complete one if at the minute he was more interested in another' (p. xxviii).

Oliver is inclined to agree with Bonnard[3] that the 'old' academic play of *Timon* borrows from Shakespeare's *Lear* and is related to his *Timon* by indebtedness to a common source. The opposite opinion is expressed by R. H. Goldsmith,[4] who shows complex interrelations between the old *Timon* and Shakespeare's two plays and argues, from analogous speeches, characters, and situations, that Shakespeare was the borrower.

Numbers 11 and 12 of the Shakespeare Quarto Facsimiles[5] are valuable additions to the

[1] *Timon of Athens*, New Arden (Methuen, 1959).
[2] 'Cast-off Copy for the First Folio of Shakespeare', *Shakespeare Quarterly*, VI, 259–73.
[3] George Bonnard, 'Note sur les sources de *Timon of Athens*', *Études Anglaises*, VII, 59–69.
[4] 'Did Shakespeare Use the Old Timon Comedy?', *Shakespeare Quarterly*, IX, 31–8.
[5] *The True Tragedy of Richard Duke of York*, 1595 (Shakespeare Quarto Facsimiles no. 11); *Richard the Third* (no. 12), (Oxford University Press, 1958, 1959).

reference shelves. In no. 11, Sir Walter Greg reproduces in excellent facsimile (the best since no. 7) the unique Bodleian copy of *The True Tragedy of Richard Duke of York* (1595). His marginal references to the Folio text of *3 Henry VI* make easier and more profitable the study of this reported text. No. 12, the first Quarto of *Richard the Third* (1597), reproduced from the Huth copy in the British Museum, is photographically inferior to its predecessor. Greg's collation of the four extant copies and one fragment of the Quarto produces only one true variant (the Folger and Yale copies read correctly 'to' instead of 'from' at II, i, 5).[1] The inclusion of a reproduction of A3 of Q2 was well advised, for the two lines (I, i, 101–2) of the received text that appear first in Q2 may well have been printed as a press correction in some copy of Q1 no longer extant. Early quartos of Shakespeare being so rare and unattainable, it is strange that more individuals have not collected these fine quarto facsimiles. They bring the reader as close to the original as it is possible to come and afford a variety of unexpected delights.

The one new Penguin title is *Pericles*,[2] with a text, writes Professor Harrison, 'considerably nearer to what the original author (or authors) wrote in 1608'. The editor finds little trace of Shakespeare's hand earlier than Act III and considers that even if the later scenes be Shakespeare, they are 'Shakespeare below his best'. In the history of the early editions, it might have been pointed out that the play entered at Stationers' Hall by Edward Blount was not just a transcript; it was the prompt-book—'A booke Called. the booke of Pericles...'—and that there was a reprint in 1609 as well as later editions in 1611 and 1619.

The Folger Library General Reader's Shakespeare has added two new titles, both edited by Louis B. Wright and Virginia A. LaMar.[3] These resemble their predecessors in format and arrangement and wealth of contemporary illustrations. The Introductions feature a short, sensible biography of Shakespeare.

The Pelican Shakespeare[4] has likewise added two titles: *Twelfth Night*, with an admirable Introduction by Charles T. Prouty, and *King Lear*, with a movingly passionate Introduction by Alfred Harbage. The texts follow the Folio closely, and appendixes give variants so that each reader may accept or reject what has been preferred by the editor.

Two of the serious problems of the editors of Shakespeare are (1) how to construct the textual stemma, and (2) what variant readings and conjectures to record. Some light is to be found in *Textual Criticism* by Paul Maas.[5] It concerns itself with classical texts and alludes but twice (pp. [v], 52–3) to Renaissance printed texts, with a reference to Shakespeare and qualified approval of the term 'substantive'. Maas thinks incisively, however, and it would be wholesome for editors of printed texts to test their principles against those found valid in the widely different field of classical manuscripts.

The intensive study of the work habits of the men who set type for the Shakespearian quartos and folios leads naturally to the examination of other books printed in the same shops. One

[1] Bad inking and loose type caused most of the apparent variations in text (see Greg, p. vi). It would have been more accurate to record the F copy as reading 'merc' at I, i, 151.

[2] G. B. Harrison, ed., *The Play of Pericles Prince of Tyre* (Harmondsworth: Penguin Books, 1958).

[3] *A Midsummer Night's Dream*, and *The Tragedy of Macbeth* (New York: Pocket Library, 1958, 1959 (P.L. 67 and 70)).

[4] Alfred Harbage, general editor, *Twelfth Night*, *King Lear* (Baltimore: Penguin Books, 1958).

[5] Paul Maas, *Textual Criticism*, transl. by Barbara Flower (Oxford University Press, 1958).

book that invites attention above all the rest is Augustine Vincent's *A Discovery of Errors* (1622), which came from Jaggard's press while the First Folio was being printed. E. R. Wood directs attention to a number of leaf cancels, paste-on cancels, and one over-printing.[1] There is no immediate Shakespearian interest, unless it be to point out that Vincent's zeal for accuracy led him to read proof and also to avail himself of corrections noted by John Selden, thus emphasizing the words of Heming and Condell about Shakespeare: 'It had bene a thing, we confesse, worthie to have bene wished, that the Author himselfe had liv'd to have set forth, and overseen his owne writings.'

Following the lead of Philip Williams, who first drew attention to the importance of Jaggard's 1619 Shakespeare Quartos in the study of the compositors, and ultimately of the copy texts, of the First Folio,[2] D. F. McKenzie has made a close study of some 3200 variants between Q1 of *The Merchant of Venice* and Q2, which was put in type by Folio compositor B.[3] It was Williams's impression that in *Lear* (1619) B gives 'little evidence of the carelessness of which he has been accused, and the few errors that he did make are not those which have been attributed to him in the F text'. The results of McKenzie's detailed tabulation and analysis of the variants in *Merchant* (1619) are to the contrary. Excluding substantial changes in stage directions and speech prefix forms, which 'appear to have all the characteristics of planned rather than impromptu editing', and a few readings that may represent press corrections of Q1 that do not appear in the sixteen or more surviving exemplars, McKenzie finds that B's attitude towards his copy and his habits of work in 1619 ('misdirected ingenuity, deliberate tampering and plain carelessness') were little different from those in 1621–3. These characteristics, though tedious to enumerate, deserve attention and suggest that the other 1619 Quartos must be scrutinized with equal care. For, as J. R. Brown wrote in his Introduction to the New Arden edition of *The Merchant*, all of the 1619 Shakespeare texts appear to have received the same kind of unauthoritative editing that he observed in that play.[4] The extent of B's mischief in F cannot be safely estimated until all the available evidence has been compiled about his work in other books.

In an essay that is as stimulating as it is important, Clifford Leech contributes to the study of the relative dates of *2* and *3 Henry VI* and *1* Henry *VI* and to an appreciation of the rapid growth in Shakespeare's artistry.[5] His discussion of the pervasive influence of Marlowe's *Tamburlaine* (a popular play followed by an unpremeditated sequel) should be read for its own sake. What is significant for Shakespearians is Leech's demonstration that *2* and *3 Henry VI*, though apparently planned as a two-part story, do not conform to the usual pattern. In *3 Henry VI* Shakespeare abandoned the rise/fall pattern and for the episodic structure of *2 Henry VI* substituted an organic design, revealing thus early some of the original qualities of his mind and his

---

[1] 'Cancels and Corrections in *A Discovery of Errors*, 1622', *The Library*, 5th series, XIII, 124–7. It may be worth noting that large-paper copies of the book seem to have been printed before the trade edition. At least this is true of sheet 4 E 1–4, for two Folger l.p. copies have the cancelland 4 E 1, while all the Folger small-paper copies have the cancellans.

[2] 'Two Problems in the Folio Text of *King Lear*', *Shakespeare Quarterly*, IV, 451–60.

[3] 'Compositor B's Role in *The Merchant of Venice* Q2 (1619)', *Studies in Bibliography*, XII, 75–90.

[4] Brown lists (p. xix, note 1) thirteen of Q2's changes that he had accepted on the assumption that Jaggard had attempted to edit the text. At least eight of these are, however, required by the context, and another, at IV, i, 394, may represent a press correction in Q1 that existed in a no longer extant copy.

[5] 'The Two-part Play. Marlowe and the Early Shakespeare', *Shakespeare-Jahrbuch*, XCIV (1958), 90–106.

architectural genius. Leech suggests that following the period of disintegration and reorganiza-
tion of acting companies in 1594, a manuscript of Strange's *Harey the vi* (written later than
Shakespeare's two plays by an unknown poet and acted as 'ne' in 1592) came into the possession
of the Chamberlain's Men and that Shakespeare reworked it so as to make it the first part of
the Henry VI trilogy. Some of the additions included the reference to Dame Eleanor Cobham
at I, i, 39 and the Margaret–Suffolk scenes (v, iii, 45–195; v, v).

Debate continues[1] about the possibility of dual authorship of *The Shrew*. The play, as E. P.
Kuhl mentioned incidentally,[2] has throughout a wealth of musical imagery appropriate to
a man of Shakespeare's knowledge. Actually, musical terms, both denotative and allusive, are
present to a degree 'unique at least in the nineties'.[3] Furthermore, according to Herbert and
Miss Waldo, both kinds occur in about the same proportion in the passages generally ascribed
to Shakespeare and those often attributed to a different author. In their quantity and in their
degree of complexity in allusion, as well as in their distribution, the musical terms suggest the
work of a single hand.

Certain cruxes in the texts invite endless speculation. One of these is in *Julius Caesar*,
IV, iii, 143–96, immediately after the quarrel between Brutus and Cassius. Although Brutus
has just told Cassius of Portia's death, the entrance of Messala brings up the subject again and
Brutus is heard to say that he has had no news of her. One hypothesis is that Shakespeare wrote
two versions, intending to cancel one, but that marks of deletion were ignored and all the lines
were put into print. Rejecting this, Brents Stirling[4] argues that emendation is unnecessary.
Shakespeare's intention was to show how a man, burdened with grief, attempts clumsily to
fend off expressions of sympathy and bury sorrow in concentration upon the military business
in hand. Another crux that provokes endless, and even acrimonious, debate is Hamlet's 'too
too sallied [solid, sullied] flesh' (I, ii, 129). In the opinion of Helge Kökeritz,[5] this 'defies an
unequivocal solution, because the phonological evidence is ambiguous, as is the context'.
The reading in Qq. 1, 2, 'sallied', may be an erroneous spelling of *sullied*, because of an a:o
misprint, or a phonetic spelling of *solid*, the reading of F (cf. *unsallied* in *L.L.L.* v, ii, 352 and
sallies—Q2—in *Hamlet* II, i, 39, where F has *sulleyes*). Kökeritz is confident that *sallied*, the
hypothetical past participle of an unrecorded verb, *sally* = to soil, is a phonological and morpho-
logical impossibility. Approaching the problem from a different direction, Samuel A. Weiss[6]
urges that the correct reading is *solid*. The passage in *Hamlet* has significant similarities, as others
have noted, to *2 Henry IV*, III, i, 45 ff., a play written only a year or two earlier. Weiss points
out what seem to him decisive duplications in the cluster imagery of the two speeches: Desire,

[1] Tommy Ruth Waldo and T. W. Herbert, 'Musical Terms in *The Taming of the Shrew*: Evidence of Single
Authorship', *Shakespeare Quarterly*, IX, 185–99.

[2] 'The Authorship of *The Taming of The Shrew*', *P.M.L.A.* XL (1925), 552.

[3] Figures for Shakespeare: *Two Gentlemen*, 63 allusive, 68 denotative; *L.L.L.* 39, 52; *Dream*, 24, 55; *Merchant*,
37, 37; *Shrew*, 84, 16; etc. For other dramatists of the nineties: Marlowe, *1 Tamburlaine*, 1, 23; *2 Tamburlaine*, 4, 24;
Faustus, 0, 9; *Jew of Malta*, 9, 27; Greene, *Alphonsus*, 2, 25; *Orlando Furioso*, 6, 20; *Friar Bacon*, 7, 9; Lodge and
Greene, *A Looking Glass for London*, 6, 27; Lodge, *Wounds of Civil War*, 2, 11; Chapman, *Blind Beggar*, 5, 14;
May Day, 0, 20; etc., etc.

[4] 'Brutus and the Death of Portia', *Shakespeare Quarterly*, IX, 211–17.

[5] 'This Sullied Solid Flesh', *Studia Neophilologica*, XXX, 3–10.

[6] '"Solid", "Sullied" and Mutability: A Study in Imagery', *Shakespeare Quarterly*, IX, 219–27.

Food and Garden, Time, Books, Storm, Clothes, Bitterness, and Tears. The cluster occurs, with variations, in *As You Like It* and also in *Troilus and Cressida*. The lines of *2 Henry IV*,

> O God that one might reade the booke of fate,
> And see the reuolution of the times,
> Make mountaines leuell, and the continent
> Weary of solide firmnesse melt it selfe
> Into the sea.[1]

are an eloquent commentary on the crux in *Hamlet*.

An equally controversial line is in the Hostess's description of Falstaff's death: 'His Nose was as sharpe as a Pen, and a Table of Greene fields.' The accuracy of Shakespeare's description of Falstaff's symptoms is attested by A. A. Mendilow[2] and Ephim G. Fogel,[3] but the former accepts Theobald's emendation 'babled', relating it to the delirious talk of victims of the fever, while the latter is adamant for 'Table'. The Hostess, he argues, is guilty, here as elsewhere, of an ellipsis. What she means to say is that 'his Nose was as sharpe as a Pen, and [it was] a Table of greene fields', a green or yellowish-green hue being one of the customary symptoms. S. F. Johnson[4] will have none of this. He thinks the F reading 'Table' is a misprint for 'talkt', which Theobald mentioned as a possibility, and cites in support a reverse error in Ford's *Loves Sacrifice*, II, i, the Quarto of which (1633) reads 'To grace our talks with your grave discourse'. All editors since Gifford (1827) have unhesitatingly emended to 'grace our *table*'.[5]

Although glossing and emending Shakespeare have been made easier and safer by the *O.E.D.*, there is no reason for complacency, for usages unrecorded there may be found in archival manuscripts that frequently preserve spoken, as contrasted with literary, language, and in proverbial expressions that have survived in fragmentary form. By recourse to such evidence, Miss Hilda M. Hulme attempts[6] to explain a number of readings that have caused trouble. The result is a new kind of conservatism. '...In interpreting Shakespeare's text,' she cautions, 'we should give more weight to internal evidence of context and situation than to external evidence set out in abstract in *NED*.... Apart from literal error, we might do well to suppose the original text authentic; if this text appears to offer evidence of usage outside the dictionary limits of date and locality, then it is our dictionaries, and not the text, which should change' (*Neophilologus*, XXI, 212). Among the passages discussed are such trouble makers as Escalus'

---

[1] Quoted from Q1. F, too, reads 'solide'.

[2] 'Falstaff's Death of a Sweat', *Shakespeare Quarterly*, IX, 479–83.

[3] '"A Table of Green Fields" A Defense of the Folio Reading', *Shakespeare Quarterly*, IX, 485–92.

[4] '"A Table of Green Fields" Once More', *Shakespeare Quarterly*, X, 450–1.

[5] According to Johnson, only G. B. Harrison has dared to print *talke*, though the revised Yale Shakespeare cites C. T. Prouty's advocacy of *talkt* and F. W. Bateson (*Essays in Criticism*, V, 94, and VII, 226) has written that *talked* is the obvious word.

[6] 'Three Notes on the Interpretation of Shakespeare's Text: *Sond, sond, sond, sond* (*Taming of the Shrew*, IV, i, 145); *Wee'll fit the kid-foxe with a penny worth* (*Much Ado*, II, iii, 45); *Retyres to chiding Fortune* (*Troilus and Cressida*, I, iii, 54)', *Neophilologus*, XXXI, 212–15. 'Three Notes: *Troilus and Cressida*, V, vii, 11; *Midsummer Night's Dream*, II, i, 54; *Measure for Measure*, II, i, 39', *J.E.G.P.* LVII, 721–6. 'Shakespeare of Stratford', *Review of English Studies*, X, 20–5. 'The Spoken Language and the Dramatic Text: Some Notes on the Interpretation of Shakespeare's Language', *Shakespeare Quarterly*, IX, 379–86.

'brakes of ice', Thersites' 'double-hennd sparrow' (Q, Spartan), Othello's 'yong affects In my defunct and proper satisfaction', and the expression, 'Ile go to bed at noone', of Lear's Fool.[1]

There is no direct contribution to Shakespeare studies in Robert K. Turner Jr.'s report on the printing of Qq. 1–2 of Thomas Tomkis' *Albumazar*, but some of the methods employed deserve attention.[2] Turner traces the sheets of these quartos through the press and assigns the work of type-setting to the compositors by tabulating the appearance of certain italic and roman types and noting certain consistent changes in spelling and then correlating the results with the pattern of the headlines. The quarto of *2 Henry IV* comes at once to mind, for in it there was abnormal need for italic *S*'s[3] and, when the supply of these was exhausted, the substitution of roman capitals.

[1] Valuable as the new-old readings are, they must not be accepted unhesitatingly. At *Merchant*, II, vi, 16, for example, Miss Hulme appears to prefer the F spelling *Hudg'd*, which she thinks may be 'more than a compositor's error' rather than Q's *hugd*. Her reason is that [dz] for [d] is common in Stratford archives. This is to overlook the fact that F is a reprint of Q, which was set from Shakespeare's foul sheets. If any Shakespearian spelling has survived in this line, it must be Q's *hugd*.

[2] 'Standing Type in *Albumazar*', *Library*, 5th series, XIII, 174–85. The use of standing type is an important part of the story of *Albumazar* that has no counterpart in Shakespeare quartos.

[3] See also sheet E of *The Merchant of Venice*, Q1.

BOOKS RECEIVED

[Inclusion of a book in this list does not preclude its review in a subsequent volume.]

ARMSTRONG, WILLIAM A. *The Elizabethan Private Theatres: Facts and Problems* (Society for Theatre Research Pamphlet Series, no. 6, 1957–8; London: Printed for the Society, 1958).

BARBER, C. L. *Shakespeare's Festive Comedy: A Study of Dramatic Form and its Relation to Social Custom* (Princeton University Press; London: Oxford University Press, 1959).

BONJOUR, A. *The Structure of 'Julius Caesar'* (Liverpool University Press, 1958).

BRIGGS, K. M. *The Anatomy of Puck* (London: Routledge and Kegan Paul, 1959).

BULLOUGH, G. *Narrative and Dramatic Sources of Shakespeare*, vol. II (London: Routledge and Kegan Paul, 1958).

COLERIDGE, S. T. *Coleridge's Writings on Shakespeare*, edited by Terence Hawkes (New York: G. P. Putnam's Sons, 1959).

DAVIS, H. and GARDNER, H. (editors). *Elizabethan and Jacobean Studies Presented to Frank Percy Wilson in Honour of his Seventieth Birthday* (Oxford: Clarendon Press, 1959).

GARDNER, HELEN. *The Business of Criticism* (Oxford: Clarendon Press, 1959).

HEGENBARTH, JOSEF. *Zeichnungen zu fünf Shakespeare-Dramen* (Cologne: Hoffman, 1957).

JOSEPH, B. *The Tragic Actor* (London: Routledge and Kegan Paul, 1959).

LEVIN, H. *The Question of Hamlet* (New York: Oxford University Press, 1959).

LITTLE, H. V. *The Gospel in Shakespeare* (London: Carey Kingsgate, 1959).

MERCHANT, W. M. *Shakespeare and the Artist* (Oxford University Press, 1959).

MUIR, K. *Shakespeare and the Tragic Pattern* (Annual Shakespeare Lecture of the British Academy, 1958; London: Oxford University Press, 1959).

POTTS, ABBIE F. *Shakespeare and the Faerie Queene* (Cornell University Press; London: Oxford University Press, 1959).

SABOL, A. J. *Songs and Dances for the Stuart Masque* (Providence: Brown University Press, 1959).

SHAKESPEARE, WILLIAM

(Folger Library General Reader's Shakespeare):

Julius Caesar, edited by Louis B. Wright and Virginia Lamar (New York, 1958).

Macbeth, edited by Louis B. Wright and Virginia Lamar (New York, 1959).

Romeo and Juliet, edited by Louis B. Wright and Virginia Lamar (New York, 1959).

(Penguin Shakespeare):

The Narrative Poems, edited by G. B. Harrison (London: Penguin Books, 1959).

(Shakespeare Quarto Facsimiles):

No. 12. *Richard the Third, 1597*, edited by W. W. Greg (Oxford: Clarendon Press, 1959).

(Translations):

KOSTETZKY, E. G. *Romeo and Juliet* (Munich: Ukrainian Shakespeare Society, 1957).

KOSTETZKY, E. G. *The Sonnets* (Munich: Ukrainian Shakespeare Society, 1958).

SEVIN, N. *Venedik Taciri*, and *Julius Caezar* (Ankara: Maarif Basimevi, 1958).

TARNAWSKI, W. *Burza* (reprint edited by S. Helsztyński; Wrocław: Ossolinski, 1958).

(Bibliography):

HAHN, WIKTOR. *Shakespeare w Polsce* (Wrocław, 1958).

BOOKS RECEIVED

SHARPE, R. B. *Irony in the Drama* (North Carolina University Press; London: Oxford University Press, 1959).

SIMPSON, R. R. *Shakespeare and Medicine* (Edinburgh: E. and S. Livingstone, 1959).

VYVYAN, JOHN. *The Shakespearean Ethic* (London: Chatto and Windus, 1959).

WADSWORTH, F. W. *The Poacher from Stratford* (Berkeley and Los Angeles: University of California Press; London: Cambridge University Press, 1959).

INDEX

Aaron, Stephen, 134
Adams, J. C., 114, 120, 122, 123, 132
　　The Globe Playhouse, 119, 120, 121
Adams, J. Q., 163
　　Chief Pre-Shakespearean Dramas, 48 n.
　　Life of Shakespeare, 88 n.
Aeschylus
　　Agamemnon, 20
　　Prometheus Bound, 70
Ahrenson, Rene, 131
Airamo, Hemmo, 126
Akrigg, G. P. V., 159
Aksimova-Vulf, I., 133
Akutagawa, Hiroshi, 130
Alden, John, 124
Alexander, Peter, *The Heritage Shakespeare* reviewed, 163
Allen, A. R., 103 n., 105 n.
Allen, D. C., *Studies in Honor of T. W Baldwin*, 152 n.
Alleyn, Edward, 111, 112
Alleyn, Joan, 112
Allio, René, 127
Alterman, Nathan, 129
Andersen, Ludwig, 125
Andrews, Keith, 80 n.
Anikst, A., 133
Annesley, Brian, 30
Aristotle, 28, 151
Armstrong, Louis, 142
Arnold, Matthew, 63, 68
Arthos, John, 151
Arthur, H. H. G., 105 n.
Atkins, Robert, 134
Australia, report on Shakespeare in, 124
Austria, report on Shakespeare in, 124

Bacon, Sir Nicholas, 104 n.
Baddeley, Angela, 141
Bailey, Benjamin, 62, 64
Bailey, F. A., 104 n.
Baker, Arthur E., *A Shakespeare Commentary*, 44, 47 n.
Baker, Ernest, 104 n.
Baldini, Gabriele, 130
Baldwin, T. W., *William Shakespeare's Small Latine and Lesse Greeke*, 89 n.
Barish, J. A., 152
Barnes, Barnabe, *The Devil's Charter*, 118
Barroll, J. Leeds, 155
Barry, Bruce, 124
Barry, James, 75, 76
Bartini, Gari, 129

Bartlett, John, *Concordance to Shakespeare*, 44
Baskervill, C. R., *The Elizabethan Jig*, 123 n.
Bateson, F. W., 168 n.
Bath, Marquis of, *see* Thynne, Henry
Baudissin, Wolf Graf, 124
Beaumont, Francis, 103
Beaumont, Francis and Fletcher, John
　　A King and No King, 119
　　Philaster, 119
　　The Captain, 116
　　Wit at Several Weapons, 114
Becker, Maria, 128
Bedford, twelfth Duke of, *see* Russell, Hastings
Beethoven, Ludwig van, 70
Belgium, report on Shakespeare in, 125
Bellamy and Robarts, 76
Benedek, Marcell, 129
Bentall, Michael, 134, 135
Bentley, G. E., *The Jacobean and Caroline Stage*, 123 n.
Berger, Ludwig, 128
Bernheimer, Richard, 159
Berry, Francis, *Poets' Grammar* reviewed, 152
Bessenyei, Ferenc, 129
Bethell, S. L., 148
Betterton, Thomas, 113
Birkinshaw, Philip, 131
Bjerke, André, 130
Blake, William, 76
Blatchley, John, 127
Bleeck, Peter van, 74
Bloch, Eduard, 80 n.
Blount, Edward, 165
Bondarenko, F., 133
Bonjour, Adrien, 131, 132
　　The Structure of Julius Caesar, 132; reviewed, 147
Bonnard, Georges, 164
Bor, Matej, 140
Bowman, J., 113
Bradbrook, M. C., 153, 158
Bradshaigh, Elizabeth, 92, 94, 95, 96
Bradshaigh, James, 92
Bradshaigh, Mary, 92, 94
Bradshaigh, Roger (1577–1641), 92, 94
Bradshaigh, Sir Roger (1628–84), 92, 93, 94, 96, 98, 104 n.
Bradshaigh, Sir Roger (1649–86), 92, 94
Bradshaigh, Sir Roger (1675–1747), 92
Brady, Leo, 125
Bradley, A. C., 1, 2, 4, 5, 11, 14, 17, 33, 69
　　Shakespearean Tragedy, 10 n., 18 n., 19 n., 45
Brathwait, Richard, *Whimsies, or A New Cast of Characters*, 114

INDEX

Brecht, Bertolt, 127
Bridge, Sir Frederick, *The Old Cryes of London*, 110 n.
Bridge, Tony Van, 126
Bridgewater, second Earl of, *see* Egerton, John
Bright, Timothy, 38
   A Treatise of Melancholy, 40 n.
Brissoni, Alessandro, 129
Brockbank, J. P., 149
Brome, Richard, *Lare Lancashire Witches* (with Heywood, Thomas), 114, 120
Brook, Peter, 70
Brooks, Cleanth, 146
Brown, Ford Madox, 78, 79
Brown, J. R., 166
Buccleuch, eighth Duke of, *see* Montague-Douglas-Scott, Walter
Buckingham, Duke of, *see* Villiers, George
Buckley, Keith, 124
Bucknill, J. C., 33
   Remarks on the Medical Knowledge of Shakespeare, 30, 39 n.
Bukhman, N., 132
Bulgaria, report on Shakespeare in, 125
Bullough, Geoffrey, *Narrative and Dramatic Sources of Shakespeare*, vol. II reviewed, 157
Burbage, Richard, 116
Burchanov, Sh., 132
Burgersdyk, L. J., 125
Burghley, Lord, *see* Cecil, William
Burney, E. F., 75
Burnim, Kalman, 80 n., 159
Bush, Geoffrey, *Shakespeare and the Natural Condition*, 10 n.
Byrne, Muriel St Clare, 160
Byron, Lord George, 49

Caddy, William, 94, 95
Cadell, Thomas, 75, 76
Calderón De La Barca, Pedro, *La vida es sueño*, 129
Caldwell, Zoe, 124, 142
Calvin, Jean, 148
Campbell, Douglas, 125
Campion, Thomas, 106
Canada, report on Shakespeare in, 125
Cardenio, 157
Carey, Denis, 125, 126
Carr, H., 110 n.
Castelnuovo-Tedesco, Mario, 129
Cecil, William, Lord Burghley, 95, 104 n.
Chamberlain, J., *Letters*, 110 n.
Chambers, Sir E. K., 114, 156, 160
   The Elizabethan Stage, 123 n., 159
Chambers, R. W., *W. P. Ker Memorial Lecture: King Lear*, 18 n.
Chapman, George
   Blind Beggar, 167 n.
   May Day, 167 n.

Charell, Erik, 145 n.
Charles II, King, 109
Charnock, Ralph, 104 n.
Charnock, Roger, 104 n.
Chaucer, Geoffrey, 158
Chekhov, Anton, *The Seagull*, 151
Chettle, Henry and Munday, Anthony, *The Downfall of Robert Earl of Huntingdon*, 107
Cibber, Mrs C., 74
Cinthio, Giraldi, 84
   Epitia, 157
   Hecatomnithi, 88 n.
Clarke, Mary Cowden, 77
Claudius Tiberius Nero, 121
Clausen, Claus, 128
Clemen, Wolfgang, 128, 129
Closson, Herman, 125
Cluny, Alain, 127
Cokayne, G. D., *Complete Baronetage*, 103 n.
Coleridge, Samuel Taylor, 50, 62, 63, 151
Colquhoun, Robert, 79, 80
Condell, Henry, 166
Cooke, Juliet, 138
Copeland, Dolley, 93
Copland, R., *The Highway to the Spital-House*, 103
Copley, Anthony, *Witts Fittes*, 158
Craig, Hardin, 42, 47 n.
Crane, Ralph, 164
Crawford, Earls of, *see* Lindsay, Alexander, James *and* David
Croft, Michael, 135
Cromek, R. H., 75
Crow, John, 146
Cutts, John P., 157, 161
Czechoslovakia, report on Shakespeare in, 126

Dahinten, Gisela, *Die Geisterszene in der Tragödie vor Shakespeare* reviewed, 155–6
Danby, J. F., *Shakespeare's Doctrine of Nature*, 18 n., 47 n.
Dandridge Sisters, The, 142
Daniel, P. A., 48 n.
Daniel, Samuel, 158
Dante Alighieri, *La Divina Commedia*, 70
Davenant, William, 137, 138, 145
   The Cruel Brother, 120
   The Cruelty of the Spaniards in Peru, 120
   The First Day's Entertainment, 120
   The Siege of Rhodes, 120
   The Unfortunate Lovers, 120
   See also Dryden, John
Davenport, Robert, *A New Trick to Cheat the Devil*, 120
Davies, C. W., 151
Deering, Richard, 107
Dekker, Thomas, 33, 103, 107
   The Honest Whore I, 33, 36, 39 n.
   The Sun's Darling (with Ford, John), 120

Delacroix, Eugéne, 78
Delaram, Francis, 101, 102
De Loutherbourg, P. J., 75
De Lullo, Giorgio, 129
De Madariaga, Salvador, *see* Madariaga, Salvador de
Demay, Henry, 127
De Nobili, Lila, 143
Deschamps, Jean, 128
Devine, George, 79, 80
De Witt, Johannes, Swan Theatre drawing, 113, 119, 120
Dilke, C. W., 66
Disney, Walt, 142
Double Falsehood, 157
Douce, Francis, 78
   Illustrations of Shakespeare, 105 n.
Drayton, Michael, 106
Dryden, John, 137, 138, 139, 140, 145, 146
   The Tempest: or the Enchanted Island (with Davenant, William), 137, 139, 142; production at Old Vic reviewed, 137–40
Dudley, Robert, first Earl of Leicester, 95, 104 n.
Dugdale, W., 103 n., 104 n.
Du Guernier, Louis, 73, 74
Dürer, Albrecht, 75, 80 n.
Duthie, G. I., 18 n.

Edinborough, Arnold, 161
Edwards, E., 75
Edwards, Philip, 149, 162
Egerton, John, second Earl of Bridgewater, 109
Ehrl, Charlotte, *Sprachstil und Charakter bei Shakespeare* reviewed, 153
Eliot, T. S., 30, 148
Elizabeth I, Queen, 37, 40 n., 104 n., 155
Elizabeth II, Queen, 130
Elliot, Eleanor, 124
Elliott, G. R., *Dramatic Providence in 'Macbeth'* reviewed, 147–8
Ellis-Fermor, Una, 146
Emmerson, Ian, 134, 136
Empson, William, 17
   The Structure of Complex Words, 18 n., 19 n., 39 n.
Enright, D. J., 150
Erasmus, Desiderius, *Colloquia*, 88, 89 n.
Esmein, A., *Le Marriage en Droit Canonique*, 89 n.
Evans, Edith, 140, 142
Evans, Henry, *see* Leyris, Pierre

Fairfax-Lucy, Alice, *Charlecote and the Lucys* reviewed, 154
Falckenberg, Otto, 128
Falk, Rossella, 129
Farquhar, H., 110 n.
Fenton, Richard, 75
Ferrero, Mario, 129

Ficino, Marsilio, 158
Finch, Arthur, 105 n.
Finkel, Simon, 129
Finland, report on Shakespeare in, 126
Finn, Christine, 137
Fischer, S., Rowohlt and Goldmann, 128
Flatter, Richard, 124, 157
Fletcher, John, 38, 117, 162
   Love's Pilgrimage, 116
   The Double Marriage, 116
   The Honest Man's Fortune, 120
   The Prophetess (with Massinger, Philip), 122
   The Two Noble Kinsmen, 38, 157
   See also Beaumont, Francis
Flower, Barbara, 165 n.
Fludd, Robert, 159
Foà, Arnoldo, 129
Foakes, R. A., 105 n.
Fogel, E. G., 168
Ford, John
   Love's Sacrifice, 168
   See also Dekker, Thomas
Four Plays in One, 120
France, report on Shakespeare in, 127
French, Leslie, 131, 135
Fripp, E. I., *Shakespeare: Man and Artist*, 88 n.
Fukada, Tsuneari, 130
Furness, H. H., Variorum edition of *King Lear*, 10 n., 39 n.
Furse, Roger, 79
Fuseli, J. H., 75, 76

Galitskii, V., 133
Gardner, Gordon, 138
Gardner, Helen, *The Business of Criticism* reviewed, 146
Garrick, David, 74, 75, 80 n., 159
Garrivier, Raymond, 127
Gee, N. C., 105
Geoffrey of Monmouth, 41, 44, 46
   Histories of the Kings of Britain, 44
George III, King, 40 n.
Germany, report on Shakespeare in, 128
Gesta Romanorum, 41, 44, 46
Gheeraedts, M., 104 n.
Gibbons, Orlando, 107, 110 n.
Gielgud, Sir John, 79
Gierow, Karl Ragnar, 131
Gifford, H., 168
Gilbert, Sir John, 77, 80 n.
Gillhouley, James, 135
Godwin, William, 76
Goethe, J. W. von, 148
Gökcer, Cüneyt, 132
Golding, Arthur, translation of Ovid's *Metamorphoses*, 39 n.

Goldsmith, R. H., 155, 164
  Wise Fools in Shakespeare, 39 n.
Goodman, Benny, 142
Gorboduc, 42, 43, 44, 45, 46, 47, 48 n.
Gorvin, Joana Maria, 128
Gosson, Stephen, 159
Granville, George, 138
Granville-Barker, H., 17
  Prefaces to Shakespeare: First Series, 18 n.
Gravelot, H. F. B., 73, 80 n.
Green, John, 154
Greene, Robert
  A Looking Glass for London (with Lodge, Thomas),
    167 n.
  Alphonsus, 122, 167 n.
  Friar Bacon, 73, 167 n.
  Orlando Furioso, 167 n.
Greg, W. W., 165
  A Bibliography of English Printed Drama to the Restoration,
    163
  Henslowe Papers 111, 112 n.
  The Editorial Problem in Shakespeare, 162
  The Shakespeare First Folio, 123 n., 162
Grieve, Thomas, 80 n.
Griffith, W., 110 n.
Guernier, Louis du, *see* Du Guernier, Louis
Guerrieri, Gerardo, 129
Guthrie, Tyrone, 129, 140, 141, 142, 145, 163

Hahn, Wiktor, *Shakespeare w Polsce* reviewed, 154
Hale, John, 136
Halkin, Simon, 129
Hall, John, 75
Hall, Peter, 135, 142, 143, 144, 145
Halliwell-Phillips, J. O., 163
  Outlines of the Life of Shakespeare, 88 n.
Hämäläinen, Ekke, 126
Hamilton, Lionel, 134
Hanmer, Sir Thomas, 73, 74, 80 n.
Hanuš, Jan, 126
Harbage, Alfred, 165
Harding, D. P., 86, 88 n., 89 n.
Harding, Edward, 76
Hardy, Barbara, 151
Hardy, Robert, 140
Harker, J., 79
Harrington, William, 83
  Commendacions of matrymony, 83, 88 n.
Harris, Bernard, 155
Harrison, G. B., 165, 168 n.
Harsnett, Samuel, 34, 36, 39
  A Declaration of Egregious Popish Impostures, 39
Harvey, Gabriel, 110 n.
Harvey, G. H., 78, 80 n.
Harwood, Frank, 135
Hatton, Sir Christopher, 104 n.

Hauser, Frank, 135
Hawes, Craven, 79
Hawkes, A. J., 103 n.
Hawkes, Terry, 153, 158
Haydon, Benjamin Robert, 61, 68 n.
Hayman, Francis, 73, 74, 80 n., 159
Heilman, R. B., *This Great Stage*, 18 n.
Helpmann, Robert, 80
Helsztyński, Stanisław, 154
Heming, John, 166
Hemingway, S. B., 163
Henry VIII, King, 37, 40 n., 76, 105 n.
Henslowe, Philip, 111, 112, 160
Hepton, Bernard, 134
Herbert, T. W., 167
Herbert, William, Earl of Pembroke, 155
Herlie, Eileen, 125
Herrick, Robert, 106
Heywood, Thomas, 100
  A Maidenhead Well Lost, 99, 100, 102
  Fair Maid of the Exchange, 105 n.
  Fortune by Land and Sea (with Rowley, William), 122
  Rape of Lucrece, 107
  See also Brome, Richard
Higgins, George, 103 n.
Higgins, John, *Queen Cordila*, 41, 44, 45, 46
Hill, R. F., 152
Hilliard, Nicholas, 104 n., 143
Hindley, Charles, *History of the Cries of London*, 110 n.
Hinman, C. K., 161, 164
Hoby, Sir Edward, 156
Hodges, C. Walter, *The Globe Restored*, 120, 123 n.
Hodges, M. K., 104 n., 105 n.
Hoffmann, Friedrich, 156
Hogan, C. B., *Shakespeare in the Theatre*, 145 n.
Holbein, Hans the Younger, 76
Holinshed, Raphael, 30, 41, 44, 45, 46
Holland, Norman N., 161
Holland, Philomen, translation of Pliny, 158
Holles, G., *Memorials of the Holles Family, 1439–1656*, 104 n.
Holm, Ian, 144
Homer, 61
Hooper, John, 87
  Later Writings of Bishop Hooper, 89 n.
Hoppe, Harry, 163
Hornyold-Strickland, H., 105 n.
Horton, Priscilla, 77
Hosley, Richard, 160
Hotson, Leslie, 73, 97, 98
  Shakespeare's Motley, 80 n., 104 n., 105 n.
  The Commonwealth and Restoration Stage, 120
Houghton, Alexander, 104 n.
Howard, Frank, 75, 76
  *The Spirit of the Plays of Shakespeare, Exhibited in a Series
    of Outline Plates*, 76
Hubler, Edward, 148

Huddleston, Bridget, 92, 104 n.
Huddleston, Sir Ferdinand, 92, 97, 104 n.
Huddleston, Sir William, 92, 104 n.
Hulme, Hilda, 154, 168, 169 n.
Hungary, report on Shakespeare in, 129
Hunt, Hugh, 124
Hunt, Leigh, 59, 65, 68 n.
Hunter, G. K., 163
Hurry, Leslie, 79
Hutchinson, Robin, 105 n.
Hutchinson, W., *The History of the County of Cumberland*, 104 n.
Hutchison, Neil, 124
Hyde, John, 135

Inchbald, Elizabeth, 139
Irving, Sir Henry, 79
Israel, report on Shakespeare in, 129
Italy, report on Shakespeare in, 129

Jacob, Rik, 125
Jacquot, Jean, 160
Jaggard, Isaac, 163, 166
James I, King, 104 n.
James, D. G., 17, 18, 30
  The Dream of Learning, 18 n., 19 n.
  The Life of Reason, 39 n.
James, Finlay, 139
Japan, report on Shakespeare in, 130
Jennen, Charles, 74
Jewkes, Wilfred T., *Act Division in Elizabethan and Jacobean Plays*, 117
Johan Johan, 153
Johnson, Gloria E., 161
Johnson, S. F., 168
Jonson, Ben, 153
  Bartholomew Fair, 107
  Cynthia's Revels, 123 n.
  Epicœne, 120
  Everyman out of his Humour, 102, 116
  The Alchemist, 130
Jorden, Edward, *Brief Discourse of a Disease Called the Suffocation of the Mother*, 34
Jouve, Pierre Jean, 154
Judges, A. V., *The Elizabethan Underworld*, 105 n.
Jurkka, Jussi, 126

Kaděrávek, Emil, 126
Karapetian, O., 132
Kasimov, N., 132
Kaufman, Edward K., 156 n.
Kean, Charles, 77, 78
Kean, Edmund, 77
Keats, John, 58–68
  Endymion, 59, 61, 65
  Hyperion, 66, 67

On sitting down to read King Lear once again, 64
On the Sea, 58–9
Poems 1817, 59
To Autumn, 66
Keats, Thomas, 59, 66
Kemble, John Philip, 76, 139, 145 n.
Kenter, Yildiz, 132
Keynes, Sir Geoffrey, 76
Khodshaev, K., 132
King Leir, 30, 41, 43, 44, 45, 48 n., 158
Kirkman, Francis, *The Witts* frontispiece, 114, 115
Kiss, Ferenc, 129
Klatzkin, Raphael, 129
Knight, Charles, *Pictorial Shakespeare*, 77, 78, 80 n.
Knight, G. Wilson, 146, 148
  The Sovereign Flower reviewed, 147
Knights, L. C., 81, 84
Kökeritz, Helge, 167
Kortner, Fritz, 128
Kostetzk, E. G.
  translation of *Romeo and Juliet* reviewed, 154
  translation of *Sonnets* reviewed, 154
Krauss, Werner, 124
Kuznetson, V., 133
Kyd, Thomas, *The Spanish Tragedy*, 33

Lady Alimony, 123
Lafforgue, R., 127
Laine, Edvin, 126
LaMar, Virginia A., 165
Lamb, Charles, 5, 80
  Tales from Shakespeare, 76
Lamentable Song of the Death of King Lear and his Three Daughters, A, 41, 44, 45, 46, 47
Langham, Michael, 125
Langland, William, *Piers Plowman*, 106
Laseur, producer at Haagse Comedie, 130
Lasso, Orlando di, 161
Laugh and Lie Downe, 103
Laughton, Charles, 144
Lawrence, Jordan, 135
Lawrence, L. A., 110 n.
Lawrence, W. J.
  The Elizabethan Playhouse, 113, 123 n.
  Pre-Restoration Stage Studies, 123 n.
Lawrence, W. W., 88 n., 153
Leach, Francis, 110 n.
LeClaire, Guy, 124
Leech, Clifford, 149, 152, 156, 166
Lehto, Leo, 126
Leicester, first Earl of, *see* Dudley, Robert
Leigh, Vivien, 70
Leyris, Pierre and Evans, Henry, *Œuvres Complètes de Shakespeare* reviewed, 153–4
Libraries
  Birmingham Public, 77, 80 n.

Libraries (*cont.*)
  Bodleian, 109, 165
  Bridgewater, 108–9, 110 n.
  British Museum, 80 n., 105 n., 107, 108, 109, 110 n., 165
  Folger, 74, 80 n., 105 n., 159, 163
  Huntington, 108, 109, 110 n.
  John Rylands, 104 n., 105 n.
  Pepys, 106, 108, 109
  University College, Cardiff, 80 n.
  Victoria and Albert Museum, 80 n.
  Wigan Public, 105 n.
Liliev, N., 125
Lindsay, Alexander, twenty-fifth Earl of Crawford, 92, 104 n.
Lindsay, David, twenty-eighth Earl of Crawford, 90, 105 n.
Lindsay, James, twenty-fourth Earl of Crawford, 92, 96
Lindtberg, Leopold, 124, 125
Locrine, 156
Lodge, Thomas
  Wounds of Civil War, 167 n.
  See also Greene, Robert
Lodovici, Caesare Vico, 129
Lomax, Harry, 135
London Lickpenny, 106
Love's Changelings Change, 120
Lucy, Sir Thomas, 154
Lullo, Giorgio de, *see* De Lullo, Giorgio
Lupton, Donald, *London and the Country Carbonadoed*, 106
Lydgate, John, 160
Lyons, Clifford P., 153

Maas, Paul, *Textual Criticism* reviewed, 165
Macready, William Charles, 77, 80 n.
Madariaga, Salvador de, 148
Maeterlinck, Maurice, 30, 31
  Life and Flowers, 39 n.
Maitland, F. W., *see* Pollock, F.
Major, T., 129
Malleson, Miles, 139
Malone, Edmund, 113
Manning, Barbara, 124
Marlowe, Christopher
  Dr Faustus, 167 n.
  Jew of Malta, 167 n.
  Tamburlaine, 156, 166, 167 n.
Marston, John
  Antonio and Mellida, 156
  Antonio's Revenge, 156
  Sophonisba, 113
  The Malcontent, 116, 119
Mary, Queen, 104 n.
Mason, W., *Caractacus*, 49

Massinger, Philip
  A Very Woman, 115
  The Bashful Lover, 115
  The Bondman, 120
  The City Madam, 115, 120
  The Duke of Milan, 115
  The Emperor of the East, 115
  The Fatal Dowry, 115, 120
  The Guardian, 115
  The Roman Actor, 115, 120
  See also Fletcher, John
Mauri, Glauco, 130
Maurstad, Toralv, 130
May, Val, 134
McArdell, J., 74
McCallin, Clement, 124
McDougall, Roger, 124
McKelvey, John, 134
McKenzie, D. F., 166
McKerrow, R. B., 163
McLure, N. E., 110 n.
McManaway, J. G., 156, 163
McNeal, Thomas, H., 158
Mendilow, A. A., 168
Merchant, W. M., 80 n., 160
  Shakespeare and the Artist, 80 n.; reviewed, 158–9
Meri, G., 133
Meskin, Aaron, 129
Messalaar, Gerard, 130
Messalina, title-page engraving, 114, 115, 120
Middleton, Thomas, 117
  A Chaste Maid in Cheapside, 113, 119
  The Spanish Gipsy (with Rowley, William), 120
  The Witch, 157
Mikhoels, S., 133
Milton, John, 58, 65, 105 n.
  Paradise Lost, 62, 65
Minetti, Bernhard, 128
Mirror for Magistrates, A, 30
Moiseiwitsch, Tanya, 129
Monnet, Gabriel, 160
Montague-Douglas-Scott, Walter, eighth Duke of Buccleuch, 104 n.
Moody, John, 134, 135
Mordvinov, N., 133
Morgan, Priscilla, 141
Mörk, Lennart, 131
Morris, B. R., 156
Morris, Harry, 156
Moudoués, Rose-Marie, 128
Muir, Kenneth, 39 n., 40 n., 132, 157, 158, 162
  Shakespeare's Sources, 157
Mulready, William, 76
Munday, Anthony
  Fedele and Fortunio, 116
  See also Chettle, Henry

Munro, J. J., *The London Shakespeare* reviewed, 162–3
Murray, Henry, 92
Myriell, Thomas, 107

Nagler, A. M., *Shakespeare's Stage* reviewed, 160
Nestroy, Johann, 125
Netherlands, The, report on Shakespeare in, 130
Newton, Mrs Eric, 80 n.
Nicholls, Anthony, 142, 144
Nicoll, Allardyce, 128, 159
    The English Theatre, 114
Nijhoff, Martinus, 130
Nobili, Lila de, *see* De Nobili, Lila
Noguchi, Isamu, 79
Norman, A. M. Z., 158
Norway, report on Shakespeare in, 130
Nosworthy, J. M., 161

Obertello, Alfredo, 130
Ognyanov, Lyubomir, 125
Okes, Nicholas, 99
Oliver, H. J., 164
Olivier, Sir Lawrence, 70, 79, 128, 161
O'Riordan, Adam, 135
Orwell, George, 31
    Selected Essays, 39 n.
Ost, Geoffrey, 134
Otway, Thomas, 38
    Venice Preserved, 38
Overton, Henry, 110 n.
Overton, John, 109, 110 n.
Ovid, 36
    Art of Love, 159
    Metamorphoses (trans. Golding), 39 n.

Paavola, Jouko, 126
Pafford, J. H. P., 152
Palmer, W. T., *The Verge of Western Lakeland*, 104 n.
Parenti, Franco, 129
Parry, Natasha, 138
Partridge, Bernard, 79
Patch, Cardinal Wolsey's Fool, 100, 104 n.
Paul, Henry N., *The Royal Play of 'Macbeth'*, 40 n., 163
Paul, St, *Epistle to the Romans*, 84
Payne, R., 134
Peele, George, *Soliman and Perseda*, 110 n.
Pembroke, Earl of, *see* Herbert, William
Pennington, Heloise, 97
Pennington, John, Lord Muncaster, 92
Pennington, Joseph, 92, 93
Pennington, Maria Margaret Frances, 92
Pennington, Nicholas, 93, 94
Pennington, William (d. 1652), 92
Pennington, Sir William (1655–1730), 92, 93, 96, 104 n.
Pennington-Ramsden, Sir William, 90, 104 n., 105 n.

Pepys, Samuel, 108, 113, 119
Percy, Bishop Thomas, *Reliques of Ancient English Poetry*, 47 n.
Percy, William, *The Faerie Pastoral*, 120
Perkins, William, 85
    Christian Oeconomie, 88 n.
Phelps, Samuel, 77
Phialas, Peter G., 156
Philip, Prince, 130
Philip II, King, 104 n.
Pierfederico, Tonino, 129
Piper, David, 105 n.
Pizer, Lois D., 156 n.
Planchon, René, 127
Pleasant History of the Life and Death of Will Summers, A, 99, 101, 102, 105 n.
Pliny, *see* Holland, Philomen
Plummer, Christopher, 125
Plutarch, 61, 151
Pollard, A. W. and Redgrave, G. R., *A Short-Title Catalogue*, 109
Pollock, F. and Maitland, F. W., *The History of English Law*, 88 n.
Polonsky, Norma, 124
Pope, Alexander, translation of Homer, 61
Potts, Abbie Findlay, *Shakespeare and the Faerie Queene* reviewed, 157–8
Poussin, Nicolas, 158
Preston, Elizabeth, 92
Preston, Thomas, 92
Price, Cecil, 68 n.
Pricke, R., 109
Productions of Shakespeare's plays, *see* Shakespeare, William, plays
Prouty, Charles T., 165, 168 n.
Prucha, Jaroslav, 126
Purcell, Henry, 137
Pythagoras, 36

Quayle, Anthony, 70

Racine, Jean, 151
Raimund, Ferdinand, 125
Ranin, Matti, 126
Ravenscroft, Thomas
    Deuteromelia, 107, 110 n.
    Melismata, 107
    Pammelia, 107
Ravid, Shoshanna, 129
Rawling, Henry, 94
Redgrave, G. R., *see* Pollard, A. W.
Rees, B., 134
Rees-Jones, S., 105 n.
Reinhardt, Max, 142, 145 n.
Rembrandt van Rijn, 75
Renard, Christopher, 135

Rétoré, Guy, 127

Reynolds, George F., *The Staging of Elizabethan Plays at the Red Bull Theater*, 122–3

Reynolds, Jane, 68 n.

Reynolds, John Hamilton, 58, 61, 68 n.

Reynolds, Sir Joshua, 80 n.

Richardson, Tony, 135, 140

Ridler, Anne, 148 n.

Riuttu, Leo, 126

Rivington, F. and C., *Shakespeare*, 75

Roach, John, 76

Robards, Jason, Jr., 125

Robarts, *see* Bellamy

Robin, Armand, 154

Rogers, Paul, 124

Romney, George, 80 n.

Rosati, Salvatore, *Il Giro Della Ruota* reviewed, 147

Ross, Lawrence J., 156

Rostova, I., 133

Rothe, Hans, 128, 131, 140

Rothwell, W. F., 116

Rott, Adolf, 124

Rowe, Nicholas, 73

Rowlands, S., *Greene's Ghost*, 110 n.

Rowlandson, Thomas, 108

Rowley, William
   A Shoemaker a Gentleman, 113, 119
   See also Webster, John *and* Heywood, Thomas

Roxana, title-page drawing, 113

Runciman, Alexander, 74, 75

Runciman, John, 74, 75, 76

Rush, David, 134

Russell, Hastings, twelfth Duke of Bedford, 104 n.

Rylands, George, 163

Rylands, John, 138

Sabol, Andrew J., *Songs and Dances for the Stuart Masque* reviewed, 161

Sahinbas, Irfan, 132

Salingar, L. G., 153

Sandby, Paul, 108

Saudek, E. A., 126

Scase, David, 134, 136

Scharf, George, *Recollections of the Scenic Effects of Covent Garden Theatre, 1838–9*, 77

Schiavonetti, Luigi, 76

Schiller, J. C. F. von, 128

Schirmer, Walter F., 128

Schlegel, A. W. von, and Tieck, Ludwig, translation of Shakespeare, 131

Schluter, Kurt, *Shakespeares Dramatische Erzählkunst* reviewed, 153

Schrevelius, Cornelius, 88

Schücking, L. L., 32, 33
   Character Problems in Shakespeare's Plays, 10 n., 39 n.

Scott, Reginald, 39

Scott, Richard, 134

Scott, William, 136

Seale, Douglas, 134, 135, 136, 139

Secchi, Nicolò, *L'Interesse*, 157

Sehrt, Ernst Theodor, 128

Selden, John, 166

Seldes, Gilbert, 145 n.

Semmelroth, Wilhelm, 128

Sen, Sailendra Kumar, 151

Seng, Peter J., 161

Sevin, Nureddin
   Julius Caezar reviewed, 154
   Venedik Taciri reviewed, 154

Shaaber, M. A., 163

Shakerley, Sir Geoffrey, 92

Shakerley, Katherine, 92

Shakerley, Peter, 92, 94, 104 n.

Shakespeare, Joan, 39 n.

Shakespeare, Mary, 39 n.

Shakespeare, William
  plays
   All's Well, 31, 39 n., 118, 147; productions, 128, at Memorial Theatre (1959), 140–2; Arden edition reviewed, 163–4
   Antony and Cleopatra, 1, 41, 50, 118, 133, 151, 158; productions, 132, 136; translation, 130
   As You Like It, 157, 168; productions, 124, 126, 128, 131, 134, 135
   Comedy of Errors, 30, 39
   Coriolanus, 1, 151, 158; production, 145; translation, 130
   Cymbeline, 149
   Hamlet, 1, 7, 8, 9, 30, 31, 38, 39 n., 49, 50, 58, 64, 69, 78, 79, 80, 146, 148, 149, 151, 152, 156, 160, 161, 167, 168; productions, 124, 128, 132, 133, 134, 135, 136; translation, 130
   1 Henry IV, 41, 120, 152, 163; productions, 124, 125, 127, 134
   2 Henry IV, 156, 161, 163, 167, 168, 169; production, 134
   Henry V, 41; productions, 124, 134
   Henry VI (3 parts), 41, 116, 120, 156, 158, 165, 166
   Henry VIII, 74, 119, 120, 149, 158, 160, 162; production, 135; Arden edition, 105 n.
   John, 30; productions, 127, 134
   Julius Caesar, 30, 41, 116, 118, 147, 160, 167; productions, 126, 131, 135; translations, 129, 130, 132, 154
   Lear, passim; criticism, 1–10, 11–19, 20–9, 30–9, 147, 152, 165; costumes and illustration, 72–80; imagery, 41–7; influence on Keats, 58–68; productions, 69, 74, 75, 76, 77, 79, 124, 125, 126, 127, 128, 129, 132, 133, 134, 145; sources, 30, 39, 41–7, 107; staging, 69–71, 75, 159, 161; style, 49–57; translation, 126
   Love's Labour's Lost, 167; production, 134

Shakespeare, William, plays (*cont.*)

   Macbeth, 17, 20, 30, 37, 38, 40 n., 49, 69, 81, 118, 146, 148, 151, 152, 157, 160, 163; productions, 126, 127, 130, 132, 134, 135, 136; Folger General Reader's edition, 165; translation, 154

   Measure for Measure, 31, 81–9, 116, 153; productions, 124, 131; translation, 130

   Merchant of Venice, 138, 166, 167 n., 169 n.; productions, 124, 125, 129, 130, 132, 134, 135; translation, 154

   Merry Wives of Windsor, 153, 157; productions, 129, 132, 133

   Midsummer Night's Dream, 119, 167 n.; productions, 125, 126, 127, 128, 130, 131, 132, 135, 136, at Memorial Theatre (1959), 142–5; Folger General Reader's edition, 165

   Much Ado, 153, 157; productions, 125, 128, 131, 132, 134, 135

   Othello, 7, 9, 20, 49, 50, 58, 69, 116, 118, 148, 149, 151, 155, 158, 159; productions, 125, 126, 128, 129, 132, 135; translation, 154

   Pericles, 38, 58, 149, 162; production, 135; Penguin edition reviewed, 165

   Richard II, 41, 153, 156; productions, 124, 127, 131

   Richard III, 41, 156; Shakespeare Quarto Facsimile reviewed, 164–5; production, 131

   Romeo and Juliet, 7, 8, 58, 153; productions, 125, 126, 129, 134, 135, 136; translations, 130, 154

   Taming of the Shrew, 153, 167 and n.; productions, 125, 128, 130, 131, 132, 135

   Tempest, 30, 39 n., 58, 59, 61, 137–8, 139, 142; productions, 70, 127, 128, 130; Dryden's adaptation, 137–40; translation, 154

   Timon of Athens, 1, 31, 49–50, 51, 52, 158, 160; Arden edition reviewed, 164

   Titus Andronicus, 30, 156; productions, 70, 124

   Troilus and Cressida, 31, 43, 156, 157, 158, 168; productions, 132, 135

   Twelfth Night, 30, 39, 153, 159; Pelican edition reviewed, 165; productions, 125, 128, 131, 132, 134, 135

   Two Gentlemen of Verona, 167 n.

   Winter's Tale, 107, 119, 149; productions, 125, 126, 131, 132

  poems

   Passionate Pilgrim, 161, 163

   Sonnets, 31, 155; translations, 126, 130, 154

Shakespeare's England, 83, 88 n.

Shapiro, I. A., 156

Sharpe, Ella Freeman, *Collected Papers on Psycho-Analysis*, 30, 39 n.

Shaw, Glen Byam, 134, 135

Sheridan, Richard, 38

Shroeder, John W., *The Great Folio of 1623*, 163 n., 164

Siddons, Sarah, 76

Sidney, Sir Philip, *Arcadia*, 30, 42, 44, 45

Siegel, Paul N., *Shakespearean Tragedy and the Elizabethan Compromise* reviewed, 148

Simpson, R. R., *Shakespeare and Medicine* reviewed, 155

Sir Clyomon and Clamydes, 157

Sisson, C. J., 155

Sjöberg, Alf, 131

Skelton, Tom, 90–105

Sládek, Josef Václav, 126

Smeaton, Oliphant, *The Life and Works of William Shakespeare*, 48 n.

Smirke, Robert, 76

Smirnov, A., 133

Smith, John Harrington, 156 n.

Smith, Warren D., 155

Smuts, Jan C., 141

Soellner, Rolf, 155

Somerville, H., 39 n.

   Madness in Shakespearian Tragedy, 30

Sonnenberg, Cecilia, 131

Sophocles, *Oedipus Rex*, 9, 71

Sotheby and Wilkinson, 68 n.

South Africa, report on Shakespeare in, 131

Southern, Richard, 123 n., 160

Spencer, B. T., 151

Spencer, Theodore, 42

   Shakespeare and the Nature of Man, 47 n., 48 n.

Spenser, Edmund, 30, 110 n.

   The Faerie Queene, 41, 44, 46, 157

Spivak, Bernard, *Shakespeare and the Allegory of Evil* reviewed, 150–1

Sprague, A. C., 74

   Shakespearian Players and Performances, 80 n.

Spurgeon, Caroline, 58, 66

   Keats's Shakespeare, 68 n.

   Shakespeare's Imagery, 45

Stamm, Rudolf, 131

Staunton, Howard, *Shakespeare*, 80 n.

Stemmer, J. P., 131

Štěpánek, Zdeněk, 126

Sternfeld, Frederick W., 161

Stirling, Brents, 167

Stoker, Willard, 134

Stothard, Thomas, 76

Strehler, Giorgio, 151

Stříbrný, Zdeněk, *Shakespeare's History Plays* reviewed, 152

Stroud, T. A., 151

Stroux, Karl Heinz, 128

Sullivan, Maxine, 142

Summers, Will, 100, 101, 102, 105 n.

Supervielle, Jean-Louis, 127

Supervielle, Jules, 127

Sweden, report on Shakespeare in, 131

Swinburne, Henry, 84, 85, 86

   Treatise on Spousals, 83, 88 n., 89 n.

Switzerland, report on Shakespeare in, 131

INDEX

Tait, J., *Parish Registers of Wigan*, 104 n.
Tarnawski, Władysław, *Burza* reviewed, 154
Tate, Nahum, 73, 74
Taylor, Dick, Jnr., 155
Thackeray, William Makepeace, 77
Theatre, Elizabethan
  companies
    Chamberlain's Men, 117, 119, 167
    King's Men, 117, 118, 119
    Paul's Boys, 120
    Strange's Men, 167
  theatres
    Blackfriars, 113, 115, 116, 117, 118, 119, 121, 122, 123 n., 160
    Fortune, 112, 119
    Globe, 113–23, 158, 160
    Red Bull, 113, 116, 119
    Rose, 112
    Swan, 112, 113, 116, 119
    Whitefriars, 120
Theatres
  London Old Vic, 79, 125, 137, 138, 139, 160
  Memorial Theatre, Stratford-upon-Avon, 70, 74, 75, 79, 137, 140, 145, 160
  See International Notes *for theatres abroad*
Theobald, L., 157, 168
Thomas, Sidney, 103, 105 n.
Thorp, Margaret Farrand, 161
Thurston, John, 76
Thynne, Henry, sixth Marquis of Bath, 104 n.
Tieck, Ludwig, *see* Schlegel, A. W. von
Tietze, H., *Dürer Catalogue*, 80 n.
Tillyard, E. M. W., 153
Tomkis, Thomas, *Albumazar*, 169
Tomlinson, T. B., 151
Trnka, Jiří, 126
Trougton, Henry, 94
True Tragedy of Richard Duke of York, The, Shakespeare Quarto Facsimile reviewed, 164
Tsarev, M., 133
Turkey, report on Shakespeare in, 132
Turner, R. K., 169
Turner, Thomas, 93, 94, 95
Turner, William, 106
Two Noble Kinsmen, The, 38, 157

Underhill, Arthur, in *Shakespeare's England*, 83
Ure, Mary, 144
U.S.A., report on Shakespeare in, 132
U.S.S.R., report on Shakespeare in, 132

Valk, Diana, *Shylock for a Summer*, 126
Valk, Frederick, 126
Valli, Romolo, 129
Van Dyck, Anthony, 74
Veinstein, André, 160

Venne, Van der, 123 n.
Verdi, Guiseppe, 128
Vilar, Jean, 127
Villiers, George, Duke of Buckingham, 110
Vincent, Augustine, *A Discovery of Errors*, 166
Vladislav, Jan, 126
Vočadlo, Otakar, 126
Voeten, Bert, 125, 130
Voorbergh, Cruys, 130
Vos, Erik, 130
Vyvyan, John, *The Shakespearean Ethic* reviewed, 149–50

Waingrow, Marshall, 152
Waite, James, 94
Waite, Ralph, 93, 94
Waldo, Tommy Ruth, 167
Walker, Roy, 160
Warner, G. F., *Catalogue of the Manuscripts and Muniments of Alleyn's College of God's Gift at Dulwich*, 112 n.
Warning for Fair Women, A, 118
Warre, Michael, 130
Waterhouse, Ellis, *Painting in Britain*, 80 n.
Watkins, Ronald, 135
Watteau, Jean Antoine, 73
Webster, John, 33, 116, 119
  The Duchess of Malfi, 38
  The Thracian Wonder (with Rowley, William), 115
  The White Devil, 38
Webster, Margaret, *Shakespeare Today*, 69
Weelkes, Thomas, 107
Weiss, Samuel A., 167
Welsford, E., *The Fool*, 39 n., 104 n.
West, Benjamin, 61, 62, 75
West, Rebecca, *The Court and the Castle* reviewed, 148
Wharton, Joseph, 34
Wheatley, Francis, 108
Whetstone, George, 84
  An Heptameron of Ciuill Discourses, 88 n.
Whitney, Geoffrey, *Choice of Embleme*, 73
Whittaker, Herbert, *Stratford, the First Five Years*, 126
Wickham, Glynne, 162
  Early English Stages, vol. 1 reviewed, 159–60
Widgren, Olof, 131
Wilkins, George, *The Painful Adventures of Pericles Prince of Tyre*, 162
Wilkinson, *see* Sotheby and Wilkinson
Williams, Charles, *The Image of the City and Other Essays* reviewed, 148
Williams, John, 104 n.
Williams, Philip, 166
Will of Whitbeck, 97
Wilson, A., *The History of Great Britain*, 110 n.

INDEX

Wilson, Benjamin, 74, 80 n.

Wilson, Georges, 128

Wilson, Harold S., *On the Design of Shakespearean Tragedy*, 10 n.

Wilson, Robert, *The Three Ladies of London*, 103, 107

Witt, Johannes de, *see* De Witt, Johannes

Wolfe, John, 109, 110 n.

Wolsey, Thomas, 100, 105 n.

Wood, A. C., 104 n.

Wood, E. R., 166

Wordsworth, William, 63

Wright, Louis B., 122, 165

Young, G. M., *Shakespeare and the Termers*, 39 n.

Zaradski, Iu., 133

Zeleński, Tadeusz Boy, 69

Zitner, S. P., 159

Zoffany, Johann, 74, 80 n.

Zubov, K., 133